DATE DUE

Liberty after Liberalism

Liberty after Liberalism

Civic Republicanism in a Global Age

Lawrence Quill

palgrave
macmillan

First published 2006 by
PALGRAVE MACMILLAN
Houndmills, Basingstoke, Hampshire RG21 6XS and
175 Fifth Avenue, New York, N.Y. 10010
Companies and representatives throughout the world

PALGRAVE MACMILLAN is the global academic imprint of the Palgrave Macmillan division of St. Martin's Press, LLC and of Palgrave Macmillan Ltd. Macmillan® is a registered trademark in the United States, United Kingdom and other countries. Palgrave is a registered trademark in the European Union and other countries.

ISBN-13: 978-1-4039-4249-4 hardback
ISBN-10: 1-4039-4249-8 hardback

This book is printed on paper suitable for recycling and made from fully managed and sustained forest sources.

A catalogue record for this book is available from the British Library.

Library of Congress Cataloging-in-Publication Data
Quill, Lawrence, 1971–
    Liberty after liberalism : civic republicanism in a global age / Lawrence Quill.
       p.   cm.
    Includes bibliographical references and index.
    ISBN 1–4039–4249–8 (cloth)
    1. Common good.   2. Public interest.   3. Republicanism.   4. Liberty.
    JC330.15.Q55 2005
    320′.01′1—dc22   2005049577

10   9   8   7   6   5   4   3   2   1
15   14   13   12   11   10   09   08   07   06
Printed and bound in Great Britain by
Antony Rowe Ltd, Chippenham and Eastbourne

For Haleema-Jazmin, who remains the reason

Contents

Preface

This book has been long in the making, beginning life as a doctoral dissertation at the University of Essex, UK (1996–2000). I would like to thank my dissertation advisor Dr Barry Clarke for his constant support and good humor during the years of research and writing. I would also like to thank the members of my dissertation committee, Dr Michael Freeman and Dr Aletta Norval, my internal examiner, Dr David Howarth, and my external examiner, Dr Adrian Oldfield, for their generous advice and suggestions for improving the text.

I owe a special debt of thanks to the undergraduate students at the University of California, Santa Cruz, with whom I shared many long and fruitful conversations about life, politics and surf. Members of the Heidegger Reading Group, notably Nicole Wernimont and Jessica Rutberg, and those truly remarkable students from my courses in the history of political thought, especially Greg Ferenstein, during the years 2001–2003. All contributed to the current volume and were further proof, if proof were needed, that the most important study occurs outside of the classroom or lecture hall.

I would also like to thank Dr Hasmet Uluorta whose enthusiasm for learning is matched only by his brilliance, and John M. Pollard, a dear friend these many years, whose uncommon sense and good humor continue to provide both instruction and inspiration. Special thanks also go to my mother, Thelma Ann Caldera, who has shown time and again that kindness is the greatest virtue and to the late Ronald Lawrence Palmer without whom none of this would have been possible.

1
Introduction: From Polis to Cosmopolis

> Political philosophy has hitherto been concerned with the polis and has devised its questions and concepts accordingly. It defies imagination to contemplate what change political philosophy will need to undergo when the cosmopolis replaces the polis as its primary framework of reference.
>
> – Parekh, 1982, p. 201

1.1 Introduction: Republican liberty and political space

The title of the present work, *Liberty after Liberalism*, was chosen to reflect the deep ambiguity of the present political condition – both for liberalism and for the citizens of liberal-democratic states. Citizens today, not by any means all but a significant and growing number, are presented with opportunities for political participation that were largely absent less than a generation ago. As they exercise this freedom, often in defense of their liberal rights and protections, they do so beyond the confines of the liberal political space – the nation-state.

This, then, is a special kind of freedom; a freedom that is both ancient and distinctly *post*modern. It is ancient because it is one of the earliest kinds of political freedom. It is probably not the first example of this kind of freedom in human history – cities, where it originated, existed in Mesopotamia for thousands of years before the urban and socio-economic preconditions that enable this kind of freedom emerged in the West. It is postmodern because something like this experience of freedom is being exercised today but in an entirely new context, beyond both the ancient city-state where it began and the modern state and nation where its appearance has been infrequent.

The philosopher Hannah Arendt understood well this idea of freedom and the ambiguous position it occupied in modernity and in modernity's political space, the nation-state. Indeed, for her it was the 'lost treasure' that was occasionally reclaimed, the 'miracle' of collective action that when it burst upon the scene had the potential to alter political and social reality.

In a discussion of the Resistance movement in France during World War II, she described this freedom in the following terms:

> The collapse of France, to them [the Resistance] a totally unexpected event, had emptied, from one day to the next, the political scene of their country, leaving it to the puppet-like antics of knaves or fools, and they who as a matter of course had never participated in the official business of the Third Republic were sucked into politics as though with the force of a vacuum. Thus, without premonition and probably against their conscious inclinations, they had come to constitute willy-nilly a public realm where – without the paraphernalia of officialdom and hidden from the eyes of friend or foe – all relevant business in the affairs of the country was transacted in deed and word.
>
> (Arendt, 1987, p. 3)

We can deduce a number of features peculiar to this form of liberty from this description. First, it is unpredictable, often arising at moments of crisis. Arendt could identify the emergence of this freedom when the political imaginary during the war years had been stripped away, leaving the Emperor naked and the population with a profound existential anxiety as they confronted a world they no longer recognized. Second, it is an active or positive notion of freedom (Berlin, 1969) with ontological significance, a freedom that has to be exercised to be realized by people who are not necessarily professional, expert or 'career' politicians, nor are they bureaucrats, technocrats or functionaries. Indeed, 'officialdom' is likely to be quite suspicious of this kind of political activity when qualifications for the enterprise are neither the completion of a civil service examination, the harnessing of influential pressure group influence nor the gathering of votes in an election. The only qualification for this kind of politics is that you are human, and that you value the public world.

This sort of freedom does not fit easily within the institutional structure or imaginary of an age that purposely supplants public, civic engagement for the dubious joys of technical management, control and administrative efficiency. This point was made by Arendt herself in her numerous writings (Arendt, 1958, 1968, 1972, 1973, 1987). But it has also been made in different ways by those sympathetic to her vision, and by her critics.

Arendt's unwillingness to offer a blueprint for a revived republican politics beyond the most general musings that overcome the problem of transition – how to move from a liberal, mass democracy to a vibrant republican one – has led critics to point to republicanism's limited applicability in the contemporary political environment (see Fallon, 1989). Modernity has not been kind to the idea of positive freedom.

But we no longer live in modernity. To say such a thing is not simply to engage in academic point-scoring but to describe a new reality that is unfolding in response to new crises. The task for those who value the contribution of the republican tradition and the uniquely human freedom that it describes is to catch up to a new sociology as tens of millions of people around the world participate in a growing politics of resistance, acting in parallel with and sometimes in opposition to their own governments. What was once regarded as republican liberty should properly be considered 'cosmorepublican' liberty referring to its practice today in a context beyond the state (Beck, 2000b,c).

Cosmorepublican freedoms are those freedoms already being exercised in a historically unprecedented fashion by 'communities' of individuals interested in protest and dissent, exchanging ideas and proposing policy alternatives to those offered by their own territorially based governments. That this freedom should be exercised at all, often in opposition to national governments and to other centers of global power, is extraordinary and, I would argue, consistent with some of the deepest principles of republican freedom. Indeed, Arendt might have described such action as a politics motivated by nothing less than a 'love of the world' rather than a love of the state.

This claim has important consequences for how we understand the nature of citizenship and its demands. For reasons that I explore in detail later, I think Arendt was correct not to embrace the promise of education in pursuit of the creation of republican citizens – if cosmorepublican citizens are created today they are created by happenstance and not by formal training – but mistaken in her desire to place republican freedoms within a liberal institutional context.

Arendt's dilemma – her desire to find a home for political activity in the modern world – has been articulated by numerous thinkers. Most recently, a variant of this claim has been advanced by Bohman (2001, 2004) who makes an eloquent case for 'cosmopolitan republican' freedom and the need to find an institutional home for a republican politics on a global scale. The approach I take here, however, is somewhat different.

If one takes the view that a republican politics writ large will invariably express itself as a form of dissent it is not clear that attempting to institutionalize or find a home for this dissent is the best way to keep global institutions and their representatives responsive to the demands of transnational publics. While Bohman and others are correct to point to the dangers of 'tyranny' under conditions of globalization which increase the possibility of 'potentially arbitrary authority' (2004, p. 342), the general unwillingness of governments to yield power to non-governmental groups or, worse, stifle dissent by purposefully drawing those groups within the boundaries of formal institutions must caution against an exclusively institutional response to the new global politics that is emerging.[1] Indeed, it seems sensible to suggest that exercising cosmorepublican freedoms *outside* of the formal political apparatus is necessary if the institutions of global governance are to respond to the demands of global citizens.[2]

1.2   Republicanism in context

Historians note that the dominant issues confronting political theorists in the ancient world were of territory and number: 'how far the boundaries of political space [could] be extended, how much dilution by numbers could the notion of citizen participant withstand, how minor need be the "public" aspect of decisions before the political association ceased to be political' (Wolin, 1961, p. 70). Culturally, the importance of a 'public life' also began to be supplanted by the sphere of 'private life' which overshadowed both state and society from the fifth century onwards after the collapse of the Roman Empire: 'From the court down to the lowest official, in city and countryside, in religious and professional organizations, private persons took centre stage. Wealth itself became a personal matter, and individuals sought to make everything, from their homes to their tables, private' (Aries, 1987, p. 419).

Attachment to the *polis* or *res publica* was incomprehensible after the fifth century AD because it simply did not exist in actuality or idea. After Rome there was no barbarian state but different centers of power that had no fixed borders, expanding and contracting according to the ambitions of particular warlords – a condition that would persist until the early modern period, which transformed the political geography into what we recognize today as the state.

The greater challenge, however, came from a qualitatively different kind of experience offered by a different 'imagined community' (Anderson,

1991). The 'discovery' of spiritual or inner space marked a reflexive turn to inwardness that is associated with the highly personalized theological journey of St Augustine of Hippo and more broadly with the Christian tradition. The rejection of the temporal for the spiritual – the city of men for the *City of God* – and the adoption of Christian virtues like humility instead of the Classical virtues like greatness and glory led those who subsequently wished to defend republican freedoms to rail against the stultifying effects of Church doctrine.

Although comparisons have been drawn between monastic communities and the life of the Greek polis (Mumford, 1968) it was the republican Machiavelli and his attempt to recast the ancient exhilarations of political life over the spiritual comforts offered by the Church that best illustrate a republican revival during the early modern period. Not only did Machiavelli famously proclaim that he loved his own city more than his soul but for him, religion's primary purpose was sociological. The proper function of state-controlled religion was to assist in the creation and maintenance of the civic or political virtues. The Church of Rome, however, failed on at least two counts. First, its emphasis on virtues like humility encouraged unmanly qualities. Second, the Church, due to its own internal corruption, while powerful was not powerful enough to unite Italy. Not having permitted any other power to do so, it had been the cause of Italy being prey to invasions by barbarians.

For all of Machiavelli's brilliant insights concerning the institutional requirements of political life – he turned to Sparta and the Roman Republic, its leaders and institutions for inspiration – there was at least one crucial problem with his account. Like the Greeks before him, Machiavelli made no attempt to describe a form of politics that operated beyond the fairly narrow confines of his own political space, his beloved city-state of Florence. His own theories of republican freedom, arguably the most important since Aristotle, limited themselves once again to a context that was, at the very time that he was writing, being supplanted by the emergence of the modern state. Consequently, as the relative importance of individual cities declined so too did the relevance of their freedoms.

The most obvious difference between the ancient and the modern world was, as Montesquieu and his intellectual heirs pointed out in the centuries that followed, one of *size*. Aristotle's political universe spread no further than the walls of Athens which ran for twelve miles to the port of Piraeus, while his physical universe was ultimately spherical and, more importantly, finite. Copernicus, Galileo and, of course, Newton effected their revolutions upon the heavens by expanding them infinitely and the consequences for the political world were no less critical.

Indeed, from the seventeenth century onward, a political symmetry developed between sovereignty – exclusive rule over a bounded territory – and legitimacy. The issue for states, as for Newton's universe, was one of prediction and control even if that meant that (some) freedom would ultimately be sacrificed for security. Consequently, during this period republicanism moved from being a 'live' hypothesis to a 'dead' one.

The most famous account of politics during this period appeared in Thomas Hobbes' writing. Hobbes produced a thoroughly mechanistic view of political life – influenced by his misunderstanding of Euclid's geometrical proofs – and one that was actively hostile to notions of ancient liberty. But his was only the first of a long line of attempts to apply scientific principles and order to the inherently unruly world of human affairs. In 1728, Desaguliers adapted Newton's physics to politics in his *Newtonian System of the World*. John Locke, who was a friend of Newton's and who had read his *Principia*, also asked his readers to engage in a peculiar thought experiment, to imagine a time before civil society existed and, through the application of reason alone, to construct society anew. His *Two Treatises of Government* prompted readers to reject the notion that they were subjects by birth to a particular ruler and to consider which principles might best be employed in the construction of a new political order – though not an *entirely* new one. Revolution for Locke was something that he was ready to justify only in hindsight.

The long eighteenth century was a period of profound transformation, the beginning of liberalism proper and commercialism, industrial revolution, urbanization and the end of absolutism. It was also a period of profound cognitive transformation (Porter, 2001).

At the beginning of the eighteenth century a third of the world was missing from maps while the fabled Southern Continent, which mariners had pursued since the fifteenth century based on Ptolemy's speculations and which did not in fact exist, was still there. Other areas simply read 'terra nullius' or empty lands. Yet by the end of the century, following the three voyages of James Cook who succeeded in going 'further than any man before', maps changed from being part of visual encyclopedia to becoming documents of mathematical precision. The world of the eighteenth century was larger but it was also carefully plotted and charted (Thrower, 1999).

The political philosophy of liberalism which, from its beginnings, was a tradition preoccupied by order, mirrored this development by its attempt to control the political space of the emerging state in both actuality and imagined form. The liberal political space was much like the rest of the globe, something to be mapped, its boundaries fixed with the corresponding ideas of constitutionalism, rights and law. Liberalism was ultimately territorial – hardly surprising for a philosophy whose ultimate concern was the defense of private property – the twin units of its analysis, the individual and the state. Political freedom in this context was properly understood as a property of individuals not the experience of groups as it had been for earlier generations of thinkers.

For a republican like Rousseau, who had a firm grasp of the relevance of scale in his own understanding of republican politics, the consequences of this new context, the context of the state and of the great invention of the modern period, representative government, were not lost.[3] If, in fact, it was no longer possible to sit under an oak tree and regulate the affairs of state then the only other solution, according to Rousseau, was total immersion in it – man had to be 'denatured' in order to become a thoroughly civilized citizen.

Rousseau's attempts to grapple with the related issue of character formation in the modern context lend us the third aspect of republican liberty. Rousseau could screech at the inhabitants of Geneva for not being Spartans or Athenians, rather 'just a bunch of petty, selfish merchants and artisans', because the content of their character was so different from the future republican citizen he had in mind. If citizenship was not a natural condition, and Rousseau did not think that it was, then in the modern world of nation-states citizens would have to be educated or *created*. The message for modern states was that the 'creation' of citizens was paramount: 'create citizens, and you have everything you need' (Rousseau, 1973, p. 147). The question was, however, what sort of citizen best suited the needs of the state and its rulers.

What is significantly different between a thinker like Rousseau and a contemporary republican like Arendt is that (apart from one disastrous excursion into the field of education for the latter) hardly any of the heirs to the tradition started by Aristotle offer a method of transition from the steady state of government and bureaucracy to the dynamic culture of political freedom. This may be a quirk of contemporary political theory, the reflection of a genuine unwillingness to speculate about such matters. For Arendt, as for many of her followers, it was more relevant to speak about the glories of freedom's past and to search for modern liberal institutions within which a diluted form of republican freedom might occur. As we shall see in a later chapter, in her own way, Arendt continued the search for a fabled political space in a liberal world that was well and truly mapped.[4]

1.3   Republicanism: Relevant debates

In recent debates, neither freedom, politics, nor what has been termed 'the political' provided the main focus for the many exchanges that occurred between liberals and their critics. Instead, the point around which argument revolved was the notion of 'community'. John Rawls (1971) had suggested in *A Theory of Justice* that rationally, self-motivated, calculating individuals abstracted from their actual socio-historical situation would divide the spoils of society justly and fairly from their relative positions behind a 'veil of ignorance'. A number of theorists that came to be grouped under the 'communitarian' label pointed out that the self was historically situated rather than a merely useful metaphysical construction and Rawls' metaphor was extremely limited in application. Rawls' liberal self, in their opinion, simply did not exist.

In response, liberals attempted to bring the community back in by historicizing the transcendental justification offered in the 'original position' suggesting that the Rawlsian account of justice could actually be used in concrete situations of the present moment. A text like the *Theory of Justice* was redescribed, not as a 'philosophical account of the human self, but only ... an historical-sociological description of the way we live now' (Rorty, 1991, p. 265). Michael J. Sandel's (1984) famous criticism of the Rawlsian 'unencumbered self' was defended by liberals as 'the encumbrance of our modern social condition' (Gutmann, 1985, p. 316). Even Rawls embraced this historicized rendering of liberal commitments in his later works by suggesting that most members of *reasonable* liberal societies already endorsed what he described as a 'freestanding political conception' of justice.

The move toward a more relativist version of liberalism rooted in the liberal 'community', all but disabled the communitarian critique. Some commentators saw communitarians as wholly misguided in their criticism of liberalism while others began to question whether there had ever been a debate in the first place (Beiner, 1992; Caney, 1992; Walzer, 1992). The attempt to reclaim a thicker notion of community revealed to some that the real enemy of communitarians was modernity, not liberalism, an insight that could have been applied with equal readiness to republicanism and its notion of public freedom.

While the liberal-communitarian debate raged during the last two decades of the twentieth century, the impetus for a 'republican revival' occurred much earlier, in the field of academic history in the 1960s, with a reassessment of the American Revolution and the philosophies of the founding fathers. In the process, the dominant assertions of Louis Hartz

(1955) were contested. Hartz had considered the liberal theory of John Locke as providing the paradigm of revolutionary thinking in America. Yet Hartz's reading was met with the 'republican' responses of historians such as Bailyn (1967), Wood (1969) and Pocock (1975). Each differed in the degree to which they identified or utilized the components of the republican heritage. Yet, in their own way, each offered to locate the source of revolutionary thinking in a period of intellectual history prior to Locke.

Bailyn made Locke appear an incidental figure among the revolutionary pamphleteers of the period, while Wood identified English republican writers like James Harrington as providing the theoretical heritage to the Revolution. Only Pocock would go further and identify the civic virtue and civic republicanism of Machiavelli's Florence, the commitment to public life and patriotism, as the conceptual source of the American response to British tyranny. Indeed, at times, Pocock's analysis seemed to place republicanism and liberalism in diametrically opposed positions (Pocock, 1975, p. 460).

This rediscovery of a republican heritage led scholars from other fields to look closely at republicanism and to use it as a response to the perceived deficiencies arising from the liberal-communitarian debate. The precise nature of the new republicanism was unclear, but this did not stop a number of political and legal theorists from promoting the republican cause. Republicanism was seen as a theory that offered something definitively different (and therefore good) from liberalism. It was a challenge and, in some form at least, promised a workable alternative.

The political theorist Ronald Beiner (1992) argued that the problem with the communitarian argument had been its relentless focus on the notion of community. In Beiner's opinion, the issue was not lack of *Gemeinschaft*. Instead, Beiner made the perceptive comment that the central question was one of 'vocabulary', or whether the type of moral vocabulary used to describe the social world was adequate. Liberalism, he concluded, failed to address the question of the character of the social order. What was required was a philosophical anthropology that identified the 'basic' moral and political requirements of human beings from which one might critically examine the exercise of different life choices. This neo-Aristotelian identification of virtue (*arete*) as constitutive of human flourishing was a popular approach. Yet theorists differed over whether what counted as 'human flourishing' might be regarded as particular and local or universal and cross-cultural in application.[5]

Beiner's and other's insights concerning the relevance of language use in framing the political world remain of central importance. However, the drawback to these arguments was that often no proposals emerged for how a liberal society might move toward becoming a republican one. There was, as one critic noted, a failure to address the 'transition problem' from liberalism to the new republicanism (Burtt, 1993). How was a modern, large, densely populated, heterogeneous nation-state supposed to adopt the supposed attributes of small, largely homogeneous city-states of the kind found in Aristotle's Athens or Rousseau's Geneva? Of course, one answer to this conundrum had already been provided by republican authors like Harrington and Montesquieu, albeit one that contemporary republicans tended to play down – the theory of representation.[6]

Liberal critics argued that republicans should propose alternative strategies rather than endlessly exposing liberalism's deficiencies. Republicanism had attempted to establish itself as a distinctive political theory but was it in any way a relevant one? Without at least some indication as to where republicanism might be going or what it might have to offer the modern world, there was a danger that it might be ignored altogether.

In response, those sympathetic to the idea of public freedom eventually realized that more could be gained by asserting the similarities as well as the differences between the two theories. Consequently, within academic history, responses to Pocock's analysis and the resulting shifts of position encouraged commentators to emphasize the conciliatory mood of historiography toward the events of 1776.

Similarly, legal theorists attempted to argue that liberalism and republicanism were ideal theoretical bedfellows. A 'neo-republican', rather than the exclusively republican, revival ensued so that what began as an outright rebuttal of liberalism's obsession with rights and procedural neutrality, eventually moved toward reconciliation and compromise (Michelman, 1986; Horwitz, 1987; Sunstein, 1988; Sherry, 1995). A whole new wave of writing resulted that attempted to join liberal rights together with republican virtue.

The terminology of the period reflected the obsession with compromise as neo-republican or 'liberal-republican' or 'republican-liberal' accounts were produced, with authors tending to distinguish those elements of republicanism they favored from those they did not (Lloyd, 1995; Thomas, 1997). So, an objective notion of the good might be rejected while the idea of positive freedom was proclaimed. And while political participation and self-government required a deliberative democratic framework, it was hoped that the transformative effects of such encounters – that would, moreover, eventually lead to consensus – would avoid the need to advance controversial proposals over the content of a civic education.

Within the field of political theory the spirit of the times was also evident. Martha Nussbaum claimed that we did not have to choose 'between virtue and enlightenment' although her 'thick vague theory of the good' demanded extensive social reform (Nussbaum, 1992). Jeffrey Isaac argued that, historically, republicanism had been successfully incorporated into liberalism, and Richard Dagger suggested that rights and citizenship could be better understood under the aegis of what he called 'republican-liberalism' (Isaac, 1988; Dagger, 1997). Quentin Skinner (1992) also pointed to historical circumstances in which republicanism and *negative* freedom happily coexisted. By the end of the 1990s neo-republicanism, or what was in many ways by this time a *liberalized* form of republicanism, pointed toward combining 'the fact of pluralism' and the size of the modern nation-state with the notion of a decentered society, a 'republic of republics' and a participatory view of citizenship.

Skeptics pointed out, nonetheless, that there were tensions within this hybridized theoretical project. A willingness to respect individual rights, on the one hand, combined with a reluctance to impose values of any sort on a community, on the other, led some to doubt the coherence of the new republicanism. Embracing pluralism without a common good or shared metaphysic to fall back on avoided the accusation from liberals that one was foisting an archaic metaphysic upon liberal citizens. But facing up to the hard truth of the unavoidable and significant differences that existed between groups within society without such a shared sense of common virtues and values, however, posed the very real dilemma that the differences and diversity of modern societies might actually undermine the republican enterprise (Sullivan, 1988).

Suzanne Sherry at least was clear about the implications of the neo-republican project. A system that placed a value upon a person's virtue would inevitably result in the differences among citizens being rewarded for their civic usefulness. Some version of moral certainty was also required if judgements about what was socially valuable were to be made. These involved what Sherry described as the construction of 'situated truths'. Moreover, because the vast majority of citizens were simply unprepared for a participatory model of politics an educational system was required that advocated both 'critical thinking' and 'cultural literacy' for all. Indeed, Sherry saw the best hope for a republican future by 'educating children for responsible republican citizenship' (Sherry, 1995, p. 135).

Others agreed. By itself, the reordering of social institutions would not generate a co-operative politics. But an education imagined as a continuous project rather than one that concluded with childhood could encourage the very values necessary to sustain and withstand the turbulence of political life. Education had been a concern of republicans throughout history and was seen as the key to generating the kind of political commitment to the polity and to liberty that had been largely replaced by nationalist political sentiment. An educational approach that stressed the diversity of opinions and a critical method to approaching problems rather than authoritative solutions was seen as desirable (Oldfield, 1993). Together with a meaningful form of decentralization and the opportunities to practice citizenship, advocates suggested that citizens might thus be propelled toward political action.

Nonetheless, it was quite clear that to create a republican community one had to first create republican citizens. As one advocate of 'strong democracy' noted, '[i]f the young were born literate, there would be no need to teach them literature; if they were born citizens, there would be no need to teach them civic responsibility' (Barber, 1992, p. 210).

Liberal-republicanism, for all its noble attempts at reconciliation, had ended by confusing the terms of debate. Were liberals republican or republicans liberal? Whatever the answer, any distinctive message that republicanism might have once had was all but lost in the process.

With hindsight, this outcome was not surprising. When criticizing or incorporating facets of liberalism, for example, one can choose between a version of Hobbes and that of Locke, Kant, Bentham, Mill senior and junior, to mention but a few, and in modern times between Nozick, Rawls, Scanlon, Williams, Dworkin and so on. Liberalism, as Jeremy Waldron has pointed out, is an 'umbrella concept' incorporating a number of different doctrines (Waldron, 1987, p. 127).

Yet, republicanism is also an umbrella concept. A brief typology of republicanisms would have to include Aristotle, Cicero, the Italian republicanism of Machiavelli, English republicans like Harrington, the French republicans Rousseau and Montesquieu, American republicans Jefferson, Rush and Webster and, in the modern context, Arendt, MacIntyre, Sandel and so on. Where Paine or De Tocqueville fit in this typology is rather less clear, and because of the choices available through the divergent writings of these 'republican' theorists one can choose between the various republicanisms on offer or attempt to combine some of their many different components. What republicanism is, or at least what one understands republicanism to be, will, consequently, largely depend upon what one has chosen from this theoretical bazaar.[7]

1.4 A dead hypothesis?

Until recently, the theory of republicanism seemed to have relatively little to offer contemporary political understanding. It was criticized (somewhat ingenuously) for its elitism: Milton famously described the people of the Commonwealth as 'the herd confused' – its dubious emphasis on military virtue and glory; Weber referred to the polis as a 'warrior's guild' – not to mention its explicit misogyny (Pitkin, 1981, 1984). In Athens women were excluded from the right to *politeuesthai* and for Machiavelli, 'la fortuna é donna', a characterization of the Roman goddess of fortune who favored the 'manly' and should be 'conquered by force'.

Oscar Wilde's irreverent quip about socialism – that it would take up too many afternoons – could be applied with equal candor to republicanism. Written into republicanism was a historical dependence upon large groups of people (i.e. slaves) so that a leisured class of political aristocrats might live the good life. But how were individuals to value a fully political life, of the kind Aristotle envisaged, asked one critic, 'amid the challenges of tedious jobs, limited incomes, family problems, and everyday personal tragedies and triumphs' (Burtt, 1995, p. 150)?

The decidedly ambiguous nature of the term 'republic' only deepens the problems. Even Thomas Jefferson, one of the most important and radical republican theorists of the eighteenth century, was forced to admit that the idea of the republic 'is of very vague application in every language' (Fries, 1963, p. 563).

The approach I take here is similar to Faulks (2001) who unashamedly includes within his own revised notion of liberal citizenship those elements of the tradition that he prefers – equality, individual rights, perfectionism, universal citizenship – while rejecting those he does not, the idea of the social contract and the radical opposition between man and nature. Faulks recognizes that the meaning of liberalism is overdetermined and that liberal citizenship is an idea as much as a legal reality, a contingent set of assumptions that changes as the aspirations of a people and the requirements of a particular political period change. His conception of citizenship is both liberal and explicitly postmodern in the sense that he wants to develop the notion of liberal citizenship in the light of the effects of the new economy and sociology of the postmodern period.

It will come as no surprise that, following Faulks, my account of 'cosmorepublicanism' will reject some of the more dubious elements of the republican heritage. There is no place for misogyny or the military virtues[8] in my version of cosmorepublican citizenship, though both a disdain for women and military expansionism are elements of the tradition that echo down the centuries. Equally, cosmorepublicanism must reject its attachment to the polis and to an inward-looking patriotism as political activity increasingly finds itself involved in a dialectical process shifting back and forth between local, national and international spheres and to multiple points of political contact and interaction.

Cosmorepublican citizenship will be active in many spheres. Cosmorepublican citizens will be autonomous, skeptical, critical of the idolatry of government and officials – the cult of personality in politics in the age of the media spectacle has more in common with the Roman circus than it does with the principles of human freedom and dignity. Cosmorepublican citizenship is best understood as a peculiarly developed form of political agency that has arisen as a result of the change in postmodern political topographies. Cosmorepublican citizens are best understood not as situated or unencumbered selves but *ironic* selves, bridge builders and networkers who participate virtually and actually in order to effect change locally and globally.

Classical republican models held a mirror up to a liberal world and found it lacking. In contrast, contemporary approaches to republicanism have attempted to couch it within the terms of a liberal political paradigm, with varying degrees of success. The former may be accused of irrelevance, the latter for failing to be distinctive. The task for a postmodern republicanism is neither one of recovery nor accommodation. Mine is not an attempt to resurrect Aristotle, or other dignitaries from republicanism's past – much as Machiavelli did in order to keep himself company in his villa in Northern Italy during a prolonged period of estrangement from court.[9] Rather, in the present work, I will try to reconstruct republicanism by acknowledging the efforts of individuals who are exercising their political freedoms in concert and in an attempt, ironically, to preserve their territorial liberties.

1.5   Overview of the argument

The next chapter will focus on the idea of the political space and related expressions of citizenship in the ancient and modern world. This is very much a foundational chapter in which I will examine the theoretical and sociological underpinning of the small political unit, be it the polis, guild, Renaissance city-state or town-hall meeting and the limits that these spatial models have imposed upon the concept of republican citizenship. In an attempt to move beyond the polis, I will consider the paradoxical problem of size – the oft-quoted reason for the demise of the Classical conception of politics – and the rise of representative government. I conclude this chapter by identifying those themes that are still 'relevant' as the concept of republican citizenship evolves today in a context beyond the nation-state.

Chapter 3 focuses on the liberal political space of the state and the corresponding, yet contradictory, notions of liberal citizenship. The topography of liberalism was an invention of the early modern period that grew in time to develop a complex apparatus of control that has changed little since the end of the nineteenth century. The consequences of this development for the notion of citizenship have been profound. Divisions within liberal society between economy and politics, and public and private life helped redefine citizenship as a legal entitlement with additional voting rights for some. Yet by the end of the twentieth century, as liberal thinkers turned to the republican vocabulary of virtue to revive notions of liberal community, it was becoming far less obvious that liberalism possessed the intellectual resources to cope with postmodern challenges. This chapter will consider the attempts that have been made to push liberalism beyond its own political space and whether, in so doing, liberal internationalism is a coherent answer to the problems posed by globalization.

Chapter 4 returns to republicanism but within the context of modernity and postmodernity. Specifically, this chapter analyzes the efforts that have been made to accommodate republican principles within liberalism and the institutional structures of the modern state. Two republican approaches are identified. The first seeks to appropriate the mechanisms of state control, the second seeks to find accommodation within the state apparatus so that a space for political activity might be carved out. In response, I point to the tension between structure and agency in the light of postmodern geographies and new technologies that have permitted outbreaks of political activity on a global scale. Sections 4.3 and 4.4 begin to sketch the dynamics of a republican form of citizenship that operates at the supra-national level by recovering the idea of the nomad as the quintessential postmodern citizen.

In an attempt to flesh out this notion, Chapter 5 considers the revival of interest in the theory of cosmopolitanism. I will begin by considering the legacy left by Kant – the thinker most often associated with contemporary variants of cosmopolitanism and a self-professed 'republican' – and its relation to contemporary advocates of cosmopolitan democratic theory. While there is much of enormous interest to be found in the latter, what I suggest is that the institutional cosmopolitanism of contemporary democratic theorists needs to be supplemented by a nomadic conception of cosmorepublican agency to be effective. This would keep global institutions dynamic but it would also add a distinctly political dimension to the cosmopolitan debate whose focus on governance has been criticized for not considering the necessity of debate and disagreement over issues of global importance.

Chapter 6 addresses 'the problem of transition' directly by examining the responses by liberals, republicans and cosmopolitans to the function of state-sanctioned education. For obvious reasons, education has remained the key to both the preservation and the transformation of an existing society. This chapter will examine the resources that each theory has provided in moving politics toward a global dimension and the problems associated with that move. It will also consider the particular strains that liberal educationists face as the fundamental algorithm of state education – education to work – starts to unravel as national economies can no longer guarantee a life time of employment for their populations.

Chapter 7 examines the notion of cosmorepublican citizenship within the context of two competing political spaces in postmodernity – the space of empire and the space of the network. My claim in this chapter is that a new political spatiality of empire is currently being constructed, one that is also being responded to via cosmorepublican spaces of resistance. These spaces encourage a new kind of political agency – which I describe as the publicly ironic character of cosmorepublican citizens – that challenges the twin theoretical pillars of modern liberalism: consent and obedience to state authority.

2
The Transformation of Political Space

> Such a government is evidently restrained to very narrow
> limits of space and population. I doubt if it would be practi-
> cable beyond the extent of a New England township.
> – Thomas Jefferson, 1963, p. 537

Francis Cornford, writing a paper on the notion of physical space a few
years after Einstein had released his *Special Theory*, suggested that physics
had made the universe appear less 'a steel structure' and more like
'India rubber' where 'the India rubber itself exists only as an arbitrary
figment of the human brain' (Cornford, 1936, p. 216). Such revolutionary thinking in the natural sciences, supported by further theoretical
advances since Einstein's breakthroughs at the beginning of the last
century, has not been matched by any such advance in political understanding or imagination. Indeed, one scholar, notably *not* a political
scientist or theorist, recently remarked upon the peculiarity of a discipline
(political science) that insists upon instructing its students on ideas that
are based upon theories that are at least three hundred years out of date
(Pinker, 2002).

As significant as the challenge of mass democracy in the seventeenth
and eighteenth centuries which heralded in new models of political space,
political life in a global context opens up a series of new possibilities
and challenges. The 'power of place' is being reconfigured as democratic
demands are made across borders around issues that no single state
actor can manage independently. While the state remains the dominant
unit of analysis for theorists, citizens are demanding and forging spontaneous alliances across borders, exercising the democratic impulse
beyond the confines of their respective territories. As one commentator
put it recently, '[d]emocracy alone has been confined to the nation

state. It stands at the national border, suitcase in hand, without a passport'
(Monbiot, 2004, p. 3).

States have, hitherto, provided the guarantees that citizens require to
safeguard their liberal liberties. Now those very same citizens are also
exercising their cosmorepublican freedom at a level beyond the state and
often in protest against the state. Increasing awareness of environmental
destruction, pollution, large-scale corruption and, most recently, opposition to the 'war against terrorism' in Afghanistan and Iraq have provided
the motivating concepts around which different civilian populations have
coalesced politically.

The boundaries to freedom that existed during the modern period
were both territorial and, of equal importance, conceptual. The invention
of national traditions, complete with the pomp and circumstance of flag,
anthem and a pantheon of national heroes forged the distinctive identities
of nationhood and nationality with which we are all too familiar. State-
sanctioned education programs from the end of the nineteenth century
taught liberal principles to future citizens in their imagined communities
that perpetuated the myth of national unity (Hobsbawm, 1992).

Contemporary republican theorists have done much to draw attention
to the weaknesses of the liberal model and the rich alternative history
of freedom that republicanism provides. However, they have been as
much a captive of their own spatial models – most notably the *polis* – as
liberals have of theirs. While many of the liberal critiques of republicanism
may be safely ignored there is considerable truth to the idea that *if* republicanism is to having something more to say about life in the postmodern
world it must move away from nostalgic attachments to the past.

The battle between ancients and moderns and their competing
conceptions of liberty needs to be re-examined. If republican critique is
to be more than lamentation for a long lost liberty, a new republicanism must be grounded in the ability to 'satisfy the deepest urges and
aspirations of the [post]*modern* human being and to meet the challenges of
the [post]*modern* age' (Parekh, 1993, p. 167). This chapter describes the
history of a series of politico-spatial transformations in the West and
their consequent impact upon the notion of republican citizenship in an
attempt to identify the normative resources that would enable republicanism to meet the challenges set by a global politics.

2.1   Political space in the early republic

Although politics did not begin with Athens it is to Greece that theorists
turn when they think of the origins of politics and democracy in the

West. The earliest expression of a political space in the West was the city-state as this emerged in Greece around the fifth century BCE. It emerged because of a subtle shift in the dynamics of power away from the private authority of the *basileis* and toward the *agora* where the power of speech was dominant.

Solon began the revolution by initiating a program of reforms in 594 BCE known as 'the shaking off of burdens' ending a system of mortgage for indebted farmers and removing the threat of slavery from those unable to pay their debts. Herodotus also notes that Cleisthenes' proposals in 509 BCE redrew the political boundaries of Attica and overhauled the political system, spreading power throughout Athenian society. 'He took the people', notes Herodotus, 'into his political club.' One of the significant features of this reform was that it gave the ordinary Athenian a sense of place. Athenians when asked who they were would give their name, the name of their father and the name of their *deme*.

Citizens shared power equally as equals. What they also shared was a general commitment to the principles of civic virtue, the subordination of private to public life, where being human and being a citizen was intimately linked. The Athenian city-state was the only location where citizenship might find its most complete expression.

On the one hand, urban design had made a social and political space possible. The central public space of the *agora*, the market place, effectively flattened the social order by pre-defining all those who entered the space as equals (much as the political space of the coffee-house in Paris and London would demand in the eighteenth century) and contrasted sharply with the religious and more private area of the Acropolis and the seclusion offered by the space of the home (Vernant, 1982, p. 125). On the other hand, it was said that wherever the Athenians went, *they* and not Athens would be a polis (in contrast to the *astu* or physical setting). Political space was not a container, a thing into which politics was put, but part of the social fabric, a living entity. Politics was the intangible space people created between them as much as it was physical architecture. Urban design, the 'spiritual universe of the polis', theories of the natural universe and of political life were all intimately related.

The result of this unique experiment in living together, as the Classical historian Moses Finley pointed out, was that although the 'men' of Athens would have held divergent views and opinions nearly all would have shared the premises of the polis, the cultural assumptions necessary to make political communication possible (Finley, 1983). Part of the cultural backdrop was the assumption that Athenian freedom which rested on one's own economic and temporal independence – freedom from work meant you had more time, more *schole* or leisure to do what you wanted to do – in turn rested on the complete and institutionalized bondage of others. No paradox was recognized for an Athenian – there are no surviving abolitionist treatises, for example – because the idea that freedom could or should be enjoyed by everyone because of their status as a human being was entirely foreign to the Greek mind. Destitution for an Athenian was the inability to own slaves and, consequently, to be unable to secure one's freedom from the burden (or *ponos*, meaning curse) of work. If there was a social tension between free men and slaves then it was a similar kind of tension as that between dominant and subordinate, the old Greek practice of antithesis, of two things in conflict, of protagonist and antagonist in Greek theater. For Greek thinkers like Aristotle and Thucydides these opposites were an example of proper natural functioning. That the stronger should rule the weak was the natural order of things.

The question of the political legitimacy of the polis together with one's obligation to it simply did not arise. The one notable exception, Crito's attempts to persuade Socrates to escape from prison and certain death, was refuted on the grounds that abiding by the law, even an unjust one, was preferable to a life away from the city. Man, in Aristotle's famous phrase, was a *zoon politikon*, and the *polis* the highest and most developed form of community. It was a unique place that, which from the time of Solon, set its own standards via the political process.[1] Those not interested in public life, as Pericles noted in his funeral oration, should simply not reside in the city-state.

However, the quest for harmony and the desire to avoid *stasis* or strife by the end of the Classical period was becoming increasingly difficult to maintain. Aristotle had noted in Book VII of his *Politics*, that his 'political animals' needed to live 'within sight of one another' if the polis was to remain an effective institution. Plato calculated in the deeply conservative *Laws* that the optimal number of citizens was 5040. But more importantly, his *Republic*, an anti-political, authoritarian tract that owed more to Sparta than to democratic Athens, dictated a strict separation of roles within the polis so that the dangers of increasing numbers of politically active citizens might be averted. Politics should be left to those who knew best – to kings who were philosophers and philosophers who were kings.

However, no solution to the spatial problem that wanted to retain public freedom *qua* political activity could avoid reconceptualizing the notion of the political space. A number of experiments with federal organizations followed the end of the Peloponnesian War in 404 BCE, notably the notion of *isopolity* where a citizen could exercise his rights in a number of different member cities. The creation of the city of Megalopolis, founded in 371 BCE by the Theban general Epaminondas, was also meant to unite all the people of ancient Arcadia in one great city in order to counter the hegemonic power of the Spartans.

One common interpretation of the polis during this period of Greek life is that while it was still generating a vibrant cultural life it was becoming politically suspect. The space of the polis was so deeply entrenched within the Greek mind that when it was no longer available in practice, Greek political theory found itself lacking a relevant context (Wolin, 1961, p. 94). Political theory was unable to negotiate the conceptual move from the national to the international sphere as political influence increasingly spread beyond the Peloponnese to Persia and Macedonia. The inability to achieve a higher unification in the face of these external threats resulted in the exhaustion of the polis as a viable form of civic life with the Athenian defeat in 338 BCE.

The republic of Rome when it emerged after the expulsion of the monarchy in 509 BCE was a political space that was geared to solving an entirely different problem – at least, initially. Early on in the republic's history it became apparent that through the struggle between the different socio-economic orders there was in fact not one republic but two. Political struggle over access to the higher offices of the Roman state resulted in a series of demands early in the republic's history from the plebs including equality before a written law, relief from debt bondage and the fair distribution of lands acquired from newly conquered territories. The consequences when these demands were not heard was one of the first acts of non-violent civil disobedience in recorded history and an interesting spatial experiment (Sharp, 1973, p. 75).

In 494 BCE the plebs seceded from Rome, walking out from the gates to a neighboring hill that left the city virtually empty. There, they established a parallel state on Janiculum Hill organized along tribal lines. They met in council and voted on propositions, which when passed were called plebiscites. This competing notion of political space, while it was eventually incorporated within the wider republic of the Patrician order, would nonetheless have an enduring impact upon how the republic was governed.

As the republic expanded so measurements were standardized and a network of roads created. A common currency was also designed to contribute to a sense of belonging within the symbolic or virtual political space. The legal reality of dual citizenship and the hypothetical and

highly moral notion of universal citizenship, with the universe imagined as a single city, also became popular. Malcolm Schofield points out
that the Stoic idea of the city as a universal, moral community was one
philosophical answer to the problem of size (Schofield, 1991, p. 73).
A city could, after all, be defined in various ways. It could refer to the
organization of buildings, as a group of men living in the same place, a
'habitation', but it could also refer to a moral space within the boundaries
of which all men lived – an idea that later cosmopolitan thinkers would
embrace.

Although Cicero and many other Romans turned to the Greeks for
guidance, for a republic that grew rapidly in size and diversity the
priorities of those few in power quickly turned to the management of
distance and the temptations of conquest. As Caesarism triumphed and
the republic descended into empire, Roman political space came to be
embodied within the figure of the ruler.[2]

Conceptions of citizenship also became increasingly inclusive at the
cost of meaning – the right to participate was transformed into the
'right to habeas corpus'. Freedom from politics became as important as
the freedom to participate politically had been for the Greeks. Politics
came to be seen as a hindrance rather than the highest expression of
the good life. Epicurus commented that 'we must free ourselves from
the prison house of affairs and politics' (cited in Wolin, 1961, p. 78).

Citizenship was transformed from an activity into a legal construct
that was used increasingly as a strategic tool to pacify an expanding
population. In AD 212 Marcus Aurelius Antoninus (Caracalla) extended
citizenship to all the peoples of the empire so that Roman rule would
gain legitimacy in the eyes of the conquered. It also meant that taxes
could be more easily collected and the need for military expansion
reduced. Rome raised the question of whether an active sense of citizenship was possible beyond the small, relatively homogeneous community
of the polis.

After the collapse of Rome, it took something like a thousand years
for a recognizable political space to re-emerge in Europe, as it did via
the guild movements and communes that arose spontaneously during
the Middle Ages between 1050 and 1250 AD. Towns during this period
were havens of liberty – offering freedom to a serf attempting to flee
from a lord, provided that residence within a town's walls could be
proven for a year and a day. Associations formed that were designed to
protect men's economic interests, their property and, ultimately, their
personal safety from the violence of nobles. Indeed, the guild with its
horizontal network of obligations was something of a revolutionary

organization. The provisions of protection to its members went so far as to advocate active retaliation against nobles who had violated the freedom of one if its members. This effectively turned the world of the Middle Ages upside down by, first, summoning a noble and if he did not appear before the commune wreaking vengeance upon him, his family and/or property – an exclusive right of nobility during the Middle Ages.

The town community, or 'commune' in North-Eastern France and 'Gemeinde' in Germany, made its own laws, appointed representatives and initiated policies of exclusion (of foreign goods, for example). Political authority lay with members of guild associations and very often their descendants. Statutes were presented before the assembly for majority approval, and while the day-to-day running of the town was usually conducted by a select number of 'honest guildsmen' all affairs were ultimately subject to approval of the entire guild membership (Black, 1984).

One of the most significant changes to the political topography of Europe, however, occurred as a result of the events that took place in Italy during the quattrocentro. The 'Italian Revival' which began two hundred years earlier with the rediscovery of Aristotle's *Politics* explored the possibilities of various forms of government. This response was made possible because of Italy's unusual status as one of the most urbanized and commercially advanced countries in Europe at the time. Cities of 200,000 people were common in Northern Italy while Paris could only muster 10,000. Large, concentrated populations permitted the development of markets and Italy's geographic position facilitated trade with the East (Jardine, 1996).

While stable monarchies like England developed proto-theories of executive power and political sovereignty,[3] Marsiglio of Padua and Leonardo Bruni argued for popular sovereignty and a division between the Church and the state in a way which permitted the possibility of independent and secular political activity, a space for politics. It was through the writings of Niccolo Machiavelli, however, that the most significant developments in spatial perspective occurred at precisely the same moment as urban design was being transformed through a proliferation of public squares and streets (Braunfels, 1988, p. 49). Architecture, not to mention a Mediterranean climate, clearly had something to do with the practice of politics.

Machiavelli pitted his notion of the city and the love he bore it against the spiritual universe of Christianity. The author of *The City of God* considered the duty of a true Christian to avert his gaze from the problems of temporal existence, to avoid the 'lust of the eye' as St John put it and to keep firmly focused on the path that leads to the Creator. Christianity's spatial orientation, while it would manifest itself in extraordinary architectural accomplishments across the continent of Europe, was designed to humble the onlooker not empower them. Spatial concerns were ultimately inward and upward.

The Christian 'turn to inwardness' had an enduring and, arguably, deleterious effect on political or public spaces and the notion of 'the public' in the West. As Richard Sennett suggests, thanks to the inward turn, 'the outside as a dimension of diversity and chaos...lost its hold upon the human mind as a dimension of moral value, in contrast to an inner space of definition' (Sennett, 1990, p. 19).

Machiavelli, who recognized the importance of a civic religion for the cultivation of the appropriate civic virtues – he was an acute observer of the power of the imagination over the actions of individuals – was deeply suspicious of the Church's influence in worldly affairs. Indeed, nothing separates Machiavelli more sharply from his medieval predecessors than his attitude to religion. The Church of Rome, in Machiavelli's opinion, was first and foremost a powerful *political* institution with the Pope, a military and political commander.

This recognition led the Italian humanists to conjecture that the state was an entity that could exist independently from the person of the king or pope, such that the challenge posed to politics in a republic was how to check the power of the ruler. Consequently, politics was not regarded as an expression of the good life as it was for Aristotle, but a tool, a means by which the greatness and glory of the ancient republics might be reclaimed for a modern city if leaders could be controlled and corruption avoided by the exercise of civic virtue and liberty.

The other observation made during this period was that achieving *concord* or harmony, a primary goal for the Greeks, was impossible in political life and should not be sought after. On the contrary, disagreement and disunity was the essence of politics which demanded from each and every citizen a commitment to public duty. Participation in the political life of the city was in one's own interests, an essential element that maintained one's liberty through a perpetual struggle with the powerful magnates.

A political community that secured a free way of life and restricted the activities of a few powerful individuals (the *popolo grosso*) required vigilance and participation in the political process on the part of the many (the *popolo minuto*). Indeed the key to citizens' maintenance of their *virtu* and their liberties was through organized activity in the *ordini*, the institutions, constitutional arrangements and methods of organization within society. Like the earlier Greek experiment with republican politics, it was made possible because of urbanization and commercialization. But unlike the earlier model, the humanists argued for a politics based upon enlightened self-interest and not upon an esoteric notion of the good life for man.

Despite this fundamental philosophical difference, however, both approaches shared a fundamental spatial oversight. Like the Greeks before him, Machiavelli could not imagine life outside of the spatial boundaries of the Florentine city-state. One commentator notes that '[t]hough Machiavelli knew that the future lay with larger states and wanted Italy to become one of them, he gave almost no thought to the problem of how great a state should be governed' (Plamenatz, 1992, p. 82).

Indeed, when the theorists and practitioners who discussed and shaped the future of the French or American republics in the eighteenth century considered the form of political life most appropriate to their own times, they did not think that the wisdom of Classical theories, from which the Italian humanists drew their inspiration, was likely to solve their problems. In fact, for a thinker like Hamilton, they represented precisely what had been wrong with political life. City-states were not havens of freedom but 'little, jealous, clashing, tumultuous commonwealths, the wretched nurseries of unceasing discord and the miserable objects of universal pity and contempt' (1961, p. 73). The context for Rousseau, Montesquieu or Publius had changed. It was the state and the nation, not the polis or city-state that was the proper object of contemplation.

The problems for the Classical and Renaissance republican model when applied to the French republic or the thirteen colonies were, as Montesquieu put it, in *The Spirit of The Laws*, those of size and ethos. He might also have mentioned time. The dawn of the industrial revolution did not bode well for mass participation in political life when there was so little leisure to be had. Indeed time rather than space was the critical issue as the Abbe Sieyes had noted during the Revolution in France. Modern commercial societies, with their concentration of labor in industry, made it impossible for citizens to participate as citizens because they did not have the time. Citizens were forced to entrust government to people who did – a wealthy, leisured class with time for politics.

For Montesquieu, the modern state was not only large it was culturally diverse and, therefore, incapable of generating the shared sense of civic duty and responsibility that was integral to premodern republican societies. Self-interest, and not necessarily enlightened self-interest, had by the eighteenth century replaced virtue; legalism replaced the potency of custom and eventually patriotism would be replaced by the much weaker notion of nationalism. When Montesquieu and others like him wrote about republicanism in the eighteenth century they were writing about something that was qualitatively different from the earlier theories from which they drew their inspiration. What was being attempted was an imaginative reconstruction of republicanism replacing the old with 'a new expansive republicanism fit for the modern political world' (Shklar, 1990, p. 266).

2.2   The problem of size

The political response to population increase, expansive territories, economic take-off and the concentration of political power in the modern period – all deemed part of the inevitable evolutionary path from tribe to region to nation (Hobsbawm, 1990, p. 38) – was the theory of representation, developed initially by the authoritarian Hobbes and which was also called, thanks to the corruption of language, *republican government.*

In *Federalist 10* Madison argued that the new United States would be a republic and not a democracy. The distinction was critical. If democracy in Athens referred to a small number of citizens gathering together to administer the government in person the real difference in the modern period was '*the total* [and deliberate] *exclusion of the people in their collective capacity'* from any share in the government (1961, p. 387, emphasis in original). By this declaration it was clear that the founders were following the Roman rather than the Athenian model, were accepting of the great divisions of wealth that existed in the fledgling republic and which would only be exacerbated by commerce and industry, and proposed a moderate form of government that would secure against democratic despotism (Yates, 1987, p. 171).

While Jefferson and Tocqueville proposed their own solutions which did, in fact, underwrite popular involvement in the political process for the sake of the health of that selfsame process, representation was chosen over these alternatives because it was actually considered an improvement upon the classical small polity model. Direct democracy could offer no safeguard against faction but a representative republic, *because* of its size, could encourage enough conflicting interests to cancel one another out. 'The influence of factious leaders may kindle a flame within their particular States, but will be unable to spread a general conflagration through the other States...' (1961, p. 84).

By the eighteenth and nineteenth centuries, republicanism had, thanks largely to the work of Montesquieu and the popular writings of

Publius, been transformed into a vocabulary of governance where the *agathoi*, the good or the best, ruled the rest. The former were variously defined using different criteria that ensured their superiority notably a surplus of wisdom, virtue, patriotism or, more to the point, an excess of personal property. Yet, time and again, representatives were heralded as eminently more sensible about the true interests of the country in contrast to the ignorant and impassioned masses. For Madison, because representatives were the best sort of people they were able to 'refine and enlarge the public views... [representatives were] a chosen body of citizens, whose wisdom may discern the true interests of their country and whose patriotism, and love of justice will be least likely to sacrifice it to temporary partial considerations' (1961, p. 82).

Theories of elitism and exclusion were certainly consistent with earlier republican theories which had severely limited access to office by using various criteria for removing whole sections of the population from government. But the evident lack of personal opportunities to become involved in the modern political process made plain by the (comparative) increase in opportunities to move around *within* the social order of eighteenth- and nineteenth-century societies prompted Rousseau to question the nature of modern freedom under representation.[4] In *The Social Contract*, he pointed to the consequences of representation in England and what he considered one of the central dilemmas of modern life:

> The English people think that they are free, but in this belief they are profoundly wrong. They are free only when they are electing members of Parliament. Once the election has been completed, they revert to a condition of slavery: they are nothing. Making such use of it in these short moments of their freedom, they deserve to lose it.
> (Rousseau, 1973, p. 266)

For Madison, however, the aim of the new republic was not to create a politicized society. In 1787 in the debates over the new constitution, he pointed out how, 'In England, at this day, if elections were open to all classes of people, the property of landed proprietors would be insecure. An agrarian law would soon take place.' The purpose of government was, therefore, 'to protect the minority of the opulent against the majority' (cited in Yates, 1987, p. 170).

One of the most extraordinary accomplishments of this period was that the *res publica*, or public thing, became an almost exclusively private thing with its connection to democracy turned into a process of election which forced 'the people' to choose an aristocracy to rule them. The anti-federalists looked at this with horror as they saw the elements of the large republic come into direct conflict with the freedoms and values of the small republic which they valued. Not only was voluntary obedience to the law almost impossible in the context of large states, such that the use of force against a people was almost inevitable, but the major problem that modern republics faced was over the question of professional responsibility. The key question for the anti-federalists was how to keep representatives responsible when they were not directly answerable to their constituents (because of the infrequency of election) nor were they *like* their constituents. As a result, anti-federalists wanted to replace representatives with what they called a 'natural aristocracy', men who were genuinely like themselves, not necessarily brilliant or wise but whose interests corresponded closely to their own, the 'middling sort' or 'yeoman class' rather than rich political celebrities or 'men of genius' (Storing, 1981, p. 17).

Liberals, both political theorists and politicians, during the eighteenth and nineteenth centuries unsurprisingly shared many of the more aristocratic 'republican' sentiments. To some, including the reformer James Mill, representation was a modern marvel, the great invention of the enlightened world. It also maintained the status quo for if some portion of the community could *adequately* represent the interests of all the members, Mill thought, surely the franchise could be restricted to it. Consequently, the ancient prohibition against women's involvement in politics stood because their interests 'indisputably' coincided with those of their fathers and husbands (Mill, 1992, p. 27).

John Stuart, Mill's son, shared a similar disposition toward representation, yet he based his principle of exclusion upon intellect. Politics had to be limited to an intellectual elite, those with the most knowledge and skill. The latter, who also happened to have the most property and privilege, should not be outvoted by those with less, that is the working classes.

From the earliest discussions of representation in the sixteenth century the subject remained a controversial topic for how were representatives to represent the interests of people whom they knew very little about? This was precisely the thrust not only of anti-federalists in the United States but of Macaulay's famous criticism of James Mill. On the subject of female representation and the elder Mill's denial of the same he noted: 'Is then the interest of the Turk the same with that of the girls who compose his harem?' (Mill, 1992, p. 291).

To properly represent, one had to make manifest or to present again the interests of the people one represented. One should, accordingly, possess their feelings and interests. Yet, this was extremely unlikely because of the inequity within the economic and political system of the period. As one critic noted at the time:

> It is impossible for a few men to be acquainted with the sentiments and interests of the US, which contain many different classes or orders of people...To form a proper and true representation each order ought to have an opportunity of choosing from each a person as their representative...Only but...few of the merchants and those only of the opulent and ambitious will stand any chance...only the gentry, the rich, the well born will be elected.
>
> (Samuel Chase, cited in Manin, 1997, p. 112)

One way of overcoming this problem historically had been the use of lot – a practice that had been used since biblical times for the distribution of property (and that would be used again to distribute land taken from the Cherokee Nation in Georgia between 1805 and 1832). Lot had been a common practice of republics, often in combination with election. The republics of Rome, Venice and Florence combined both election and lot. The Italian communes of the eleventh and twelfth centuries used lot to select magistrates. Leonardo Bruni noted that the use of lot as a mechanism of choosing leaders eliminated 'the struggles that so frequently erupted among the citizens competing for election...' (Manin, 1997, p. 53).

The advantages of lot, as Montesquieu pointed out, was that it was essentially democratic whereas election was essentially aristocratic. Lot offended no-one. It was the ultimate egalitarian method of choosing an individual for public service. Yet, as one recent study of the concept of representation concludes, while lot was considered an acceptable and egalitarian method for the distribution of commodities it was considered an unacceptable practice for the distribution of office:

> Scarcely one generation after the Spirit of the Laws and the Social Contract...the idea of attributing public functions by lot had almost vanished without trace. Never was it seriously considered during the American and French revolutions. At the same time the founding fathers were declaring the equality of all citizens, they decided without the slightest hesitation to establish, on both sides of the Atlantic, the unqualified dominion of a method of selection long deemed to be aristocratic.
>
> (Manin, 1997, p. 79)

The theory of representation had less to do with overcoming the problem of size and more to do with finding a justifiable method for securing the political arena for safe governance. Lot was not considered relevant by those whose primary interest was not in participatory democracy but in controlling the political arena (Nedelsky, 1990). For Madison, representation was not about likeness, it was about superior ruling power, about the 'right sort of person' being elected to government, something that lot would not permit or, more accurately, would leave to chance.

From the first discussion of representation in English, Thomas Hobbes' *Of Persons, Authors, and Things Personated*, this was the intended form. The motivation for Hobbes' definition of representation came from an overwhelming desire for unity, a mistrust of the multitude and a vehement dislike of republican liberty. The proper scope of freedom was defined by the sovereign power who would regulate the individual's ability to 'buy, sell and otherwise contract with one another' (1992, p. 148). Hobbes preferred a freedom for citizens that was far more restricted, defining liberty as the removal of physical impediments rather than the airy notions of human excellence given it by the Aristotelian schoolmen he so chastised in *Leviathan*. Representation, along with a series of sweeping powers that he ascribed to the government including the power to control the thoughts and opinions of subjects, was part of a general theoretical trend that Hobbes articulated transforming the bonds of community from duty-based to contract-based obligations. It also demanded an absolute and unquestioning obedience to authority.

Hobbes' theory provided a justification of political obligation that left no room for revolt. Indeed, so thorough was his political logic that the man who attempted to disobey his representative would simply be failing to recognize that to do so would be to rebel against oneself which would, furthermore, be unjust. Consequently, Hobbes added:

if he that attempteth to depose his Soveraigne, be killed, or punished by him for such attempt, he is author of his own punishment, as being by the Institution, Author of all his Soveraigne shall do: And because it is injustice for a man to do any thing, for which he may be punished by his own authority, he is also upon that title unjust.

(1992, p. 122)

Later discussions of the concept reflect Hobbes' preoccupation with order and stability. They also accept that the representative space is as much about maintaining the distance between elected and their constituents as it is about overcoming the problem of physical size. Then, as now, the kind of relationship that one has with one's representative is really no relationship at all (Pitkin, 1967; Fishkin, 1995).

It is worth pointing out that there were notable exceptions to these theoretical developments. Thomas Jefferson, almost alone among the founding fathers, clung to the Classical precepts of which he was so fond. A republic, for Jefferson, meant 'purely and simply, government by its citizens in mass, acting directly and personally, according to rules established by the majority' (Fries, 1963, p. 536). The problem of 'size' was not lost on Jefferson. Yet, for him, the expansion of the size of the polity did not automatically negate the power or relevance of the theory of small states. On the contrary, it meant that an institutional apparatus needed to be developed to ensure that things remained small and therefore manageable.

In contrast to the likes of Madison and Hamilton who argued with great flourish and persistence that the country was too large for small republics, Jefferson argued that 'Our country is too large to have all its affairs directed by a single government' (1963, p. 391). The concentration of power was likely to be abused unless a 'little rebellion now and then' could be allowed to keep the republic both dynamic and corruption free.[5] What better way to do that than equip citizens with the wherewithal to keep an eye on their representatives who operated at a distance and by tutoring citizens in the ways of political decision-making locally?

Indeed, Jefferson's proposals were a highly original combination of ancient and modern thought, involving the employment of both direct and indirect democratic institutions. The general federal level of representative government might deal with external or foreign affairs, with subsequent layers of state, county and ward government allowing opportunities for direct participation in political affairs for each citizen.

> These wards, called townships in New England, are the vital principle of their governments, and have proved themselves the wisest invention ever devised by the wit of man for the perfect exercise of self-government, and for its preservation ... it is by division and subdivision of duties alone, that all matters, great and small, can be managed to perfection. And the whole is cemented by giving to every citizen, personally, a part in the administration of the public affairs.
>
> (1963, p. 542)

Jefferson could write about the division of political offices in this fashion by not only drawing on the history he knew so well but also his personal experience of pre-Revolutionary America. Few countries had ever been more fragmented than the United States of America in the eighteenth century. As one commentator notes of the period, 'Even before the revolution, America had the posts to train half the population in the delights of politics' (Everdell, 2000, p. 155).

In the early days of the republic, Alexis de Tocqueville's observations on town hall meetings and the like suggested that they served an essential complementary function to the modern representational institutions of an extended republic. He considered intermediary or secondary institutions in the public sphere, which incorporated more than the exclusive political concerns of national government, to be of first importance and allowed himself when writing about America to imagine the possibilities of a democratic republic, one that he hoped would be transferred to France. It was, or could be, 'a society in which all men, regarding the law as their common work, would love it and submit to it without difficulty... Understanding its own interests, the people would appreciate that in order to enjoy the benefits of society one must shoulder its obligations.' Consequently, the 'free association of the citizens could... take the place of the individual authority of the nobles, and the state would be protected both from tyranny and from licence' (Tocqueville, 1994, p. 95).

Tocqueville's notion of political liberty depended upon the *mores* or customs and habits of a particular society, the 'habits of the heart', 'the moral and intellectual dispositions of men', and a commitment to religious faith: 'if men are to be free they must believe'. But it also depended on the exercise of citizenship. The township and local association was the place in which citizens learnt the defense of the union through the practices of their district. It was here that they were provided with 'a thousand continual reminders that they lived in society' (1994, p. 509). These secondary institutions were to liberty, he noted, 'what primary schools are to science; they put it within the people's reach; they teach people to appreciate its peaceful enjoyment and accustom them to make use of it. Without local institutions a nation may give itself a free government, but it has not got the spirit of liberty' (p. 63).

It was important for thinkers like Jefferson and Tocqueville to multiply the points of political contact where citizens could exercise their independence and autonomous judgement. Government, as a result, could be divided between those concerns that only a national legislature could decide while other 'administrative' functions could be handed down to the townships. The failure to preserve this buffer against the centralizing tendencies of government lead these thinkers to analyze democratic society in terms that are reminiscent of contemporary republican critiques of liberalism. Without the possibility of active, citizen involvement each person 'grew like the rest', 'lost in the crowd' with only 'the great imposing image of the people' remaining (Tocqueville, 1994, p. 669).

Centralization of power led to the formation of thoroughly private individuals, persons who allowed themselves to deteriorate into a state of weakness, apathy and acquiescence. Majority opinion became the true source of authority in society, as the philosopher David Hume had pointed out, as the revolution in America was in full swing. 'Nothing appears more surprising', he noted, 'than the easiness with which the many are governed by the few...' (Hume, 1951, p. 81). The culprit for Hume was control of public opinion, something he referred to as the true source of government authority.

By the middle of the nineteenth century the republican past and its relevance to contemporary politics had been consigned to myth. The rise of the centralized state and the expansion of capitalist markets, creation of standing armies and the concentration of political power in relatively few hands all contributed to the demise of the autonomous city and its style of politics.

The new political myth was that of government of, by and for the people. Abraham Lincoln, author of these famous words and a man who revered the political activities of the revolutionaries, men whom he considered 'the pillars of the temple of liberty', feared the consequences of their like returning to America in his own century. The world of the nineteenth century required, in Lincoln's opinion, the passion of revolution to be replaced by unimpassioned reason if peace was to be maintained. His solution, building on the practice of representative democracy instituted by the founders, was to make a 'political religion' out of the US Constitution, its laws and, one might reasonably argue, the presidency itself. In so doing he consigned the revolution, and its politics, to ancient history.[6]

2.3 The irrelevance of republican citizenship?

The theory of representation did not solve the problem of size. It merely reconfigured what was thought possible and desirable politically thereby containing the urge to exercise dynamic and potentially revolutionary political freedoms. Ideas of civic friendship and duty were replaced with notions of contractual agreement between citizen-subjects and their government. The notion of a mixed constitution, a central pillar of republican theory from Aristotle to Machiavelli, was not considered relevant for modern 'republics' because it was argued that the difference between rich and poor did not require any institutional recognition.

Mixed government had been Machiavelli's adopted answer in the *Discourses* to the natural antagonisms between rich and poor which, he thought, could never permanently be eliminated and, moreover, ought not to be. A blanket condemnation of the quarrels between the Roman nobility and the plebs would overlook the good effects that were produced. The proper ends of legislation addressed the different dispositions of rich and poor and created laws that brought about a constructive clash of opinion between them (Machiavelli, 1970, p. 113). Later accounts of political life, however, replaced organized tumult and the figure of the active citizen with individuals pursuing their own interests facilitated by the mechanism of the free market, a notion that was proselytized with an almost religious fervor.

Corruption, furthermore, was not a problem to be solved by the people but by the institutional framework of modern government. The separation of powers, checks and balances would disable faction and maintain equilibrium between competing elements within a free state. Government was therefore regarded as effective, 'whenever its institutions are strong, and corrupt when its machinery fails to function adequately' (Skinner, 1978, p. 44).

The Jeffersonian notion, that the task of preserving freedom and avoiding dependence must fall to the individual citizens themselves, thereby requiring them to be ever vigilant for signs of corruption and ever watchful for the abuse of power, was not advanced. If civic virtue was to be exercised it was not in the oversight of government but in the choosing of political leaders. Madison noted that '[t]o suppose that any form of government will secure liberty or happiness without any virtue in the people, is a chimerical idea' (Kloppenburg, 1987–8, p. 27). Yet, at the same time, he was convinced that sufficient virtue existed in the community so that the people would choose the right sort of political leader.

Had Jefferson's republic come to pass, a very different kind of politics and a very different kind of citizen would have arisen within the bounded territories of liberal-representative democracies. To accept an active role for the people would have been to accept, more broadly, the notion that political corruption was a problem rather than simply an inevitable and acceptable function of elite management. That many contemporary social scientists see corruption not in terms of the deleterious effects to a democratic polity but as part of the functionality of successful elite competition illustrates the degree to which contemporary thought has moved from the early republican concerns like those expressed by Jefferson (Ball, 1988, p. 243).

The rejection of the active notion of republican citizenship for the more muted, passive liberal version also spoke volumes about how one understood what was, or rather, ought to be thought possible in the political world. The discussion by liberal theorists concerning the proper scope of citizenship, the place of the economy in human life and the basic requirements of education, reflected and continue to reflect a fundamentally conservative outlook concerning the proper relation between subordinates and their betters.

Blair Worden has commented that '[i]t is as a politics of virtue that republicanism most clearly defines itself' (1994, p. 47). By the eighteenth century, however, the political virtues had passed out of fashion. For Machiavelli, the key to the citizens' maintenance of their *virtu* had been through organized activity in the 'ordini', the institutions and political organizations in a society. Citizen *virtu* kept the powerful and ambitious in check and the *ordini* made sure a citizen was in no doubt about what was in his best interests. Each and every citizen would be imbued with such a strong sense of civic virtue that they could not be bribed or coerced and thereby undermine the common good. The civic institutions of religion, law and education would all be enlisted so that citizens might place the good of their community above their own selfish interests, for their own better good.

Nearly all descriptions of virtue equate it with particular qualities of character. Indeed, the concept of corruption was often associated with the corruption of the self. A failure to identify one's interests with those of the political community was a sign of personal failure. But by the end of the eighteenth century, politics had a much reduced need for virtuous citizens. Thanks to Mandeville's account of private vices and public benefits in his *Fable of the Bees*, one that shocked but resonated with financial opportunists provided by the 'new economy' of the early eighteenth century, corruption actually appeared to possess a property that benefited the new economic system of laissez-faire economics (Balen, 2003). According to Mandeville, the paradox of modern society – 'All trades and places knew some Cheat, No calling was without Deceit' – was that it actually required vice while maintaining the pretence of a morality of virtue. Vice was necessary, he argued, if civilizations were to prosper.

The introduction of standing armies, increasing dependence upon commerce rather than more pastoral pursuits, and the rejection of heroic and manly virtues in the eighteenth century for the virtue of institutions rather than individuals seemed to identify republicanism as, at best, a premodern political theory. The consequence was that, if he could no longer engage directly in the activity and equality of ruling and being ruled, but had to depute his government and defence to specialised and professional representatives, [a citizen] was more than compensated for his loss of antique virtue by an indefinite and perhaps infinite enrichment of his personality, the product of multiplying relationships, with both things and persons, in which he became progressively involved. Since these new relationships were not political in character, the capacities which they led the individual to develop were called not 'virtues' but 'manners'...

(Pocock, 1981, p. 360)

Another weakness was republicanism's attitude toward the economy. The Classical model of political life, though it depended on a slave class, rejected the relevance of manual labor which was regarded as a curse from theoretical discussions of civic life. As Aristotle noted in the *Politics*, 'the good man and...the good citizen ought not to learn the crafts of inferiors except for their own occasional use; if they habitually practise them, there will cease to be a distinction between master and slave' (1994, p. 57).[7]

Classical republican theory asserted the predominance of politics over all other aspects of social life, especially the economy and offered no guidance for the complex, commercial systems of later ages. For those thinkers during the Revolutionary period in America who were impressed with the ancient models of political life there was, as one commentator notes, no classical language for understanding the modern commercial system that was emerging. Unlike liberalism which was supported with the extremely well-developed political economies of Ricardo and Smith, republican political theory offered no equivalent language. 'It did not help persons who sought to understand the private transactions that were determining the shape and direction of the Anglo-American economy' (Appleby, 1992, p. 355). The hostility that many republican authors displayed toward the notion of a life centred around work meant that they were, for the most part, unable to offer any workable alternative.

There were exceptions. Some republicans, like Benjamin Franklin and Thomas Paine, thought that the new economy and republicanism could unite together to provide a stable system of government.[8] Other thinkers like Rousseau and Jefferson, however, sought a more radical approach by attempting to recast the importance and significance of work within modern society. For Rousseau, unpleasant work (by which he meant activity that was dirty and labor-intensive) served an important social and political function. In the *Social Contract*, he suggested that socially necessary work might be regarded as a form of public service forming part of a national work ethic that would energize the nation. The error of modern societies was that a surplus of money could be traded for leisure, for free time away from work. In Rousseau's opinion this would be a mistake.

> In a country that is truly free, the citizens do everything with their own arms and nothing by means of money; so far from paying to be exempted from their duties, they would even pay for the privilege of fulfilling them themselves. I am far from taking the common view: I hold enforced labour to be less opposed to liberty than taxes.
>
> (Rousseau, 1973, p. 265)

For Rousseau, even if citizens did not carry out laborious work tasks in common throughout their lives, he considered exposure to the hardships of work for a limited period beneficial for developing a sense of civic obligation to others and a sense of belonging to the community at large.

Jefferson, meanwhile, advanced the case for the virtue of a simple agricultural existence. 'While we have land to labor', he noted, 'then, let us never wish to see our citizens occupied at a workbench, or twirling a distaff' (1963, p. 217). Jefferson was not oblivious to the pressing issue of the economy in post-Revolutionary America, nor was he arguing for a return to the mythical bucolic pleasures of a pre-industrial existence. He was convinced, however, that there was more to human life than industrial work. He saw the proper use of the economy as a means to preserving political liberty rather than permitting the accumulation of excessive personal fortunes for the few. What he actually saw around him were the competitive pressures of an industrial economy – pressures that damaged civic virtue as even Adam Smith noted with concern in his *Wealth of Nations*[9] – coupled with the dangers of 'banking establishments' that he considered more of a threat to political liberty than 'standing armies' (1963, p. 537).

Honest agricultural work was juxtaposed against wealth creation and the excessive concentration of political power that this created to highlight a peculiarly modern dilemma. Whether *homo politicus* was superior to *homo faber* was moot. What Rousseau and Jefferson shared was a suspicion that once a concentration of economic power occurred, political corruption would inevitably follow. Indeed, Jefferson was acutely aware that economic dependence amongst a people would create a situation in which their liberties could be rested from them without their even knowing it. It is worth quoting Jefferson at length on this point.

I am not among those who fear the people. They, and not the rich, are our dependence for continued freedom. And to preserve their independence, we must not let our rulers load us with perpetual debt. We must make our election between *economy and liberty*, or *profusion and servitude*. If we run into such debts, as that we must be taxed in our meat and drink, in our necessities and our comforts, in our labors and amusements, for our callings and our creeds, as the people of England are, our people, like them, must come to labor sixteen hours in the twenty-four, give the earnings of fifteen of those to the government for their debts and daily expenses; and the sixteenth being insufficient to afford us bread, we must live, as they do now, on oatmeal and potatoes; have no time to think, no means of calling the mismanagers to account; but be glad to obtain subsistence by hiring ourselves to rivet their chains on the necks of our fellow sufferers...

(Jefferson, 1963, p. 543, emphasis in original)

Citizens might find themselves with formal, liberal political rights but without the ability, or 'basic capability set', to use the language of contemporary economists, required to exercise those rights in any meaningful fashion. The bondage created by debt and by an economic system that permitted the accumulation of wealth for the few and dependence for the many had no room for liberties that could be exercised in common. Such a system was an anathema to meaningful and mindful political activity. It left citizens without the time to be vigilant and in a perpetual state of exhaustion such that what time was available to them would likely not be spent in thinking about politics.

2.4 Conclusion

This chapter has sought to address the age-old complaints made against republicans in an attempt to see the problems they face a little more clearly. If we accept that 'the problem of size' was more accurately a problem of management coupled with an unwillingness on the part of representatives and theorists to restructure political communities to allow for public discussion, then republicanism is not in quite such bad shape. Moreover, we might interpret the 'absence' of a 'relevant' political economy to republicanism not so much as a deficiency as more a form of protest made by republicans against the worse effects of the commercial economy. Indeed, if we add to this our own contemporary sociological experience, most critically, the end of *work* as the raison d'être of human existence – either by choice or otherwise – the relation between citizens and their liberal governments becomes problematized (Rifkin, 1995). As it does so, the room for politics – republican style – grows.

Thanks to the effects of globalization, today, citizens find themselves in a unique situation, one where they are likely to be far more conscious of the relative merits of their own political systems and their own personal and political relation to a much broader community of individuals. Perhaps the single most revolutionary feature of globalization is that citizens have access to a vast array of alternative sources of information (Deibert, 1997).

Modern day coffee-houses, the virtual ones made possible by new information technologies, have enabled citizens to disturb the peace by placing them on the same information level as their leaders – a unique sociological feature of postmodernity (Giddens, 2000). One of the largest and most successful demonstrations against the effects of international trade liberalization – the campaign against the Multilateral Agreement on Investment in 1999 – was organized internationally using the same information technologies that had made trade liberalization possible. Protests against the most recent war in the Middle East in 2003 were organized using similar technologies. International non-governmental groups, whose numbers have increased exponentially over the past decade, possess a distinct advantage over nation-states today as they respond to issues and mobilize large numbers of people swiftly and with minimal cost.

The connection between agency and technological transformation should not be underestimated. If the industrial revolution formed the relation between man and machine into one of dependence, the techno-logical revolution of the late twentieth century has freed the individual citizen from information dependence. The ability of governments to control the flow of information and to construct social and political reality is far more difficult now than ever before.[10]

Does this mean that republicanism can be revived? A recent discussion of the history of republicanism in Europe noted the following: 'One question that cannot be ignored in discussion about our republican heritage is how far we are confronting a usable past' (Skinner, 2002, p. 6). If republicanism is to be revived today, it will be done so piecemeal. For much of its history republicanism was more a language of protest than a systematic theoretical approach to understanding political life. Similarly, republican authors tended to draw haphazardly on the varied elements of a classical heritage in order to vent their concerns about the existing order of things or in an attempt to make their idea of republicanism, most often expressed in an attachment to a particular author, fit inside that order.

I suggest that what a global form of republicanism can best provide is an alternative political vocabulary for change, one that draws upon notions of vigilance and agency, and that offers a compelling description of liberty and of political communities however the latter are to be defined. Now, more than at any other time in recent history, citizens can choose to do something to effect political change, locally, nationally and, perhaps, even globally. Politics, to paraphrase Giddens, is only the click of a mouse away (Giddens, 2000).[11]

Crucially, the state is now recognized as only one actor among many. The political space of the postmodern era is both 'the empire' and 'the network', as citizens find their liberties curtailed in the former while they exercise their 'virtual' freedoms in ways that allow them to negotiate 'the social, cultural, and political meanings of their joint enterprise' (Keck, 1998, p. 3). That citizens should seek political expression in arenas that are non-territorial is not without precedent and is an understandable reaction to an increasing distrust of politicians together with a suspicion of corruption in government at the highest levels.

Cosmorepublicanism is, ultimately, a politics of protest and because its actions are often aimed at the state, this invariably makes it a politics of disobedience as well. Some of the greatest threats to human life in the previous century were from acts of obedience to unjust, but not necessarily illegitimate authority (see Kelman and Hamilton, 1989). Postmodern citizens find themselves in the unenviable position of being asked to decide how much they wish to be implicated in the decisions made by their own distant representatives, decisions that are, nonetheless, made in their name and for which they are, to some ill-defined degree, responsible.

3
The State We Are (No Longer) In

This fortress built by Nature for herself
Against infection and the hand of war.
This happy breed of men, this little world,
This precious stone set in the silver sea,
Which serves it in the office of a wall
Or as a moat defensive to a house
Against the envy of less happier lands.

– *Richard II*, Act II, Scene I

Contemporary social and political life is most closely associated with
the state, in actuality and idea. The state, more properly that collection
of institutions that we call 'the state', regulates all types of human
activity from cradle to grave. It provides protection for individual citizens and their property via a permanent and professional police force,
excludes those who violate its laws by removing them physically from
the rest of society, and has defined geographical borders that it moni-
tors and defends by a professional and permanent standing army, navy
and air force. John of Gaunt's description of England as a 'fortress' and
'little world', one that was supposed to be happier than other less
impervious states is a good description of the state as a protective
container, a description of political isolationalism and insularity that
still finds resonance today in some quarters.

States lay claim to our lived existence and our mental lives. It is no
accident that Hobbes described the state in quasi-theological terms as
a 'Mortal God' who judges what is right and what is wrong. States wield
tremendous institutional powers and also a cognitive power such that we
can still talk meaningfully in the twenty-first century of 'civic religion' – of

the office of the President in the United States and constitutional monarchy in the United Kingdom (see Bellah, 1970). That the idea of 'the nation' and the secular religions of nationalism – 'the most widespread, the most unthinking and the most immediate political disposition of all at least among the literate populations of the modern world' – should hold sway over our mental lives and influence our attitude to 'foreigners' is remarkable but not altogether surprising (Dunn, 1993, p. 57).

It is equally uncontroversial, however, to note that the actuality and the idea of the state and the nation today are under strain. A strict correspondence between society, economy and politics within a bounded territory no longer exists if, in fact, it ever did. Giddens' (2000) description of globalization as a 'runaway world' and Beck's (1992, 1999) analysis of modern society as 'risk society' are apt characterizations of a new political, social and economic context in which the activities and transactions that occur do so at a level that transcends the boundaries of regions and national frontiers. The phenomenon of 'globality', argues Beck, 'means that from now on nothing which happens on our planet is only a limited local event; all inventions, victories and catastrophes affect the whole world, and we must reorient and reorganize our lives and actions, our organizations and institutions, along a "local–global" axis' (1999, p. 11).

The territorial principle which has underwritten the modern state since its inception is under direct challenge because of a deficit in the ability to control the activities of multiple actors in the global context. The most obvious example of this today is international, non-state sponsored 'terrorism', a phenomenon that is almost impossible to control except through increasingly anarchic acts of state violence in the international arena. The resultant loss or curtailing of liberties at home is regrettable but understandable if one pursues state-centric logic. The very raison d'être of the modern state – to provide security for individual citizens in exchange for certain 'natural' liberties – is under assault. The result, as Hobbes noted, is that '[t]he Obligation of Subjects to the Sovereign, is understood to last *as long, and no longer, than the power that lasteth, by which he is able to protect them*' (1992, p. 153, my emphasis). In other words, if the sovereign can no longer offer protection to its subjects then it is permissible, indeed desirable, to remove one Leviathan and replace it with another.

While many discussions of the effects of globalization upon states often speak of the latter as if they were irrelevant, it would be more accurate to say that, under the conditions of globalization, they are but one political actor among many other state and non-state entities including corporations, non-governmental organizations (NGOs) and international non-governmental organizations (INGOs). States' formal powers are being reconfigured as immunity from international standards of behavior is challenged in the law courts as citizens find themselves with rights and duties that transcend their obligations to their home state.

Claiming exemption from such treatises runs the risk of political embarrassment for elites particularly when conflicts are couched in dubious moral terms and politicians' decision-making is suspected for being self-serving rather than in the interests of the worst off. The human rights agenda, used selectively by political elites is, however, taken seriously by electorates. It will be interesting to see how persuasive arguments that refer to the importance of state sovereignty remain as institutions like the International Criminal Court or European Court of Human Rights are used by individual citizens in cases against national governments (Carrell, 2004).

The policy of states and the business practices of corporations are being held to public account by individual citizens who are in a position to make claims against their own governments or perceive an obligation, in many instances to others, that transcends national boundaries and national obligations. This chapter will consider whether liberalism possesses the resources to cope with these structural and cognitive transformations.

3.1   The liberal political space

Modern states are the product of a struggle that occurred between competing interests within the societies of Western Europe between the seventeenth and the nineteenth centuries, although the origins of state development can be traced back much further. From its beginnings, liberalism was a tradition preoccupied by order, and by the control of the political space of the state – a space that had to be mapped, its boundaries fixed with its corresponding ideas of constitutionalism, rights and law.

As liberalism developed, so different areas of concern came to light: the space of protections that were accorded the citizen via the territorial notion of individual rights; the space of civil society, the private associations that mediated between individuals and the state apparatus; the geographic region of the state, the territory over which a government claimed sovereignty; the space of the nation understood as a distinctive ethnic and cultural group; and the international arena, populated by other states, which was an anarchic space with limited controls over individual state power.[1]

Early liberal theorists like Hobbes negotiated uneasily between these spaces, advocating a curious but contemporary blend of absolutism, obedience to authority, individual freedom and security. Locke and later liberals such as Bentham, James Mill and his son John Stuart Mill each established, in their own way, the notion of the liberal state as the guarantor of individual liberties. The state was an artificial creation, a necessary evil, and although it might be possible to offer grounds for its legitimate interference in the lives of individuals, in defense of property for example, its fundamental raison d'être was to safeguard the liberties of individuals as a 'nightwatchman'. Beyond these basic safeguards, the state's activities were supposed to be restricted.

Liberal-democratic theorists sought to justify the sovereign power of the state while also placing limits on that power. This was Hobbes' dilemma and it remains the oft-quoted 'key question' for citizens in liberal-democracies today – how much liberty should one be prepared to sacrifice for the sake of those unique protections offered by the state. Whether that is, in fact, the key question is a moot point given that states are ambiguous creations at once minimal in their attempt to stay out of the affairs of citizens, while at the same time interventionist by regulating the behavior of the disobedient, coordinating state-sanctioned policy, funding state organized education programs, and so on. They are, moreover, extremely secretive collections of institutions that are keen to manage the public perception of government at home and abroad which makes any attempt to offer a sensible answer to Hobbes' dilemma difficult if not impossible.

Modern states' distinctive contemporary form is a result of a turbulent evolutionary process. Rather than a 'natural' and inevitable political outcome the form of the modern state is the result of centuries of conflict between groups within society and a series of economic and political trade-offs that have resulted in elite power-sharing and the (reluctant) extension of rights to ordinary citizens. The expansion of the franchise in the nineteenth and early twentieth centuries together with a growth in administrative reach, functions and capability – Max Weber's infamous term for this was *rationalization* – has resulted in different explanatory approaches that speak to the proper purpose and function of the state.

The following sections will focus on the space of the state and its negotiated relationship between the market, politics and citizenship. In Section 3.2, which examines the development of the liberal state over time, I will be following Macpherson's (1977) use of models that illustrate a different dimension of liberalism: protective, developmental and bureaucratic. Section 3.3 will focus on attempts by contemporary liberal thinkers to (unsuccessfully) co-opt the language of republican virtue and apply it to liberal citizenship. Section 3.4 will consider recent attempts that have been made by liberal theorists to extend liberalism beyond the confines of the state and into the international arena.

3.2   Protective, developmental and bureaucratic spaces

During the eighteenth and nineteenth centuries, two related concerns dominated liberal thought about the modern state and its proper function in the lives of ordinary citizens. Indeed, the ancient and modern question of 'how to restrain those in government from abusing their power' was complicated by the sociological fact of an expanding electorate. Hence, to the perennial question of political philosophy was added 'who should be allowed to vote?'

'All of the difficult questions of government', James Mill noted, 'relate to the means of restraining those in whose hands are lodged the powers necessary for the protection of all from making bad use of it' (1992, p. 6). To ensure that government pursued the community's interests, Mill thought that it must be made accountable to the community at large. 'It is very evident', he wrote in his *Essay on Government*, that 'if the community itself were the choosing body, the interest of the community and that of the choosing body would be the same' (1992, p. 27). However, the proper composition of the choosing body, the electorate, was by no means obvious. Indeed, for Mill, it automatically excluded children and women whose interests, he thought, could be made to coincide perfectly with those of their husbands and fathers.

Bentham addressed this issue of the expanding franchise directly by advocating what has been described as a model of 'protective democracy', though who was actually being protected and from what remains a matter of debate. Bentham advocated four goals for government: 'to provide subsistence', 'produce abundance', 'favour equality' and 'maintain security'.[2] However, in a manner reminiscent of John Locke's earlier attempts to subvert his own 'subsistence condition' – whereby 'enough and as good as' for everyone was trumped by the ability to hoard vast amounts of money instead – Bentham was careful to qualify his egalitarian leanings by arguing that there should be no direct legal guarantees to produce enough for everyone but only indirect ones so that the ability to sell one's labor in the employment market ought to be protected. As Macpherson (1977) points out in his discussion of Bentham, in a society like Britain's whose productive techniques were sufficient to produce enough for all far beyond the level of subsistence, Bentham's 'protections' for the laborer and the fruits of their labor amounted to 'an implicit support for a system which was based upon the power of a property owning class and the relative political impotence of a property-less one in which one had to sell their physical labor or starve to death' (p. 27). Government 'protections' amounted to a situation in which those in a position of relative economic and hence political power could exploit their advantage.

As a young man, Bentham was willing to sweep aside the established and befuddled traditions of legal theorizing in favor of clarity based upon what he considered the latest scientific advances (Bentham, 1988). In politics, however, his ambition was more muted. By drawing on the fundamental utilitarian principles of pleasure and pain, Bentham argued that redistributing wealth across society would be to misdiagnose the proper function of government and philosophically suspect to boot.

On the one hand, Bentham's commitments to theories of liberal political economy required government to advance the case for a free market society. His commitment to liberal egalitarianism, however, suggested that citizens ought to be protected from the market's inherently rapacious nature. Protection against the latter hinged upon extension of the franchise, secret ballot, frequent elections and freedom of the press.

But this left unanswered the question as to whether the poor, the uneducated and women should be left out of the political process. Was there a point in their own mental and moral development, he wondered, that would permit them access to the power of the ballot? Should they be admitted to political life once they could be trusted not to destroy the property of the landed? Should the franchise be extended only to those who own property – namely male householders? Or should it exclude those who were unable to read (Macpherson, 1977, pp. 35–7)?

All great reforming programs faced the 'transition problem', that is how to determine the best and most efficacious way of achieving the required changes. Mill and Bentham both identified the key problem of democracy: how to protect its members from the misuse of power by government functionaries. They also recognized the cause of unchecked political power which was the result of removing 'the people' from the business of government. Yet neither thought that most of the people were ready for the responsibilities of political decision-making nor would they be for some time.

It was John Stuart Mill who grabbed the theoretical nettle by describing liberalism as a progressive philosophy. If liberal societies were to function, then the character of liberal citizens would need to be 'developed'. His 'developmental model' of liberal politics emerged for reasons that were pragmatic as much as they were philosophically grounded.

By the middle of the nineteenth century working-class movements were becoming a significant political force in state politics. After the revolutions of 1848 in Europe – events that appalled and frightened political elites across the continent – and, in particular, the rise of the Chartist Movement in England during the same period, liberal theorists were forced to amend their political priorities. Mass involvement in politics was no longer a purely philosophical dilemma but a practical concern. Increased literacy among the working classes, access to local and national newspapers, and the ability of ordinary people to organize politically resulted in two Reform Acts in Britain, in 1867 and 1883, effectively quadrupling the electorate.

Mill was acutely sensitive to this change, which resulted in his own intellectual progress toward a qualified form of socialism.[3] As a consequence, he argued that it was the responsibility of states to see to the well-being of their citizens, replacing their condition of avoidable dependency with one of self-sufficiency. While still displaying a degree of paternalism common to liberal theorists at the time – 'The prospect of the future depends upon the degree in which they [the working class] can be made rational beings' – Mill recognized that citizens ought to be regarded as equals in society and not degraded simply because of their condition of labor (Mill, 1985, p. 123). In any case, they were unlikely to be content to 'know their place' for very much longer. Consequently, room should be made for them at the political table.

Mill's philosophical attachment to the notion of 'man as a progressive being' resulted in a somewhat ambiguous stance toward state intervention in the lives of individual citizens. Human dignity could be threatened in a society if a people's opportunities to participate in the regulation of public affairs were absent. But requiring or enforcing such participation was out of the question.

Mill was a believer in the benefits of liberal democracy to the moral development of individuals. He also thought that people were quite capable without instruction of defending their own interests. He wrote approvingly, for example, about New England townships at the end of *On Liberty*. Yet, his fascination with the latter did not extend, as it had with Jefferson, to embracing a more substantive view of political life.

Indeed, he explicitly contrasted his view of liberalism with the patriotic liberty and politics exercised in 'old times' by citizens who had to be mindful of the power of rulers and its misuse. Yet that was the past. The liberal-democratic present, he asserted, was such a time when men 'in the progress of human affairs' changed their minds about this relationship, and moved toward a form of leadership as tenancy, where these tenants if they misbehaved might have to forfeit their hold on power (1985, pp. 60–1).

For Mill, the greatest threat to individual freedom was not located in the figure of the tyrant, but from the collective mediocrity of majority opinion. To be 'self governing' was to be able to resist the vagaries of fashion within a modern society. It was necessary to educate people, but educate them so that they would recognize the benefits of representative government, a laissez-faire approach in economic relations and a sense of the public good. The proper purpose of government was to educate the working classes to attain the 'maturity of their faculties' and to develop the 'noble sentiments' which corresponded to socially useful feelings of altruism (1991, pp. 140–5).

Nonetheless, Mill was aware that the state still posed a threat to individual liberty. He desired people to fulfill their potential as 'progressive beings' and to become rational enough to accept the laws of liberal political economy. But he wanted them not just to be legally protected from the evils of government by institutional means. He wanted them to be equipped mentally and morally to defend themselves. 'Human beings', he noted, 'are only secure from evil at the hands of others, in proportion as they have the power of being, and are, self protecting' (1991, p. 245).

However, the philosopher turned politician[4] also noted that the chances of this being achieved were slight. Like Bentham (and Marx) before him, he recognized that in industrial society people simply did not have the time or opportunity to develop a 'cultivated mind' (1985, p. 145). He also recognized that the economic inequalities and dependencies within society that conspired against political freedoms were a result of historical accident, the unjust, often violent conquest of landowners in the past who still benefited from this thievery in the present to the detriment of others. And in his *Autobiography*, he made the profound observation that it simply would not be in the interest of a political elite to sponsor any sort of educational program that might conceivably threaten to reduce its power in the long run (1990, p. 103).[5]

Mill persisted, however, in his consideration of how intellectual and moral improvement could come about by asking what, if anything, government could or should do about it. If state-sponsored education programs would be taken as a threat to the ruling-elite then some other means of education would have to be found to provide the intellectual defenses he deemed necessary. To this end, other institutions would, Mill thought, provide the stimulus to criticism of the government – the press, juries and workers' cooperatives. By participation in these activities citizens could gain the experience necessary for 'a correct judgement of great practical affairs' (1985, p. 184).

Unfortunately if everyone had the vote as conditions stood, with self-interest dominating all the classes in society, the result was hardly likely to be enlightened. Therefore, those who were already enlightened, thanks to their own good fortune, were deserving of a greater number of votes than the unenlightened who were generally more numerous. This translated into the middle classes, employers, businessmen and professionals having more votes than wage earners. In his *Thoughts on Parliamentary Reform*, Mill suggested that 'if an unskilled labourer should have one vote, a skilled labourer should have two; a foreman perhaps three; a farmer, manufacturer, or trader, three or four; a professional or literary man, an artist, a public functionary, a university graduate, and an elected member of a learned society, five or six' (cited in Macpherson, 1977, p. 58).

Mill's philosophical commitments advocated radical reforms that he did not think were possible so he fell back on those measures practically available to him to move the slow process of education along. This was necessary for the growth of the independence of mind he valued so highly, the more so as the modern state threatened to 'dwarf its citizens' as he put it at the end of *On Liberty*.

Indeed, in addition to the threat of collective mediocrity the other great peril of modern living for Mill was the expanding bureaucratic reach of the modern state. As governments grew in size so their desire to collect more and more detailed information about individual citizens in order to perform efficiently and effectively would also expand. In time, the routine of organizational life would substitute for the power and activities of individual themselves; under these conditions, creative mental activity and the potential progressiveness of the governing body as well as the governed would also become stifled (1985, p. 184).

If Mill was one of the first to identify the problem of bureaucratic reach it was another nineteenth-century liberal, Max Weber, who proposed the solution. Consequently, it is to Weber that we turn to consider the final space, the 'bureaucratic space', of the liberal state and its antidote.

Weber offered one of the most influential liberal theories of the modern state based on the twin fundamentals of territory and violence. And like Mill, he thought that the age of the polis was long gone. Writing at the end of the nineteenth century in a period marked by the rapid development of industrial economies, large-scale migrations across the European continent, the extension of the franchise, mass parties, the growth of trade unions and the revolutionary events of the Paris Commune of 1871, it was evident to Weber that the city-state was not the modern state. Indeed, in a letter he wrote in 1906, Weber suggested that it was 'utterly ridiculous to see any connection between the high capitalism of today...with democracy or freedom in any sense of these words' (Gerth and Mills, 1946, p. 71). What was relevant, however, was the relation between capitalism, bureaucracy and the freedom of the individual. Capitalism and bureaucracy were connected because:

> the inner foundation of the modern capitalist business is calculation. In order to exist, it requires a system of justice and administration which, in principle at any rate, function in a rationally calculable manner according to stable, general norms, just as one calculates the predictable performance of a machine.
>
> (Weber, 1994, p. 148)

But what was the connection between bureaucracy and freedom? Weber addressed this question by asking how human beings could exercise their freedom when the development of modern state administrations directly challenged liberal freedoms on an epistemological as well as a political level. Traditional liberals like Hobbes or Locke might appeal to 'natural law' or 'natural right' to justify their theories of freedom and the state. But in an age marked by what he called 'disenchantment', the fate of a society 'which has eaten of the tree of knowledge' could hardly appeal to natural law.

If liberalism could not rely on the persuasions of a liberal metaphysics the alternative was justification based upon procedure, one guaranteed by law which in turn was supported by the state's power. People obeyed the state because the state's power, backed up by violence, was regarded as legitimate and this legitimacy extended to state officials. There was obedience because of the virtue of legality, a belief in the validity of legal statute and competence based on rationally created rules.

The size of modern states, Weber thought, demanded impersonal structures of authority, the bureaucracies with their hierarchies and rules of procedure, qualifying examinations that employed individuals based on their technical skill, competence and efficiency. Yet the not inconsiderable power that was granted to bureaucrats through their expertise and access to secret information posed a real dilemma for Weber as it had for Mill before him.[6] The institutions of modern states were necessary but the dangers to freedom were considerable. Rule by bureaucrat was a distinct possibility unless there existed a suitable countervailing power.

Weber's solution, for all his appeal to a justification beyond metaphysics, was institutional and esoteric. A strong parliament was required which would create a competitive training ground for politicians and because of the very nature of politics – its spontaneity and unpredictability – a counterweight to bureaucratic power. Political decisions were concerned with compromise rather than driven by efficiency, and successful politicians were chosen on the basis of their oratorical skill and the magical qualities of 'charisma' rather than technical prowess. The choice was clear: either a state would be run by officials so that the mass of citizens was left without freedom or rights in a bureaucratic, authoritarian political space, or citizens would be integrated into the state by making them its 'co-rulers'. Weber's liberal project was to create 'a nation of masters' (1994, p. 129).

The extent of this 'co-rulership', however, extended only as far as the ballot box. Weber referred to representative democracy as 'plebiscitary leadership democracy', and political leadership as an 'elected dictatorship'. Unlike Mill's earlier commitment to the development of the moral and intellectual resources required of all citizens, democracy for Weber was best understood as the mechanism which ensured the selection of effective national leadership through periodic voting. The function of elections and the purpose of citizenship were to choose leaders and the mass party machine would mobilize the electorate in favor of one candidate or another. During such occasions, it became 'the specific function of the leading economic and political strata to be the bearer's of the nation's sense of political purpose. In fact this is the only political justification for their existence' (1994, p. 21).

Weber attempted to find an effective balance between legitimate authority, talented leadership and competent administration. His was a restrictive theory of democracy – restrictive because democracy's function was simply the efficient choosing of political leaders and because any extension of the electorate's role in public affairs was considered undesirable. The masses were dangerous because they lacked political maturity. They were politically uneducated 'philistines' who confused ethics with politics.

High emotions did not make for good judgement *except* when it came to choosing leaders. Ordinary voters were, Weber thought, able to make a choice between different candidates, although they might not be able to discriminate among complex policy options. Democracy in the modern sense then was about providing politicians with opportunities to 'impress' the electorate by appeal to emotion rather than reason, thereby weeding out the bores from those most able to win the struggle for votes and power.

To offset the tendency toward rule by official, Weber put his faith in charismatic political leaders rather than the masses, extraordinary individuals who could inspire members of their own party and the electorate toward great things. The elite would necessarily be wealthy – politics, he said, needed to be dominated by people who live for it and not from it (p. 319) – and, quite naturally, this increased the propensity toward hubris and corruption. 'There has never been', says Weber, 'a social stratum which did not do this one way or another' (p. 319). Effective leadership required a rare combination of passion, judgement and a sense of personal and public responsibility, the ability to make difficult decisions, even unethical decisions, and to stand by them. Because politics was a vocation rather than a career, one that was inherently corrupting, few would be either willing or able to deal with what Weber described as the 'diabolical powers' that came with the management of state violence (p. 365).

Weber provides the first thoroughly modern and recognizable description of liberal democracy, the kind of democracy that is prevalent in most developed nations in the twenty-first century. Unlike John Stuart Mill, the desired transition was not from an unenlightened to an enlightened electorate but the discovery of talented and visionary politicians – a benign elite – who would lead a country into historic greatness. That Weber did not think that such individuals existed or were, at least, extremely rare finds added a profound and pessimistic sense to his political vision for the future.[7]

Subsequent authors, notably Joseph Schumpeter's realist interpretation of politics and Robert Dahl's pluralist model of democracy have built on Weber's observations but the fundamental thrust of the argument has remained the same. Democracy in the modern world cannot mean rule by the people in any obvious sense of the term 'people' and 'rule' (Schumpeter, 1976, p. 284). Democracy has come to mean 'the rule of the politician' and the function of the electorate (who are generally held in extremely low regard as little more than emotionally immature political illiterates who descend to an even lower form of mental activity when politics is mentioned) who are and should be easily fooled by the ruling elite. History, for Schumpeter,

> consists of a succession of short run situations that may alter the course of events for good. If all the people can in the short run be 'fooled' step by step into something they do not really want, and if this is not an exceptional case which we could afford to neglect, then no amount of retrospective common sense will alter the fact that in reality they neither raise nor decide issues but that the issues that shape their fate are normally raised and decided for them.
>
> (1976, p. 264)

Both Weber and Schumpeter were not describing a situation that they wished to change. They were describing one they wished to defend. The essence of liberal democracy for these thinkers, indeed for all liberal theorists who tend to fear the spectre of democracy which, in some form or other, must mean dissent from established political authority, is to circumscribe civic activity so that civic ability is limited to replacing one set of governing officials with another. To suggest otherwise, would be to suggest that democracy in the modern world possesses a meaning which, in fact, it does not – although to openly admit this, as one commentator points out, would be tantamount to professional suicide (Posner, 2003). To persist in the advocacy of those 'airy myths of direct democracy' would be to endorse a political model that would invariably lead to 'hyperresponsiveness' on the part of politicians – as they pander to the whims of a suspect electorate – and to create a recipe for inefficient government (King, 1997, p. 166).

3.3　The virtues of being a liberal citizen

The essentially passive role accorded the liberal citizen in much liberal-democratic theory has not restrained contemporary thinkers from attempting to expand the notion wherever possible. Citizenship is a dynamic, evolutionary concept affording state protections and guaranteeing formal liberties. It is also a human right as the National Assembly of France declared in 1789 and the UN Declaration of Human Rights of 1948 stipulated in Article 15.1. In its modern liberal form, it includes a minimal but nonetheless significant notion of political equality and autonomy, whose legal safeguards provide a space for the individual to pursue their interests free from interference.

In the twentieth century, the language of liberal citizenship provided enormous discursive support to formerly disenfranchised groups who have turned to the liberal language of rights, both individual and (somewhat controversially) group rights, to make their claims upon states. However, while some commentators rightly point to the internal logic of citizenship, whose benefits (arguably) 'become ever more universal and egalitarian' (Faulks, 2001, p. 3) the abstract nature of much of the discussion concerning liberal citizenship has, argue critics, provided much of the cover for the enormous inequalities that persist within developed societies.

For many liberals, the very hallmark of the human individual was freedom of the will, autonomy rather than heteronomy. As a consequence, in a political context, the question invariably arose as to why one autonomous will would submit to another. In Rousseau's immortal phrase, 'how can one enter into a society with others and remain as free as before?'

The short answer to that deceptively simple question for liberal thinkers was provided by redefining political freedom as consent to legitimate authority, rather than participation in political life. By abstracting from the actual society in which one lived to an imagined society governed by reason alone an imaginary society was created, populated by abstract individuals who possessed formal political freedoms, who were motivated by self-interest and who competed with one another within an economic *and* political marketplace. This imaginary state of nature and social contract provided the background conditions that justified the limits placed upon the liberal practice of citizenship ensuring that it was confined to voting in elections and obeying legitimate authority.

All liberal citizens were and are equal, formally, before the law. Yet much has been made of the limitations of formal equality when gross economic disparities severely restrict access to educational opportunity, health care and, ultimately, political office. What is required, some argue, is a substantive notion of equality to supplement the formal notion which would in turn require real, not to mention revolutionary, reform of liberal institutions (Sen, 1987; Nussbaum, 1990, 1992).

The contradictions of liberal-democratic theory are clearly highlighted within the political sphere, where the electorate is considered too stupid to make informed political choices but just clever enough to choose good leadership. This paradox of liberal-democratic citizenship is present because of the different expectations that occur within liberalism itself. It is simply unclear whether it is intended as a theory that advocates the regulation of self-interested individuals within a free market or one that ensures that all of its members are able to realize their individual potential as progressive beings, or some combination of the two. Indeed, more than one commentator has noted that at the heart of liberal citizenship there is a huge contradiction: 'the more it encourages an active and critical democratic citizenship, the more it shifts the polity away from liberal values towards more democratic ones' (Macpherson, 1977; Stokes and Carter, 2002, p. 31). There is a tension, then, within liberal democracy between liberalism in some form and democracy.

To be clear, liberal democracy *was* a revolutionary program, but a program that was devised to cope with the political problems of seventeenth-century English society. It was radical in its attempt to disable kingly power. The legacy of Charles I's beheading – during the time of the first and only English republic – lead to Habeas Corpus (1679), the Bill of Rights (1689) and the Act of Settlement (1701) which effectively rested independent power away from the monarch and entrusted it to parliament.

However, the kind of democracy parliament favored was always a qualified, *liberalized* one (Parekh, 1993). John Locke, hero of the glorious revolution of 1688 and intellectual godfather of the American Revolution, may have given all citizens an imaginary, natural right to property and to resist tyranny. But a close reading of Locke's *Second Treatise* shows that both were severely compromised. The social contract was a fiction, a rationalization of the existing order based on the uneven distribution of property ownership within English society. And Locke certainly did not want to endanger the existence of an institution – the institution of property – that he had spent so much intellectual labor defending (Zinn, 1990). This feature of Natural Rights doctrine was not lost upon those American revolutionaries who read Locke and who feared both political innovation and the rise of democracy.

Since the end of World War II the contradictions of liberal democracy have become more acute for a number of reasons both domestic and international. Consequently, the role of the state and the role of the citizen have been reexamined and to some extent redefined.

The question that many liberal theorists have turned to in recent times is the *character* of liberal citizenship. Much of the writing on this subject has been penned by North American authors who have responded less to the challenge of citizenship in a global age and more to the demands that liberal societies face in increasingly multicultural contexts. Nonetheless, the adoption by liberal theorists of the quintes-sentially republican notion of virtue (understood as a form of character education) is significant and reveals much about the shortcomings of the liberal model of citizenship as it was traditionally conceived.

The conceptual transformation that occurred in the eighteenth century, from the virtues of citizens, a republican idea, to the virtues of institutions of government, has to some degree been reversed by contemporary advocates of the 'liberal virtues' who specifically acknowledge the requirements of citizen virtue in at least some form. One commentator notes that:

> the operation of liberal institutions is affected in important ways by the character of citizens (and leaders)...at some point, the attenuation of individual virtue will create pathologies with which liberal political contrivances, however technically perfect their design, simply cannot cope. To an extent difficult to measure but impossible to ignore, the viability of liberal society depends on its ability to engender a virtuous citizenry.
>
> (Galston, 1991, p. 217)

These modern day virtues, however, retain their liberal credentials by being defined within the arena of liberal *society* rather than as an integral feature of a substantive liberal 'political community', a context supportive of private rather than public freedoms. It is, furthermore, quite clear that the 'liberal virtues' are intended as a response to some of the criticisms that were voiced against liberalism by their critics and that appeared in books like Alasdair MacIntyre's *After Virtue*. Indeed, this project appears to be part of a more assertive liberalism that seeks to incorporate within its philosophy concepts normally considered extraneous to the paradigm. The result has been a description of the virtuous liberal citizen with a distinctive liberal character, possessing just those virtues – of tolerance, independence, self-reflection and a sense of justice – required of an individual living in a complex, heterogeneous society.

At the outset, theorists of liberal virtue introduce a sense of 'realism' into their accounts that they charge their republican critics with ignoring. They point out that the fabled city-state community, from which the notion of civic virtue is derived, is very different from the context of the nation-state. The philosophy of liberalism is, moreover, very different from the republican who might have included the notion of a civic education, enforced participation in public affairs, military training and a 'love of country' within a theory of virtue.

A tradition of individual protective rights, a non-participatory political culture, nationalism rather than patriotism, and the fact of ethical pluralism within modern societies means that for many liberal theorists, civic virtue cannot be taught by the state. Instead, liberal theorists begin by asking what may be expected from un-virtuous yet *reasonable* liberal citizens in modern constitutional states, and what resources might 'realistically' be available for the generation of the necessary virtues. Crucially, the latter must be achieved without the sacrifice of liberal rights. In this section, I will examine three such accounts by prominent liberal theorists.

William Galston in his account provides a full list of the liberal virtues. There are virtues for the economy, society and politics of which independence and tolerance, imagination, initiative, drive, courage, self-restraint and the capacity to discern the talent in those running for office are all included. Galston is wary of a public-oriented conception of virtue preferring instead to see the liberal virtues generated within the private environment of the home, or the semi-private/public context of civil society. He also contends that an important side effect of living within a liberal culture is that it is almost inevitable that illiberal practices should become more liberal as a result. This is a common assumption, what might be termed the 'liberalism by osmosis' thesis, that is shared by nearly all liberal thinkers who write on this subject.

In Galston's view, liberalism is a distinctive and non-neutral political philosophy. It is, however, minimally perfectionist by providing what he regards as the functional basics for living in a modern liberal society falling short of a full definition of the good life.[8] While liberalism does possess a theory of the good it may be defined by identifying the *summum malum*, those things within a society, such as poverty and malnutrition, that nearly all would agree are bad and ought to be reduced (1991, p. 182). What is made perfectly clear, however, is that liberalism specifically restricts identifying 'a good' and then coercively introducing that good into liberal society via the state.

The question of 'how one should live' is left entirely up to the individual, and any move beyond what is functionally required by the state is, in Galston's opinion, unacceptably intrusive. Hence, the promotion of autonomy, the quintessential liberal ideal that we find in liberal thinkers like Kant and John Stuart Mill and that they regarded as so essential to the moral and political well-being of an individual, is not included in Galston's program. He states:

> Liberalism is about the protection of diversity, not the valorization of choice. To place an ideal of autonomous choice at the core of liberalism is in fact to narrow the range of possibilities available

within liberal societies. It is a drive toward a kind of uniformity, disguised in the language of liberal diversity.

(Galston, fn. 12, p. 359)

What liberalism is about, in Galston's account, is the protection of diversity. By taking this idea as definitive of the liberal state he argues that it is just and fair to respect and tolerate an individual or group who considers the non-autonomous or unreflective life worth living.

Stephen Macedo holds the conviction, much as Galston does, that the acquisition of liberal virtue occurs through the unconscious effects of living within a liberal culture. Isolated, illiberal groups of citizens within this environment cannot escape the pervasive influence of liberalism, and even someone as illiberal as a Nazi, Macedo suggests, will have to 'play' at being a Nazi because it is just impossible to be a *real* Nazi in liberal society without being punished (1990, p. 260).

However, because Macedo wishes to provide a response to republican/ communitarian criticisms of liberalism his virtues are part of a more substantive notion of liberalism and liberal 'community'. Macedo argues in *Liberal Virtue*, that the system of laws generated and supported by a liberal political system, the notion of 'public justification' that refers to legislators providing public reasons for their actions by appealing to the shared convictions of the citizenry, and the liberal virtues that he assumes are largely already present throughout society, form a sufficient platform from which the notion of liberal community may be advanced. Macedo suggests that liberalism embraces certain, widely shared and accepted moral values and these values serve as the basis for a substantive notion of community.

Macedo identifies the liberal virtues of impartiality, a willingness to engage with those people with whom one disagrees, independence and initiative, and suggests that these are cultivated by the liberal state's political processes. Yet these virtues require a degree of personal commitment, an allegiance to a liberal public good and to liberal public reasons and principles. This is important if dialogue in the political realm, which Macedo calls 'the realm of last resort', is to remain 'reasonable'. Politics is an activity, contra Machiavelli, in which people are encouraged not to display their differences but to highlight their commonalities, to set their deepest convictions to one side in order to form a consensus of some sort. The ability to do this is, for Macedo, part of what makes up the character of a good liberal citizen and what makes liberal politics so different from the republican version. The inability or unwillingness to embrace this form of politics will result in exclusion from the political process, asserts Macedo, and will invoke criticism from those citizens who are good liberals. 'People who disagree about religious beliefs or other commitments must regard common political principles as regulative of all their interactions with others. Liberalism requires, therefore, not merely an overlapping consensus but a consensus that practically overrides all competing values' (1990, p. 53).

Macedo wishes to advocate a form of 'political community' that encourages the development of a minimal set of character traits in its citizens, while, as far as possible, leaving people alone to pursue their own conceptions of the good. His is a more assertive approach rejecting what he regards as the tendency of liberals 'to minimize what they stand for and to evade their ultimate commitments' (pp. 50–1). Indeed, the community he wishes to advocate would necessarily undermine illiberal, hierarchical ways of living including the practices of some religious groups. The liberal public virtues, he notes, inevitably attenuate the 'devotion to one's own projects and allegiances' encouraging a 'degree of superficiality' (p. 247).

Because liberal virtue is civic *and* personal in Macedo's account, authorities of all kinds come into question (except liberal ones) and other character traits such as deference to authority and humility are sacrificed. Perhaps, most distinctive of all, Macedo's politics is exclusive. It excludes those who are either unwilling or unable to play by the rules defined by liberals and it does so in order to maintain stability and order within the political realm. In fact, so constrained might liberal politics become that it is unclear what sort of political discussion, beyond a technical discussion, might be permissible in Macedo's account as substantive discussion is likely to inflame those passions that Macedo wants to suppress. Moreover, it is not clear whether exercising a high degree of restraint within political life is the best approach to achieving anything more than a superficial and frustrated consensus within society.

Nonetheless, this account of liberal citizenship is intriguing not least because it expands the notion beyond the minimal requirements of protective democracy yet, like Galston's account, it resists moving toward a developmental model with the subsequent institutional changes that it would require. Indeed, without significant reform of the institutions of liberal society, like education for example, it is highly questionable that taking people 'as they are' is going to lead to the kind of tolerant, open-minded liberal community that Macedo desires.

A somewhat different approach, and the final example of liberal virtue to be considered here, is advanced by Shelley Burtt. Burtt's argument starts from the assumption that liberal civic virtue simply cannot base itself upon the traditional republican techniques of virtue inculcation, programs of civic education or a notion of civic duty that emphasizes the public good over private interest. The latter fails because of what Burtt considers an unacceptable notion of a 'love of country', which she interprets as selfless sacrifice to a public good. The former fails because she contends that modern states seem to have enough difficulty educating citizens to a decent standard of literacy without also having to consider the merits of civic duty and public service. To attempt to alter the scenario in favor of an education of virtue would require the focus of resources and political power toward a highly controversial end and Burtt, quite rightly, considers this most unlikely (1990, p. 26).

Her solution is an appeal to a normative psychology of self-interest, something that she considers both relevant and uncontroversial, a suitable conceptual basis for the liberal virtues. In the writings of De Tocqueville, Harrington, and Gordon and Trenchard (joint authors of *Cato's Letters*) she finds a theoretical model suited to the modern, liberal environment – one that interestingly enough borrows from authors from the republican tradition who were interested in constitutional solutions to political problems. In these examples, virtue is generated by self-interested individuals compelled to act when their interests are threatened. Their combining together to form associations to oppose an external threat consequently extends and expands the notion of self-interest with which people enter the association. In this form, the solutions to the problem of generating virtue rely on making the public good matter to individuals, thereby drawing it closer to private interests.

Burtt describes the application of self-interest to virtue as the 'privatization of virtue' in contrast to theories that emphasize or educate citizens toward allegiance to an identifiable public or common good. Combining self-interest and social action seems to hold the key to liberal virtue. And of course, this private virtue is still public in the important sense that the transformative qualities of the 'public' arena of secondary associations remain crucial to the development of enlightened self-interest and the liberal virtues.

Burtt expects to find self-interested individuals within liberal society. Her hope is that an enlightened form of self-interest will generate liberal virtues via the interactions that occur within institutions *already* in existence in liberal society. 'The media, the schools, voluntary associations, local political organizations, family and church can all reinforce the understanding of a self as a bearer of political rights that deserve realizations' (p. 365).

Criticisms of these liberal virtues and the institutions that support them can, Burtt suggests, be safely rejected particularly when the critics are of a neo-Aristotelian persuasion. 'How will Americans be brought to see, amid the challenges of tedious jobs, limited incomes, family problems, and everyday personal tragedies and triumphs, the value of a full political life in the Aristotelian sense?' (1995, p. 150).

However, although many of Burtt's criticisms of republicanism hit the mark, the choice of Aristotle is somewhat ingenuous given the theoretical depth of the republican tradition and the varied themes that exist within it. Moreover, a model of self-interest unless it is heavily qualified by a consideration of the motives, commitments and values of individuals is likely to have little explanatory power. Without some consideration of the influence of personal and public ethics upon self-interest, the power of this concept to explain and predict individual or group action is seriously diminished. The power of emotional attachments, group affiliation and personal belief are all factors that are likely to influence how one assesses and identifies one's own self-interests. It is equally problematic to suggest that economic self-interest is somehow a more natural condition in which humanity finds itself, selfish genes notwithstanding.

The notion of virtue as a result of enlightened self-interest worked well theoretically and was evident as a practical possibility in both de Tocqueville's and Cato's America. Yet this owed its success to the very public political culture that prefigured and to some degree remained with America after the revolution.[9] Tocqueville's analysis included the necessary institutional supports and practices to make the exercise of enlightened self-interest a possibility, and avoid its decline into egoism. Religion was also a central element, as was enforced jury duty, active (voluntary) participation in associations, education, and a particular view of womanhood and the family which modern liberals might find unappealing.[10]

Relying upon the liberalizing effects of contemporary liberal societies also begins to look suspect under closer examination. Burtt's list included the media, schools, voluntary associations, local political organizations, the family and church. There is some empirical evidence for the positive influence of the media upon individuals (Budge, 1996, pp. 19–20). Yet there is a vast amount of competing evidence to suggest that the media cannot be relied upon to promote the liberal virtues, particularly when so much of it is owned by a dozen or so individuals whose ends are not clearly defined, but are almost certainly aimed 'downmarket' (McChesney, 1998).

Schools provide an important (political) space of opportunity for the virtues to be encouraged, yet here too there is evidence to suggest that they may be undermined by business interests in public education coupled with a severe lack of investment. The family too can no longer be automatically expected to offer the traditional supports it once did to notions of virtue for a variety of reasons.[11]

Local neighborhood organizations, often seen as the interface between individuals and the outside world, definitely perform an important function with respect to the creation of virtue. Yet as one commentator recently pointed out, there has been a tendency for the purposes of local organizations to get lost. 'Instead of the local community organization that mediates between individual families and the wider society, we now have privatized individuals, on the one hand, and national non-profit bureaucracies on the other hand that try to drum up support from an uninterested public through telethons and mass mailings' (Wuthnow, 1991, p. 299).

Burtt's, Macedo's and Galston's analyses all reveal a profound conservatism in the advocacy of the liberal virtues. While they strive to co-opt the language of republicanism to expand their own notions of liberal citizenship they shy away from the institutional reforms that would be required to generate the virtues. Instead, they prefer to rely on the same self-interested psychology advanced by earlier classical liberal thinkers together with questionable empirical assumptions about the pervasiveness of their own set of liberal values and the transformative capacity of secondary liberal institutions in civil society. In addition, all of them share the additional fear of a form of politics that is turbulent, that considers the fundamental questions of communal life – how should we live? – in favor of polite, technical discussions that do not challenge the raison d'être of the state.

'Like all liberals', noted George Orwell of Bertrand Russell in 1939, 'he is better at pointing out what is desirable than at explaining how to achieve it. He sees clearly enough that the essential problem of to-day is "the taming of power" and that no system except democracy can be trusted to save us from unspeakable horrors ... But unfortunately he does not tell us how we are to set about getting these things; he merely utters what amounts to a pious hope that the present state of things will not endure' (1998, pp. 311–12).

Could the same be said of contemporary liberal scholarship? That conclusion would be harsh. But it is clear from the analysis offered here that the concerns of liberal theorists tend to be highly conservative and state-centric. The concept of virtue for liberal thinkers is enlisted in order to defend the existing liberal order, not alter it. Liberal virtues are not the virtues of politically active citizens. It is, therefore, at least questionable whether the concept of liberal citizenship and the liberal virtues as they currently stand possess the necessary resources to face the challenges posed by global political and economic crises.

3.4 After the liberal state?

The question that preoccupied liberals like Weber at the end of the nineteenth century was how to find a justification for the existence of liberalism when the traditional metaphysical supports provided by natural law were no longer compelling. That question has continued to preoccupy liberal thinkers up to the present time.

The main target of a work like John Rawls' *Political Liberalism*, for example, was metaphysical liberalism of the kind found in Locke, Kant or Mill. Rawls and his followers attempted to replace philosophically suspect notions like autonomy for concepts that they assumed all liberal citizens share, though this empirical assumption has come under severe scrutiny (Gray, 1993). Instead, they advocate principles for a just liberal order that they assume would be considered uncontroversial within what they regard as 'reasonable pluralist' societies.

Few appear to recognize the contingency of liberal citizenship, its historically specific characteristics or the existential challenge of living in a global environment. Efforts that have been made to transfer political liberalism to the global level have struggled with the structural consequences of an international order that systematically fails to give members of different peoples equal chances to influence the decisions that shape their fate (Rawls, 2001). Indeed, the failure by liberalism to account for the fact that international social and economic inequalities have the greatest impact upon the world's worst-off persons has led some to consider such accounts of a global liberal order simply 'implausible' (Pogge, 1992, 1994, 2001; Beitz, 2000).

Nonetheless, the liberal state and liberal citizenship are changing in actuality even if liberal theorists persist in working within the imagined space of the nation-state. Indeed, how could it be otherwise, given the comparative decrease in state power over social and economic policy since the collapse of the Bretton Woods agreement in the early 1970s; the corresponding neo-liberal revolution in the 1980s which directly challenged the authority of states by requiring the import restrictions and regulations on foreign borrowing to be relaxed; and severe restrictions on policy options for domestic governments in the 1990s that, in

some cases, resulted in economic sanction and political turmoil
(Bauman, 2000, p. 186)?

The consequences of this pattern of development have been summarized by Rodrik (2002) who notes that the continued development of
the global economy – thanks in large part to the growth in the 1990s of
'the Washington consensus', a model of economic development that
crowded out other alternative theoretical models – poses a very real
'political trilemma' to the existence of the liberal state and, consequently,
liberal citizenship in its current form. Rodrik argues:

> If we want to push global economic integration much further, we
> have to give up on either the nation state or mass politics. If we want
> to maintain and deepen democracy, we have to choose between the
> nation state and international economic integration. And if we want
> to keep the nation state, we have to choose between democracy and
> international economic integration.
>
> (2002, p. 13)

Access to political power, which was already restricted within liberal
democracies, is being further removed from ordinary citizens as political
and economic policy goals are made in secret by unelected and largely
unaccountable officials. Once these institutions have set the agenda for
national policy, domestic groups access to, and their control over, national
economic policy-making is limited thereby ensuring that competing
demands are not brought to the table. The distance between electors,
elected officials and unelected officials with enormous unchecked
powers grows as economic interdependency increases, empowering
some and not others.

The cartography of the liberal nation-state offers no way out of this
scenario. To move beyond the problem one must move beyond the
confines of liberalism and its political space.

Understanding the concept of citizenship afresh has become an
increasingly pressing problem precisely because it has become so difficult
to ignore the global dimensions of liberty and equality as well as excru-
ciating poverty and disempowerment. At the same time, conventional
ideas of liberty and equality are under assault from governments that
wish to remain 'competitive' economically or wish to restrain the exercise
of freedom expressed in protest against government in a period of
perpetual war (Vidal, 2002). This scenario requires a move away from
the methodological territorialism of the state toward a new non-
territorial cartography of political life (Scholte, 1999).

3.5 Conclusion

Change the context, as Jeremy Bentham once noted, and you change the opportunities for involvement in the political process. When the young Bentham said this he was referring to the injustices and corruption of eighteenth-century England and to a system of governance that assumed that people were uninterested in political life because they were poor and, therefore, stupid. But as Bentham pointed out, the poor were 'ignorant' because they were 'nailed to the work board' and had no leisure to act or think. They could hardly be blamed for being oblivious to worldly affairs as a result of their poverty. In fact, the poor should be given more time to think, more leisure, not simply because it would make for a more worthwhile existence but for an eminently sensible political reason – if you have no time to think about what the government is doing in your name then your goodwill may be taken advantage of. Indeed, says Bentham, if you are unable to determine whether those who govern do so in their interests or yours, 'what then is the difference between this and being governed by one's enemies?' (1988, p. 122).

The reforms that Bentham and other reformist liberals initiated in the eighteenth and nineteenth centuries developed into an institutional architecture that, outbreaks of democracy notwithstanding, has changed remarkably little. Government from Bentham's time on was regarded as an essentially technical operation, requiring skilled and experienced leadership with specialized training, an idea that has its origins in anti-democratic dialogues like Plato's *Republic*.

Yet, it is now clear that the mechanisms of government cannot continue to operate as they have done for the past three hundred years because the context has changed again. 'The closed space of national politics', argues one commentator, 'no longer exists. Society and the public realm are constituted out of conflictual spaces that are at once individualized, transnationally open and defined in opposition to one another. It is in these spaces that each cultural group tests and lives out its hybrid' (Beck, 2000a, p. 173).

Like republicanism in the modern period, the issue for liberalism in the *post*modern epoch is one of *size*. 'How far can the boundaries of the nation-state extend before they cease to make sense?' 'How far do the duties of citizens reach when their loyalties and allegiances are multiple?'

4
Republicanism Revisited

> Thus not in vain the power of the intellect... that dischargeth
> us from the fetters of a most narrow kingdom and promoteth
> us to the freedom of a truly august realm, which freeth us from
> an imagined poverty and straineth to the possession of the
> myriad riches of so vast a space, of so worthy a field of so many
> cultivated worlds...
>
> – Giordano Bruno, cited in Koyre, 1957, p. 42

The previous chapter examined the political space of liberalism and it is to that context we return now to examine the approach taken by contemporary republican authors. To date, the latter have tended to adopt a conciliatory tone. All too conscious of the more outmoded and dubious elements of their own tradition, contemporary republicans approach modern political dilemmas by adopting a preferred republican principle or idea – for example, the principle of non-domination or a program of active citizenship – and apply it to the context of the liberal nation-state in an attempt to show that republicanism is still relevant.

This chapter begins by examining the revival of republicanism within the context of liberalism but moves quickly toward a consideration of non-state forms of citizen activity as an expression of a distinctively postmodern form of politics, one that operates at different levels within and beyond the state. The plurality of political spaces in postmodernity and the nature of economic, social and political life in the contemporary environment demand that republicanism not simply accommodate itself within existing liberal structures but provide a description of how 'the many' (cosmorepublican citizens) can check 'the few' (elected representatives; unelected officials in transnational organizations). In so doing, it should be possible to reverse the modern understanding of politics as essentially a technique of control toward an understanding of politics as the active practice of resistance.

4.1 Bringing the state back in

Historically, the kind of small-scale political activity of which republicans speak was, as we have seen, toward the end of the nineteenth century, being dropped from political discourse with increasing regularity. The centralized state was fast becoming the proper subject of study and many theorists have continued with this trend at the expense, some have argued, of both civil society and politics (Sandel, 1988).

As a consequence, it has often been suggested that taking charge of the state arena is necessary; though quite how this is to happen is left unclear. One approach has been to suggest that the idea of the state's proper function, the extent of its reach into civil society and the semi-private realm of the corporation, should be appropriated in order to defend a republican conception of freedom.

If being unfree consists in 'being subject to the potentially capricious will or the potentially idiosyncratic judgement of another' (Pettit, 1999, p. 5) then freedom requires real defenses from arbitrary interference in *all* of the spheres of a citizen's life and not just the formal guarantees offered by liberal constitutional government. The proper purpose of the state, if liberal ideals are to have any real meaning, is not only to protect citizens from unjust or unnecessary interference as they go about pursuing their own personal goals, it is also to ensure that citizens do not fall into a condition of avoidable dependence. Indeed, Quentin Skinner has gone so far as to say that the state has a duty to each and every citizen to liberate them, 'from such personal exploitation and dependence, [and, moreover] to prevent its own agents...from behaving arbitrarily in the course of imposing the rules that govern our common life' (1998, p. 119).

In a similar vein, Philip Pettit has attempted to reconfigure elements from the republican tradition and transform what was, in most cases, an essentially elite program of freedom for 'mainstream males with property' to a universal ideal for all members of a contemporary, democratic society with existing liberal-democratic institutions. Working out the implications of such a view is his declared purpose and he suggests that the motivating principle of republican 'freedom as non domination' provides the legitimacy for increased state involvement in society and the economy.

Domination for Pettit includes the 'capacity to interfere, on an arbitrary basis, in certain choices that the other is in a position to make' (1997, pp. 4, 52). Republican freedom counters this by arguing that the practice of domination occurs within society and that it is a problem that needs to be acknowledged as it undermines the exercise of other liberal freedoms. Liberal thinkers fail to make this connection, suggests Pettit, because they do not recognize that a difference in social, economic and political power can be inimical to freedom. Consequently, they see 'nothing inherently oppressive about some people having dominating power over others... This relative indifference to power or domination has made liberalism tolerant of relationships in the home, in the workplace, in the electorate, and elsewhere, that the republican must denounce as paradigms of domination and unfreedom' (p. 9).

If domination is the problem for Pettit, then the state is cast as the solution. Indeed, what Pettit recommends is a degree of state involvement that liberals would probably reject as undue interference in the lives of individual citizens but that republicans concerned with non-domination regard as essential to improving and safeguarding the exercise of liberty. In short, the version of republicanism that Pettit advances is for a model of a welfare-state which would exert considerable influence in both the economy and society in the name of non-domination, requiring considerable expertise to boot.

In related vein, David Miller also offers a state-centric interpretation of republicanism but his project, while sharing some similarities with Pettit's, addresses the issue of the centrality of the nation and the importance of nationalism to the citizen psyche. Miller's fundamental observation is that nationalism is important to the modern psyche because for most people it is perceived to be important and generally has an enormous impact on the lives of ordinary citizens. Indeed, nationality, for Miller, is *the* political identity required before political discussion within diverse multicultural communities and between transnational 'communities' can begin. It is the core commitment, Miller argues, which requires a prior allegiance to the public good of a bounded, territorial community.

The motivation for individuals to participate politically comes, Miller thinks, from the notion that one might make a contribution to the cultural development of a particular polity. In order to make this possible, Miller expands the classical notion of republicanism, with its emphasis on exclusivity, to include a space for widespread contributions by individuals to the national character or 'common public culture' (1995, p. 450).

The aim of Miller's approach is to recast nationalism as cultural bilingualism. His intention is to show that different cultures can not only enjoy peaceful coexistence within a given territory but feel at home in their adopted society in a way that they currently do not. Crucially, the latter is achieved by each and every individual possessing the ability to contribute to the public conversation ultimately redefining that society in the process. National identity, according to Miller, is a precursor to this 'conversation', 'an addition to rather than a replacement for ethnic consciousness' (1995, p. 138).

The flip side of this argument is that if minority groups within a society wish to persuade the majority to change their views over a particular policy or principle, according to Miller, '[they] must first know what view [the majority] now hold, and this demands knowledge of their culture, history, and practices' (1995, p. 180). To give a specific example, Muslim primary schools in Britain were recently allocated state funding on the grounds, not of cultural integrity, but through a publicly recognized right of the equal access of religious groups to public funds after British Muslims lobbied parliament. Other denominations, including Catholic and Jewish schools, had received state support for some time. So here, there was an appeal by the Muslim community to widely held principles rather than a claim made on behalf of a particular culture.[1] This example illustrates the approach Miller's republican citizens might take when making claims in the political arena. While particular concerns and interests are advanced, they must be made in a manner suitable to the public realm, taking into account the principles by which the polity is governed and couched in the language of citizenship.

Nationality, then, is the mechanism for an expanded notion of republican citizenship for Miller because he thinks that people believe nationality matters. Republican citizenship, for that matter any theory of citizenship, must acknowledge this fact since nationality provides a sense of obligation to others which would otherwise, in his opinion, reduce the notion of community to an empty form of contractarianism – the reduction of a community to the sum of those actions that arise between self-interested individuals. Without this communitarian commitment, Miller contends, states would be little more than minimalist arrangements that provide only basic security for their members.

Both Pettit and Miller's arguments are provocative contributions and advance the case for republicanism within the context of liberal states. Both should be commended for their attempt to make republicanism relevant within a liberal context. But perhaps because both theories are so firmly rooted within the liberal political space, difficulties arise with both of their arguments. Pettit's attempt to reconsider the relation between the state and republicanism leads him to reinforce the division of labor theory of politics and rule by expert, at a time when discussions of subsidiarity, the devolution of political powers, increased transparency of political decision-making and a greater need for democratic account-ability are all on the political agenda. With this in mind, Pettit's further emphasis on the need for a state elite to oversee the republic and monitor the promotion of the principle of freedom as non-domination, while consistent with his own understanding of the theory, seems to be out of step with the times.[2]

Pettit declares that 'people must be willing to accept an inevitable degree of reliance on the public authorities, trusting ultimately in the virtue of those officials' (1997, p. 266). But it is not obvious why they should. Indeed, Pettit's own model seems to grant an inordinate amount of power to state officials without seriously contemplating the corrupti-bility of those officials – a notable feature of contemporary life that makes Pettit's theory that much harder to swallow. Indeed, there is little if any room in Pettit's constitutional theory of republicanism for any notion of opposition or active citizenship to government.

Pettit is surely right to point out that the state ought to be involved in areas of civic life that liberal theorists have hitherto considered out of bounds. The economy is the most obvious example of exploitation and dependency within modern society that actively undermines a meaningful and freedom-centered notion of citizenship. For the republican state to fulfill its remit it must, according to Pettit, concern itself '... with the level of employment and the stability of the financial system ... others things being equal, the state will concern itself with providing a good infrastructure for industry and commerce, with facilitating productivity in the workplace, with fostering market development and choice, and with establishing trade linkages with other countries' (1997, p. 163). These are all admirable sentiments and goals. But it is hard to see how plausible they are in a climate of trade liberalization when the very safeguards provided by the state are being dismantled to the mantra of the free market. Keeping non-domination in mind as a necessary addendum to formal liberal freedoms is a positive step forward. Indeed, many socially inclined liberals would probably agree with Pettit's pragmatism – he describes his approach as 'gas and water-works republicanism' reflecting his overriding concern with practical realities. Yet his argument faces at least two charges which, even if they are not fatal, are damaging.

On the one hand, Pettit's advocacy of a benign political elite justified on the basis of the division of labor is closer to the republicanism of Plato than to that of Machiavelli or a Jefferson. That this happens to be

Pettit's choice is perfectly reasonable. Yet, it requires some acknowledgement of the dangers of corruption in politics and the chance of less-than-benign-elite rulership albeit in the name of freedom as non-domination. Such a scenario is not, alas, that far-fetched.

On the other hand, Pettit's theory may simply be regarded as irrelevant. How can one advocate greater state involvement in society – something akin to a model of social democracy – when the centrifugal tendencies of globalization push in the opposite direction? The consequences of 'uneven development' throughout the global economy are well noted: worker insecurity, a limited degree of autonomy for states and, most importantly, a developing antagonism between democracy, accountability and the free market. In such a broader context it seems hopeful to recommend greater state involvement as part of a defense of civic freedoms.

Miller's argument offers some real insights into a thoroughly modern, state-centric notion of republican citizenship. First, he is surely correct to point out that 'active citizenship' will be occasional, different citizens responding at different times to issues that concern them (1995, 448). What provokes engagement in the political process will be a matter of personal choice.

Unlike most other contemporary republican theorists, he is also brave enough to directly address the prerequisites of citizenship in the form of a civic education – a move that liberal theorists, as we saw in the previous chapter, are generally unwilling to make. School, for Miller, is cast as the counterbalance to traditional family values. It is a place which prepares children for the responsibilities and opportunities of democratic citizenship under the guidance of a national curriculum (1995, p. 143). For Miller, it is clear that citizenship is not a 'natural' condition but one that has to be taught.

Miller concedes that it might be possible to imagine a situation where people will behave responsibly at a level beyond the state as 'world citizens'. But, he argues, the trouble generally with persons who are motivated to pursue a cause at the transnational level is that without any corresponding loyalty to a particular community or the prerequisites of democratic dialogue learned as part of a national curriculum, the world citizen or 'citizen pilgrim' is unlikely to be able to find a basis for agreement with others who are unfamiliar and unlike them. Citizen pilgrims are unsophisticated and do not play well with others who fail to share their worldview. Condemning the single-mindedness of the 'activist', Miller contends that '[i]f confronted by individuals who do not share her commitment to the cause' citizen pilgrims are simply unable to hold a reasonable conversation with them. They must, as a true believer, either 'convert them or oppose them by whatever means she has at her disposal' (1999, p. 78).

The difficulty with both Miller and Pettit's argument is that both rely to a considerable degree on the notion of the 'bounded community' whose existence cannot safely be assumed any more. Their exclusively statist conception of citizenship, moreover, raises a question mark over the effectiveness of government-inspired policies within the economic sphere.

Pettit's republican constitutionalism and Miller's republican nationalism offer some of the most persuasive arguments for a revitalized form of republicanism within the context of the nation-state. Yet neither addresses how the latter and its notion of citizenship will fare under conditions of globalization that apply pressures to the state from above and below. International organizations place limits on the decision-making capacities of national government that even the most powerful must accept while pressures from within the state, from citizens who experience the energizing effects of dual membership (membership in the UK and the EU, for example) and form *ad hoc* allegiances across national boundaries in the name of a particular cause, challenges the concept of nationhood and nationality as this has been traditionally conceived. Increasingly, citizenship is less about 'knowing one's place' and more about recognizing the contingency of one's own identity and the power one can exercise with others, as activist, consumer and voter in relation to the traditional authorities of party and state.

4.2   The polis within the state

If both Miller and Pettit advocate a role for republican citizenship within the context of the nation-state, Hannah Arendt offers a somewhat different perspective on the possibilities of republican politics in the modern world. Arendt is, perhaps, the most famous and challenging republican theorist of the last century. Her unique blend of republicanism draws upon Aristotelian, Heideggerian, Nietzschean and Augustinian sources providing a highly developed and influential contribution to republican thought and, in particular, to the notion of 'political space'.[3] She was an especially acute observer of the changing political spatial dynamics of modernity, an ability nurtured by education and accident – as a Jewish 'pariah' in her native Germany during Hitler's rise to power, her removal to Paris for eighteen years as a stateless refugee, then as an émigré to the United States. Her work reveals an ambiguity toward the state and the possibility of politics which she never fully resolved.

Arendt was convinced that the public or political realm had been lost and that the reasons for this loss were directly connected with the experiences of modernity and the rise of what she called 'society'. In contrast to the social space that was populated by a society of 'laborers' and 'workers', Arendt's theoretical public realm, like the Greek *polis*, was that physical and spiritual phenomenon that made politics possible. It enabled the 'plurality of men' to form relationships as equals and to transcend the 'normality' and 'sameness' of their everyday existence. Politics was a distinct (and the highest) form of what she termed the *vita activa* whose purpose was the exercise of public freedom. The political space provided the arena for political activity – something altogether different from the isolated act of voting (1972, p. 232) – acting as, in her terminology, an 'in-between' separating and relating people at the same time, gathering people together while making certain that they did not collide. The strange loss of the public realm in modernity was, Arendt suggested, like a 'magic trick' that had made the common world disappear leaving nothing tangible around which people might gather (1958, p. 52).

In a late essay, 'Public Rights and Private Interests', Arendt reiterated some of these themes in a slightly different manner, this time by suggesting that:

> The possibility for enjoying 'public happiness' has decreased in modern life because during the last two centuries the public sphere has shrunk. The voting booth can hardly be called a public place; indeed, *the only way in which a citizen today can still function as a citizen is as member of a jury.*
>
> (Arendt, 1977, p. 104, my emphasis)

That Arendt should use the example of the jury is not surprising. Alexis de Tocqueville, whom Arendt admired, had written in *Democracy in America* that 'the jury is above all a political institution' with the ability 'to make all men feel that they have duties toward society and that they take a share in its government' (1994, p. 273). In addition, biographical details reveal that Arendt's claim followed both the occasion of her own jury service in New York, and from the positive impression she had formed of the Supreme Court Judges during the Watergate hearings (Young-Bruehl, 1982, p. 457).

To support her claims for the importance and uniqueness of political life and political space, Arendt argued that '[m]an moves in two different orders of existence . . . within what is his own . . . [and] in a sphere that is *common* to him and his fellow men' (Arendt, 1977, p. 104). In the conditions of contemporary mass society, the private realm of 'intimacy' and 'individual rights' had encroached on the public realm of 'impartiality' and the 'public rights' of citizens to such an extent that to speak of a 'common good' no longer made sense. It could not, much as Tocqueville had hoped, be equated with individual 'enlightened self interest'.

The 'common' or 'public' good proper was neither the sum of individual preferences nor some version of the general will. It was a 'plural' good, one that somehow reflected the many differences between individuals and their multiple and differing perspectives rather than simply reducing or assimilating them. The loss of the public realm made talk of a 'common good', in Arendt's view, absurd because the political imagination and impartiality it demanded was something that could only be exercised along with one's equals in the space of the public realm. Quite simply, if you were not present in the public realm you were not engaging in politics.

The latter was, for Arendt, the 'intangible' dimension of political activity or 'web of relationships'. Yet this was complemented by a second but no less important 'physical' dimension – the 'world' – which provided support and a home for her fragile politics.

In *The Human Condition* she noted that the political realm of the *polis*:

> properly speaking, is not the city state in its physical location; it is the organisation of the people as it arises out of acting and speaking together, and its true space lies between people living together for this purpose, no matter where they happen to be.
>
> (Arendt, 1958, p. 198)

This was a point reiterated by Arendt through her numerous historical examples of spontaneous revolutionary activity, and through the activities of the resistance movement in France during World War II. Indeed, her perceived flexibility toward politics is a point that has not been overlooked by critics of liberalism or advocates of postmodern political alternatives, who see democratic politics in which plurality, conflict and difference as constitutive elements rather than something that should be minimized and avoided.

The metaphor of the 'web' she used to describe the interactions between individuals in her polis was used to help define the indefinable quality of political activity as she imagined it. The concept of 'power' that she spoke of so often to describe the 'potential' that exists whenever and wherever people come together to speak about some matter was, moreover, actualized in a non-violent fashion – a point of considerable importance that I shall return to later. Arendt notes:

> only where word and deed have not parted company, where words are not empty and deeds not brutal, where words are not used to veil intentions but to disclose realities, and deeds are not used to violate and destroy but to establish relations and create new realities.
>
> (Arendt, 1958, p. 200)

In addition, Arendt included a second, equally important dimension of her politics, the 'world', as distinguished from the 'earth' or 'nature'. The world was an artificial environment created by *homo faber* to provide a home for mankind and to record the outstanding activities of political individuals for posterity. Although there does appear to have been some shift in Arendt's thought about what elements constitute 'the world' she fairly consistently put the case that it may be regarded as the buildings and institutions that bring a sense of security and durability to the extraordinary, the spontaneous and 'fleeting moments of action' that occurred in the public realm (Canovan, 1985). The world is both arena and reference point,

> related to the human artefact, the fabrication of human hands, as well as to affairs which go on among those who inhabit the man made world together. To live together in the world means essentially that a world of things is between those who have it in common, as a table is located between those who sit around it; the world, like every in-between, relates and separates men at the same time.
>
> (Arendt, 1958, p. 52)

The trouble with spontaneous outbreaks of political activity, unless they were able to find a method of maintaining themselves while preserving their elements of spontaneity, was that they simply did not last. As one commentator has noted, there is an inevitable air of futility that surrounds Arendt's politics. The loss of politics was unavoidable because the revolutionary moment would always pass and be replaced by the semi-permanent structures of political authority that would, necessarily, restrain revolutionary freedoms (Keenan, 1994).

Some critics have seen this unresolved paradox as extremely damaging to Arendt's project. Yet, the fragility of politics was less a problem for Arendt than the failure to make things endure. Modern individuals were concerned with vanity rather than with the pursuit of the immortal. 'Public admiration', when it arose for individuals and their deeds, became part of the consumption process of society and therefore failed to constitute 'a space in which things are saved from destruction by time' (1958, p. 57).

For Arendt, novelty required stability. In an article she wrote on civil disobedience, she noted that '[n]either man's capacity for change nor his capacity for preservation is boundless . . . Man's urge for change and his need for stability have always balanced and checked each other . . .' (1972, pp. 78–9) The paradox of freedom and the stability of political institutions was less a problem to be solved and more a delicate balancing act between two necessarily opposed forces. As politics needed protection from the stultifying tendencies of modern life so the 'world' needed protection from the unpredictability of the 'new', of politics and its spontaneous and unpredictable beginning, lest it be destroyed. Both elements were required in Arendt's formulation and were interdependent:

> without being talked about by men and without housing them, the world would not be a human artifice but a heap of unrelated things . . . without the human artifice to house them, human affairs would be as floating, as futile and vain, as the wanderings of nomad tribes.
>
> (Arendt, 1958, p. 183)

As a result of this formulation, Arendt described 'voluntary associations' as exercising 'public rights', the 'right of people peaceably to assemble'. Yet, she would not describe them as public or political spaces because on her terms they lacked *worldliness*. Without a guaranteed, stable public realm freedom lacked the worldly space to make its appearance.

Voluntary associations were *ad hoc* organizations that pursued short-term goals, disappearing when the goal had been reached and this she regarded as a weakness. Some, notably pressure groups, had become institutionalized and reached a degree of influence sufficient to be regarded as 'assistant government' (1972, p. 96).[4] Crucially, she also noted that there was a strong political case for the voluntary associations of the kind involved in 'civil disobedience' movement of the 1960s in the United States to become a permanent feature of the institutions of government (Arendt, 1972, p. 99). Yet, Arendt made clear why she could claim the jury as the last arena of the diminished public realm:

> No civilization – the man made artefact to house successive genera-
> tions – would ever have been possible without a framework of
> stability, to provide the wherein for the flux of change. Foremost
> among the stabilising factors, more enduring than customs, manners
> and traditions, *are the legal systems that regulate our life in the world
> and our daily affairs with each other.*
>
> (Arendt, 1972, p. 79, my emphasis)

The public realm required a mixture of elements if it was to satisfy Arendt's criteria for publicness – permanence and durability for successive generations, together with spontaneity, unpredictability and equality, the inherent features of action. The former guaranteed an enduring space for people to appear, one that was also free from interference by 'bureaucracies' and 'party machines' – phenomena that Arendt had identified as having caused the destruction of the revolutionary 'council system' throughout history (Arendt, 1963). The voluntary asso-ciation was too transient a phenomenon, she thought, the town-hall meeting perhaps less so, but in 'Public Rights and Private Interests' Arendt was certain that the jury was the last public space.

Although to the modern ear this sounds surprising, within the context of Arendt's unique appropriation of the republican tradition it makes a lot of sense. Her choice of the jury as the last political space reflected her assumptions about the human capacity for 'new begin-nings' together with the political requirement for worldly 'stability'. More broadly it also reflected those theoretical divisions that she regarded as existing between the sphere of what she called 'the intimate and private' and its opposite, 'the glaring illumination of the public world'.[5]

Arendt was perceptive enough to note the paradox of the state's relation to politics, that it was at once the guarantor of political space, providing a home for the essentially fragile and transitory, but also very often the instrument of its destruction. States were necessary for liberty, securing those safeties denied the refugee and the stateless person, but jealous of political freedoms that might be exercised spontaneously by its citizens which it therefore sought to check. States were the protectors of human rights yet also their greatest violators. That a new model of the state was required was clear but perhaps because she saw now ways of achieving this, her theory assumed a tendency toward the esoteric and utopian.[6]

Arendt was able to discern the cataclysmic impact that World War I had had on European societies and the nineteenth-century model of the nation-state. Its collapse under inflationary pressures, civil war and the mass migrations of peoples led inexorably to totalitarianism. The problem of refugees that she identified then remains a problem today – with 17.1 million stateless people in 2003, according to the UNHCR. As the number of states have grown so too have the stateless. The unwanted exist now in a world that is now completely mapped with nowhere left for the stateless to be sent and where border controls are becoming increasingly stringent (Bauman, 2000).

However, at least one perceptive commentator has also noted that Arendt underestimated the appeal of human rights, and the financial and political efforts of international non-governmental organizations like Amnesty International – with more than one million members in over 150 countries[7] – and Human Rights Watch to become permanent actors on the political stage and to bring human rights violators to justice (Power, 2004, p. 36).

Arendt did not design the public realm and the vita activa as component features of a blueprint for 'the new society'. They were meant to act as a critique of what she saw as an essentially action-less one. Politics, as she imagined it might occur in the public realm, was the only human activity that was unconditioned by social conformity and the functionality of employment. It was spontaneous and unpredictable and revealed the self of the acting agent to others in ways that were not possible in society or the private, hidden spaces of the family. Importantly, the model of the public realm was a response to a time of crises, which in Arendt's case not only reflected the contemporary crises of the post-war period in the United States but also the experience of the Holocaust in Europe and the tradition of *Existenz* philosophy, and subsequently existentialism, that developed as an answer to it. The consequence of this line of thinking, however, as Margaret Canovan has noted, is that her efforts were similar to those of 'an architect over reacting against modern functionalism, and concentrating so hard on making his buildings beautiful that he needs to make them habitable' (Canovan, 1985, p. 642).

Do Arendt's political animals, then, simply have nowhere to dwell? Is this homelessness the fault of 'society' or of Arendt's too rigid analysis? I would argue that the latter is the more likely culprit, the consequence of Arendt's attempts to uphold a rigid set of neo-Classical dividers within her own thought in order to preserve a permanent space for an impermanent activity. In so doing, she advanced the case for the survival of genuinely political activity within modern society while simultaneously turning potential actors out of that space by regarding their activity as non-political or failing to recognize action that was political when she saw it. Ironically, in pursuing politics within the context of the modern state Arendt rendered her citizens homeless.

4.3 Re-imagining political community

Republicans like Pettit and Miller embrace the state in an effort to make republicanism relevant. Both approaches reflect an attempt to address the problem of state power. Pettit's 'protective republicanism' (Stokes and Carter, 2002) tips the balance away from active notions of democracy and toward knowledgeable and (hopefully) trustworthy public leadership. Miller embraces nationalism and ties it to a notion of active republican citizenship understood as 'cultural bilingualism' in order to keep the public culture dynamic and responsive to the needs of a modern, liberal, multicultural society.

Arendt offers a unique but ultimately unsatisfactory perspective on the prospects for political activity – a pessimism that she shares with a large number of postmodern theorists (see Harvey, 1989; Schatzki, 1993). In common with the assumptions of both Pettit and Miller's arguments hers is also an argument for stability. The modern polis must be secure. It must find refuge within the state and away from the turbulence of human affairs that could destroy it. The delicate balance between liberty and security is no less important for Arendt, although different in kind, than it was and remains for liberal thinkers.

The value of postmodern arguments about the nature of space and political community is that they challenge these static models in favor of spatial models that are both plural and autonomous. There is not one space or center but spaces and centers at the national and transnational level that enjoy a relative autonomy from the state's bureaucratic and often violent reach (Derrida, 2001). Orienting oneself in the postmodern environment requires a new ability to map 'the world' as the spaces supplied by new technologies are infinite and spread unevenly across the globe. If modernity shrunk the world by mapping and charting the position of every continent and island, postmodern space alters our perception of space and its relation to time by challenging our under-standing of politics and its relation to mobility. Following Virilio we might say that the nature of politics has largely been misunderstood historically. The most important concept politically, the idea of mobility, has been buried 'under the vast scaffolding of urban construction, obscuring the fundamental anthropological side of revolution... the migratory phenomenon' (1977, p. 6). Politics is not only about location. It is also about movement.

As one commentator notes, the notion of the postmodern political space, thanks to the immediacy with which technologies shrink distance, frees it from reliance upon the traditional understandings of location, of points fixed in space and the phenomenological immediacy of interacting within a given context. 'There are a variety of ways in which people communicate with each other and across a range of time scales that make the idea of the immediacy of presentation and the immediacy of the present somewhat notional. A notional, or even in some cases virtual, present might be nonetheless effective as a basis for communication and for agonistic, if spatially and temporally distant, relations' (Clarke, 1999, p. 105). The 'post-modern condition' has ushered in a new preoccupation with space *and* time that is central to any new conception of politics (Foucault, 1986; Massey, 1993; Castells, 1994).

Writing in *The Discarded Image*, the author and theologian C.S. Lewis illustrated the change from premodern to modern conceptions of space in the following way:

> To look up at the towering medieval universe is much more like looking at a great building. The 'space' of modern astronomy may arouse terror, or bewilderment or vague reverie; the spheres of the old present us with an object in which the mind can rest, overwhelming in its greatness but satisfying in its harmony.
>
> (Lewis, 1995, p. 99)

When moderns gaze at the postmodern universe the pattern is, by and large, repeated. Postmodern space seems to convey a feeling that is both exhilarating and terrifying at different moments. The feudal space was one of orders, of top–down relationships. The modern space was far more horizontal, though barriers to social mobility still existed.

Postmodern space is replete with 'non-spaces', spaces that encourage, on the one hand, a peculiar kind of solitude, anomie and 'solitary contractuality' with other equally anonymous individuals (Auge, 1995, p. 94). For thinkers attempting to blend postmodern cultural critique with a neo-Marxist analysis of liberal political economy, the cultural and social spaces of postmodernity exhibit all the vertiginous qualities that accompany late capitalism's obsession with consumerism and the fragmentation of value as 'all that was once solid melts into air'. If the citizen is present in such a void, the citizen is consumer and victim, homeless and powerless (Jameson, 1991).

Yet for others, the new spaces of postmodernity are, above all, 'relational' as increased mobility, be it virtual or otherwise, facilitates communication, signifying a return to the world of connections. As Soja notes in his discussion of postmodern space, '... spatiality is socially produced and, like society itself, exists in both substantial forms (concrete spatialities) and as a set of relations between individuals and groups, an "embodiment" and medium of social life itself' (1989, p. 120). For the first time in nearly two millennia the question 'who is the state?' is being reinvested with significance, just as it was at the outset for Thucydides who claimed that 'the people are the polis'. The potential for increased opportunity for citizen involvement and action occurs when 'politics' and 'community' are found not in formal institutions but wherever there are individuals who take the practice of citizenship seriously (Oldfield, 1991; Keck and Sikkink, 1998). Such 'communities' are contingent, the products of individual choices and the recognition of both shared responsibilities and new opportunities for political expression.

'Who' one is rather than 'what' one does becomes important as fixed notions of citizenship are transformed into what might be described as a new nomadology. Indeed, the figure of the nomad, far from being the irrelevance that it was for Arendt, is a description of a new kind of civic experience.

To the premodern and the modern world this claim would have made no sense at all. Early cities developed agricultural economies and profited from the domestication of animals that freed individuals from dependence upon the seasons for their subsistence. The anthropology of nomadic lifestyles shows that such peoples were often compelled to move, rather than chose to move, and this had a deleterious impact upon the management of time and, consequently, the development of culture and technology. The peculiarly modern nomad, the refugee, is also compelled to move not by seasonal changes but under the direction of state authorities who see within this nomadic tendency a drain on state resources.

Yet while these features of the nomadic existence are undeniable, nomads were also feared because of the kind of freedom they possessed beyond the city walls. According to one of the earliest descriptions of the nomadic lifestyle by Herodotus, '... this people has no settled cities or forts; they carry their houses with them and shoot with bows from horseback; they live off herds of cattle, not from tillage, and their dwellings are on their wagons. How then can they fail to be invincible and inaccessible for others?' (1987, IV, p. 46). Nomads were a reminder of an alternative way of living at odds with civilization which, while it promised and delivered much, produced its own paradoxes. An early critic, Diogenes, pointed out that while the city walls provided safety they also provided an opportunity to victimize one's fellows. Safe behind their city walls, citizens could commit every outrage against one another as if this had been the sole reason for their coming together in the first place (Chatwin, 1996, p. 85).

While there is no doubt that the figure of the nomad has been romanticized the idea of the nomad as a wanderer who transgresses boundaries remains a potent symbol of freedom (Laughlin, 1999). Nomads promise an alternative idea of freedom and one that reminds us of the restrictions placed upon those who live a civic life. While few of us would trade the pleasures of a settled existence and the comforts this brings for the vagaries of real nomad lives, postmodern nomads, sometimes called 'digital nomads' (Makimoto and Manners, 1997), perform the important service of reminding us of Diogenes' early observations and offer an alternative model of civic agency.

4.4   Citizen-nomads and citizen-*ships*[8]

On 10 October 2003 the Greenpeace ship, *Esperanza*, received an email from the Assistant Port Director of Miami, Florida, denying Greenpeace's berthing request for the vessel. In subsequent correspondence, the port authorities pointed out that as a consequence of two Greenpeace activists boarding and protesting a vessel, the *Jade*, some fifteen months earlier for attempting to illegally import wood, the *Esperanza* posed an undue security risk. This denial was issued as a result of what the *New York Times* described as an 'unusual prosecution'.[9] The activities of the protestors aboard the *Jade* – they had unfurled a banner which read 'President Bush: Stop Illegal Logging' – resulted in the entire organization being charged in July 2003 under a law, last used in 1890, that was designed to prohibit landlords from bullying sailors aboard vessels as they came into port.[10]

This particular example of offshore protest and the response by land-based authorities is instructive on a number of different levels and a good example of cosmorepublican political activity within a postmodern political space. That space and the citizens that inhabit it, I have suggested, are essentially mobile and part of a broader overlapping network of interests and affiliations. The ship, moreover, is an example of a space that moves and as such is both a symbolic and a physical expression of a new form of political life.

Michel Foucault noted of the idea and actuality of the boat – 'a floating piece of space, a place without a place, that exists by itself, that closed in on itself and at the same time is given over to the infinity of the sea' – was central to the political imaginary of Western civilization (1986, p. 27). The actuality of the ship, a floating factory and machine of empire, was also coupled with the idea of the ship that provided an alternative imaginary, a site of possibility, for land-locked citizens. While formal liberal freedoms were guaranteed by territorial belonging, real freedom occurred beyond the confines of such territories. Ships were a special kind of space in Foucault's terms, heterotopic spaces which opened up the possibility of social change. They were:

real places – places that do exist and that are formed in the very founding of society – which are something like counter-sites, a kind of effectively enacted utopia in which the real sites, all the other real sites that can be found within the culture, are simultaneously represented, contested, and inverted.

(1986, p. 24)

Meaning literally 'other places', heterotopic spaces are sites established through incongruous spatial relations that challenge the spaces of representation and their mode of representation within society.

Heterotopic spaces do not exist *a priori* but instead are constituted through the very ordering of things that they help to create, sites in which all things displaced, marginal, rejected or ambivalent are represented. These representations become the basis for alternative modes of ordering that have the effect of offering contrasts to the dominant representation of the social order. The aim of groups such as Greenpeace is *not* state capture nor is it the replacement of the current hegemonic ideology with another. Instead, this politics of the margins presents no end game; there is no final destination. Instead, mobility and the constancy of movement are central features of this new politics. It is, moreover, a politics that is not without precedent.

As Limbaugh and Rediker (2001) note in a recent study of political resistance in seventeenth- and eighteenth-century England, the idea and the actuality of the ship offered just the sort of alternative site for political resistance and freedom that Foucault describes. Indeed, in the case of England, the absence of a radical discourse of dissent on land provided the rationale for one to develop at sea as a counter-movement to the economic ambitions of the emerging British Empire. The ship was the most potent symbol of the expansion of capital, a mobile paradigm of the division of labor and a potent symbol of Western knowledge and 'discovery'. But a combination of labor shortages at home and poor working conditions on board also turned the ship into a site of radical politics.

By the early eighteenth century, while England had essentially been depoliticized, thanks to the efforts of the Whig leader Robert Walpole, English ships increasingly came to be populated by a multinational and often politically savvy crew. The space of the ship was a place where working people from different nationalities came together, developing a distinctive transnational consciousness along with their own language – pidgin English. In contrast to the maritime imaginary of Defoe's *Robinson Crusoe*, a solitary shipwreck who embodied the spirit of individual free enterprise, closer to reality was the multicultural crew that developed its own tradition of radical politics and a maritime phonetics that set them apart from those who stayed on shore.

Limbaugh and Rediker describe the pirate ship as an environment in which the 'world was turned upside down' – itself a phrase used by the English revolutionaries of the seventeenth century who argued for democracy against the tyranny of either King or parliament. Ships were crewed by men and women reflecting a cross section of political and religious radicalism: Ranters, Quakers, X-New Model Army, Native Americans, African, French, indentured servants or escaped slaves.

The parallels between this examination of radicalized political spaces at the beginnings of modernity and our own times are striking. The most advanced technology of the modern period than permitted freedom of movement – the ship was used against the fixed interest of a landed elite and, indeed, against the powerful interests of the British Empire.

By comparison, the technology of the postmodern period, the Internet, is itself a co-opted form of government technology.[11] And while early critics dismissed its political potential as little more than hype – 'a designer utopia customised for people who believe in technical fixes and not morality or politics' (Gray, 1995, p. 10)[12] – the last ten years have shown that it can be used as an even more radicalized, yet paradoxical, form of movement. Indeed, postmodern *homo politicus* can quite easily occupy the position of *homo prostratus*. Active citizens today do not actually have to go anywhere and e-democracy and e-governance have entered the political lexicon. As Pippa Norris notes in a recent study:

> By strengthening government transparency, theories of representative democracies stress that e-governance could improve accountability via the electoral process, allowing citizens to become more informed

so that they could evaluate the collective record of the government, the work of particular elected representatives, the contents of parliamentary debates, and the alternative policy proposals of the parties and candidates standing for office. And by facilitating new forms of interaction between citizens and the state, proponents of direct democracy hope that e-governance could channel citizens' voices and priorities more effectively into the public policymaking process.

(Norris, 2003, p. 4)

Politics in such an environment has shown itself most clearly to be a politics of self-empowerment and opposition. It is mobile, transitory and capable of producing cleavages in a society that shift about and undermine traditional group affiliations. This is not the politics of the mass social movement or alternative ideology but a politics of separate 'discourses', non-statist, impermanent outbreaks of activity, a politics at the margin expressive of personal value choices as much as ideological commitment.

The state's role and function in 'communal life' is fundamentally challenged as a result. Indeed, it has been suggested that the state may be ignored altogether as a political actor through the 'politics of direct address'. The political moment occurs outside of the formal institutions of state. Political activity 'begins not with the object of constructing similarities to address rights claims to the state, but opens rather with the object of addressing such claims to each other, and to each "other," whoever and wherever they may be' (McClure, 1992, p. 123).

While much of this may sound fanciful there is increasing evidence (for once) that the rhetoric matches the sociology. The authors of the *Global Civil Society Yearbook* (2003/4) note the increase in transnational activity on the part of 'global citizens'.[13] Over the past three years global civil society forums – the first was in Porto Alegre in 2001, the most recent in Mumbai, India, in 2004 – have moved from being parallel summits, shadowing meetings of interstate representatives at the World Economic Forum, G8, World Bank, IMF or WTO, to independent gatherings of global civil society that are larger and better organized. Since 2002, over half have involved over 10,000 people and are coordinated across the globe, in over 70 countries, including both hemispheres. There are, moreover, more meetings in the southern hemisphere now than in the north, although the number of global civil society groups is still concentrated in Western Europe and the United States.

World Social Forums – described by Anheier and Katz (2005) as 'hyper-networks' – have moved from being opportunities to meet other civil society groups to platforms for proposing alternative policies designed to alter public opinion. Organizations like Greenpeace, Amnesty International and what was hitherto called 'the anti-capitalism movement' (now more accurately described as an umbrella organization that focuses on issues of social justice and peaceful resolutions to conflict) have been successful whenever they have managed to convince captive, state-bound populations that they defend a 'public good' and the government and/or corporations are undermining that same good.

The activities of organizations like the International Campaign to Ban Land Mines, the East Timor Action Network and scores of others indicate that we are moving into an era of 'Do-It-Yourself' (DIY) politics. This has been made possible because of the relative ease with which people can communicate, travel and purchase relatively inexpensive equipment with which to document activities and provide alternative sources of news media.[14]

Power in the international sphere is no longer exclusively the power of brute force, of aggression, military might or even economic sanction. The power of the (formerly) powerless seeks to influence policy makers by changing the terms of the debate, framing issues that a wider audience can relate to and understand.

The new political communities that form do so informally as a result of the recognition of shared risks and responsibilities (Beck, 2000b,c). They are distinct because their membership is chosen rather than imposed. Formed around ideas of right and wrong they seek to influence the international political system by relating a domestic issue in one context to an international audience, increasing support for their cause and influencing their government in the process.

4.5   Conclusion

In an analysis of the effects of increased access to and use of media such as television, Joshua Meyrowitz suggested that changing social and behavioral patterns tended to accompany the new context created by a new media. The added ingredient of television, for example, to a social environment previously without this element did not equal the old environment plus the new ingredient, but a new environment altogether (1985, p. 19). Changes in the media of messages were, he suggested, 'analogous to the study of architectural or geographical change, or to the effects of migration or urbanisation' (p. 70).

If politics is fundamentally about movement, the movement of the crowd, the movement of information, then lamenting the loss of either polis or state is to misdiagnose the twenty-first-century human condition. As radical as the notion of the changed universe was for moderns, a universe of infinite size, relative position and dynamism, so the changed political space is equally revolutionary.

When Connolly argues that the 'state' must be imagined today as one site of membership among many others both inside and outside its territorial boundaries he is describing a fact of postmodern political life – that even realists like Nye (2002) acknowledge – rather than making a dubious normative claim (1991, p. 218). Organizations whose membership and concerns cross state boundaries around issues of common concern – human rights, environmental justice, poverty – have been particularly successful at harnessing citizen enthusiasm for politics beyond borders. They are, as Richard Falk notes, an integral element of 'globalization-from-below' (1995) and the spaces they occupy are the spaces created by human relationships. As Keck and Sikkink suggest, transnational networks 'must also be understood as political spaces, in which differently situated actors negotiate – formally or informally – the social, cultural, and political meanings of their joint enterprise' (1998, p. 3).

Of course, not everyone will see the new opportunities for civic action in these terms. That the influence of *the* philosopher of fear *and* of state sovereignty, Thomas Hobbes, should return to take center stage in the light of the events of 11 September 2001 is regrettable yet understandable. As Corey Robin notes in a recent article, 'fear' as an energizing and motivating concept has made something of a comeback in recent philosophical writing (Robin, 2004). But Hobbes' philosophy is unlikely to provide the theoretical resources necessary to win the day for either liberal democracy or individual freedom. Globalization has made that impossible and global terrorism is a unique invention of the postmodern period – its global reach and flexibility shares many characteristics of the large transnational corporation – directly challenging the rationale of Hobbes' state to provide security for its citizens.

The greater reflexivity that postmodernism encourages through a combination of increased anxiety and exposure to different and often conflicting information sources sensitizes individual citizens to their relative position in relation to state power and global issues. The presence of CNN, the BBC and Al Jazeera – not to mention the hundreds of independent media sites available on the Internet – in the most recent round of state-sponsored aggression in Iraq undermines the state monopoly on information and opens up a space for contestation in the process.

If the evidence of worldwide mass protest against the most recent war in the Middle East shows anything at all, it is that many millions of people doubt the motives of politicians who would defend 'civilization' from the new 'barbarians'. 15 February 2003 was a transition for the global civil society movement, with 11 million people in over 800 cities worldwide taking to the streets in protests against the actions of the United States and its allies (Sauermann, 2003). *The New York Times* described these events as the birth of a 'second superpower'.[15]

What is uniquely postmodern about the situation is that so many individuals across the world should recognize the global consequence of such belligerence and recognize that the policy of nation-states in one part of the globe directly affects the exercise of their freedoms in another. This act of recognition on the part of global citizens is an acknowledgement of the unavoidable existential dilemmas they face whether they like it or not, as they find themselves involved in a global conflagration that is both personal and political. Cosmorepublican citizenship is, above all, a choice.

5
On the Ancient and Modern Origins of Cosmopolitanism

> What can we know of the world? What quantity of space can
> our eyes hope to take in between our birth and our death? How
> many square centimeters of Planet Earth will the soles of our
> shoes have touched?
>
> – Perec, 1998, p. 78

The historical fact that republicanism's spatial concerns and corresponding cultural prerequisites for political action have *not* been rooted
in the context of the nation-state make it a relevant theoretical
addendum to theories of global governance. As one author notes, because
of these hitherto considered structural weaknesses, in the present
context, 'this approach enjoin[s] us to consider the civic possibilities
bound up in the expansion of institutional structures, legal frameworks,
and a shared political culture, beyond the boundaries of the nation-
state' (Kenny, 2003, p. 135).

There is an obvious connection between republican freedoms – 'the
freedom of the city' – and the theory of cosmopolitanism which has
in various ways imagined the universe as a single city with all its
inhabitants, moral members. The concomitant desire to 'cultivate
humanity' arose as an expression of discontent with civilization along
with recognition of the arbitrary nature of communal membership.
However, the desire to cultivate a universal politics has been much less
advanced.

Julia Annas (2002) points out that the reason for this was probably
because the early cosmopolitan thinkers lived in a society which was
far more static and authoritarian than our own. Consequently, such
theoretical speculations on the subject of a universal politics would
have been regarded as 'merely quixotic'. If there is an historical basis for

avoiding discussion of a cosmopolitan politics, however, contemporary cosmopolitans skirt around the issues of politics for slightly different reasons. As Brassett and Higgott note:

> as currently constituted, competing cosmopolitan theories of international relations or liberal political philosophies of justice, upscaled to the global level, exhibit too little an appreciation of the dynamic(s) of the market place to offer meaningful ways of addressing the political legitimacy deficit in the global economic order.
>
> (2003, p. 30)

In the eighteenth century, the discourse of cosmopolitanism reemerged in response to the increased awareness of the connectivity between nations that was growing as a result of an emerging capitalism. Immanuel Kant's notion that all those who affect one another should form a civil constitution was proposed during a period of intense warfare, technological innovation and capitalist expansion. It is not difficult for us to draw parallels between Kant's turbulent times and our own nor is it surprising that theorists who advocate global democratic reforms should turn to Kant among the theorists of cosmopolitanism to find inspiration.

Cosmopolitan thinking may be divided into two separate approaches. The first is a concern with justice, and it is this notion, by and large, which continues to preoccupy philosophers and theorists. It is the idea enshrined by the Stoics of the concept of Natural Law and by Enlightenment thinkers like Kant that there are abstract, universal laws that are accessible to reason. It is this approach that we find embodied in statements like the UN Declaration of Human Rights and in the Charter of the United Nations. In short, this approach rejects the notion that justice can be confined only to the members of social groups that share a common history, culture, language or ethnicity.

The second line of argument deals with the issue of moral status, and makes the ambitious claim that in an important *moral* sense we are all 'citizens of the world'. Also an ancient argument, this idea is supported conceptually by imagining the universe as a single 'cosmic' city with all humanity deserving of equal status within. The implications of this view have provided the impetus for some contemporary philosophers to claim that there is no morally justifiable reason why we should care less about someone else simply because they happen to have been born into membership of another national culture. If all such membership is based on luck, rather than desert, then the fictions of nationalism provide a false sense of comfort and, more importantly, a distorted perception of a world of others (Nussbaum, 1996). Contemporary versions of cosmopolitanism along with discussions of world citizenship are seen by their advocates as antidotes to parochialism and the means for encouraging support for global political institutions like the United Nations (Hutchings and Dannreuther, 1999).

Contemporary 'political' cosmopolitan thinking may also be divided into two approaches. The first follows the dominant line in classical cosmopolitan thought by pursuing institutional solutions to global dilemmas. David Held (1995, 2000, 2002, 2004b) and others (Anheier *et al.*, 2001, 2002, 2003) have analyzed the growth of a global politics as part of a new phenomenon that marks a shift toward a system of multilayered regional and global governance. The evidence for this claim is compelling, not only in terms of the exponential increase in the number of INGOs and NGOs during the last two decades but also the increased frequency with which these organizations meet.

Global governance involves many levels and many actors. Globalists that adopt an institutionalist perspective argue that the lack of transparency and accountability of suprastate governance as it is currently exercised is a crucial factor in limiting its effectiveness and legitimacy. A desire for greater transparency, accountability and democracy in global governance; a commitment to social justice in the pursuit of a more equitable distribution of the world's resources and human security; the protection and reinvention of community at diverse levels and the regulation of the global economy through the public management of the global financial and trade flows together with the provision of global public goods are all part of the cosmopolitan agenda.

The second approach to contemporary cosmopolitanism, one that is much less discussed in the literature, is the formation of a distinctively global *political* agency. Indeed a distinctly political conception of cosmopolitanism is largely absent from the debate. Although considerable work has been conducted charting both the attitudinal shifts that have occurred over time (Inglehart, 1989), the possibilities of multiple allegiances and multiple citizenships (Heater, 1999) and extensive attempts to classify the different motivational factors that inform contemporary cosmopolitan agency (Rosenau, 2003) there is no well-developed theory of cosmo-political agency and no competing model of global citizenship.

Part of the reason for this may be due to the cosmopolitan inheritance itself. Immanuel Kant's theory, which has exerted enormous influence upon contemporary cosmopolitan theorists, considered the relevant unit of analysis the state, the great hope for mankind commerce, and the possibility of securing peace through the actions of a benign hegemon. Consequently, those heirs to the Kantian tradition who advance the case for institutional reform, and who recognize the severe handicap that global inequalities pose to a cosmopolitan democratic order, seem hesitant to grapple with the notion of political agency within the cosmopolitan framework.[1]

Contemporary cosmopolitans have provided some extraordinary insights into the complex phenomenon of globalization, yet by focusing on arguments concerning the moral status of individuals and the need for institutional reform – both relevant and worthy discussions – the by now familiar problem of transition reemerges. How precisely should one move toward a more just institutional world order without discussions of global political agency and its prerequisites?

An analysis of global political agency as a legitimate force in world politics, one that operates at the national in addition to the global level seems appropriate in this instance. Indeed, one might argue that unless a decidedly political dimension is added to contemporary discussions of cosmopolitanism and attention is shifted to the extraordinary political dynamic that is now possible between individuals on a global level, arguments for the kind of reforms that are being advanced will remain essentially 'permissive'.

Yet there is another reason for teasing out the political dimension of cosomopolitanism. With its appeals to moral universalism, and in the absence of appropriate political contestation, contemporary cosmopolitanism could face the charge of being self-serving. In the absence of political discussion and disagreement, moral universals might be perceived as little better than exercises in global self-righteousness (Dallmayr, 2003). As Gowan notes, versions of cosmopolitanism that attempt to 'spread democracy' around the globe have often translated into an institutionalized form of democracy that is little better than polyarchy (Gowan, cited in Went, 2004, p. 349). Some contemporary advocates of human rights seem to agree with this approach. Universal moral principles are unlikely to meet with universal assent which is precisely why the discourse of human rights is better understood as a starting point for discussion rather than a trump to end it (Ignatieff, 2001).

What each of these thinkers point to is a form of politics as process, where politics is understood:

> neither [as] a set of fixed principles to be realized in the near future, nor yet...a set of traditional habits to be preserved, but an activity,

a sociological activity which has the anthropological function of preserving a community grown too complicated for either tradition alone or pure arbitrary rule to preserve it without the undue use of coercion.

(Crick, 1992, p. 24)

In this novel interpretation of the politics of the polis, Crick points out that the precise relation between a common good and political activity was such that politics did not require a set of fundamental principles to be adhered to – although clearly some 'rules of discourse' were necessary – but that the very different values that pervaded a society (or societies) actually required political activity *as the medium through which a diverse community might order its affairs*. Politics, in the sense employed by Crick, *was* the common good and that good acted as a civilizing process upon the participants engaged in political activity.

When one considers for a moment the nature of 'value pluralism' within modern societies, one immediately sees the distinctiveness of this view of politics and its relevance. If we accept the validity of the notion of value pluralism, the idea of incompatible and perhaps even incommensurable versions of 'the good life', then writ large the question becomes: How can individuals with their very different and demanding group affiliations live together in political association where the latter extends beyond the borders of their own communities? Dallmayr is clear on this point:

to be properly cosmopolitan, this civic culture needs to be as inclusive as possible, that is, to embrace not only people similar to 'us' but precisely those who are different or 'other' – potentially even those who now are categorized (rashly) as 'enemies'... it is important to remedy the 'deficit' of global moralism: its tendential neglect of politics...

(2003, p. 438)

5.1 Cosmo-political space

It is somewhat ironic that the thinker most often referred to by cosmo-politan theorists today never drifted more than fifty miles from his home town in nearly eight decades. Immanuel Kant wrote about universal moral laws, articulated some of the most persistent hopes for a lasting peace for all mankind, the positive effects of international commerce, and developed a theory of the origins of the solar system which still bears his name.[2] Hannah Arendt (1982) described Kant as a 'stay at home man of the world' and a recent commentator has him 'bounded in a nutshell, and counting himself king of infinite space' (Scruton, 2001). The irony of all this was probably lost on Kant, a man not famed for his sense of humor. However, by keeping an eye on 'the starry firmament above and the moral law within' he epitomized those qualities of the modern philosopher and the cosmopolitan, a flexibility of mind that makes such a notion of citizenship incompatible with exclusively nationalist group identities.

Kant was not the first theorist to consider a solution to the problem of (early) globalisation. Dante Alighieri had advocated world government in *De Monarchia*, and Leibniz and Abbe de St Pierre both advocated plans for the possibility of a lasting peace in Europe. However, Kant's approach has retained its relevance within contemporary debates because he coupled together a realist's approach to politics within states and between states, along with an idealist's view of how states might interact at a global level.

One recent commentator has argued that Kant was different from a thinker like Dante, a cosmopolitan who pinned his hope on the benign actions of a political elite, because Kant preferred what he called republican states (by which he meant representative government) where the last word on whether or not a state should go to war resided with the citizenry (Munkler, 2004). While this is true up to a point, Kant shared the sentiment of most liberal thinkers of his age, preferring to restrict the franchise to those whom he considered economically independent and therefore worthy of what he deemed a 'civil personality'. Just in case there was any confusion as to who this excluded, Kant provided his readers with a list. Unsuitable: apprentices to merchants, tradesmen, servants, minors, women in general and everyone else who depended on someone else for their living. The woodcutter and blacksmith fell short of consideration, as did the carpenter, the tutor (Kant himself was a tutor) and the tenant who also failed to qualify because they were 'mere auxiliaries' who received orders or protection from others. They did not have, in Kant's terms, civil independence (Kant, 1991).

Kant's attachment to the idea of the social contract and the liberal defense of property rights – the purpose of the social contract is 'the need to unite the private property of all members of the people under a universal public owner' (1991, p. 147) – also resulted in his endorsement of an authoritarian mode of government. 'Simplification', he noted, 'is certainly the most rational maxim for the mechanical process of uniting the people by means of coercive laws, so long as the people are passive and obedient to a single individual above them...' (p. 162).

The proper mode for the ordinary citizen was as 'respectful spectator' one, furthermore, who was in no position to disagree with government even if the latter decided to go to war. 'Even', he says, 'if the people is at present in such an attitude or position of mind that it would refuse its consent if it were consulted' they could not refuse to obey the law. It was not their responsibility to judge the rightness of the issue (p. 79).

Kant's theory also excluded the possibility of revolution. Those who speculated about such an end were 'a menace to the state' something that could justifiably result, Kant thought, in their elimination or banishment as outlaws (p. 161). And Kant's fear of rebellion extended even further, into the international arena. In the *Metaphysics of Morals* he acknowledged that the division between inside and outside was becoming increasingly porous. Hence, in the case of an internal rebellion within a state he recommended that its suppression be supported by other monarchs. They ought to come to the aid of 'the fallen monarch', punish the people's crimes and 'restore the old [order] by forcible means' (p. 147).

The reason for the enforced passivity of the citizenry, according to Kant, was that to resist legitimate authority would involve oneself in a contradiction that threatened to undermine the existence of the state. A supreme power could not be regarded as supreme if some other power in society had the legitimacy to challenge it. The reason why it is the duty of citizens 'to tolerate even what is apparently the most intolerable misuse of supreme power' is, according to Kant, 'that it is impossible ever to conceive of their resistance to the supreme legislation as being anything other than unlawful and liable to nullify the entire legal constitution' (p. 145).

Although Kant is often interpreted as the theorist who did most to provide the conceptual framework for modern institutions like the European Union and the United Nations, it should not be forgotten that there are at least two Kants: Kant the realist and Kant the idealist. The former justified the right of states to make war, in self-defense, when there is an 'an alarming increase of power in another state' which in turn justified the right of anticipatory attack, in modern parlance a 'pre-emptive strike'. Moreover, if an 'unjust enemy', could be identified, that is a state that intended to make peace impossible by not honoring their contracts with other nations, Kant suggested that such a foe should be attacked and, when defeated, forced 'to accept a new constitution of a nature that is unlikely to encourage their warlike inclinations' (p. 170).

Kant the idealist, however, is rather different. In this guise, Kant is aware of the shrinking nature of the global environment. 'Through the spherical shape of the planet they [the earth's peoples] inhabit, nature has confined them all within an area of definite limits' (p. 172). Commerce and navigation, he hopes, will force the peoples of the earth into a political union with one another or they will forever face the threat of war and the expense of constantly preparing for war.

In '*On The Common Saying...*' Kant had argued that a world state would represent the perfection of a republican constitution and a solution to the problem of world governance. Yet, in later works, notably *Perpetual Peace*, he reconsidered this view – a world republic was out of the question because it would be impossible to govern. There was no sovereign power suitable for the world at large. What was required instead was an alliance or federation 'which can be terminated at any time, so that it has to be renewed periodically' (p. 165). For peace to be perpetual what was required was a congress of states, a 'voluntary gathering of various states which can be dissolved at any time...' (p. 171). For Kant, global governance was an essentially flexible and impermanent phenomenon.

Kant's intended audience for these thoughts, interestingly enough, were members of another republic, the republic of books, not princes and rulers but a public of enlightened citizens who shared his desire for a peaceful world order. In 1796, on the second edition of *Perpetual Peace*, he even went so far as to include an article asserting that kings and state authorities should allow philosophers 'to speak freely and publicly on universal maxims of warfare and peacemaking'. Moreover, their conversations would be part of a *secret* arrangement between philosophers and rulers because if it were known that politicians might also be consulting philosophers it would be humiliating for the former (p. 115). Philosophers should be consulted not only because of what they have to say but because of their 'incorruptible natures: they can be trusted not to disseminate propaganda because they are incapable of so doing, just as they are incapable of forming seditious factions or clubs' (p. 115).

Kant's view of morality and its relation to a politics of a perpetual peace is also worth noting. With no explicit political agenda and no mention of active citizenship, Kant puts his faith in a benign elite. Kant the moral philosopher is convinced that morality will check the excesses of politics and that the person of the 'moral politician' will provide what nature cannot, namely the will to take advantage of favorable external conditions and institute a lasting peace.

The moral politician is, he says, 'someone who conceives of the principles of political expediency in such a way that they can coexist with morality'. Working in an environment where he is surrounded by competing, and even conflicting, interests, he seeks what he thinks is in the true ethical interests of man. A political moralist on the other hand unites politics and morality in entirely the wrong way. He takes advantage of the natural desire of men to see the aims of their leaders in a moral light to create an ethic which merely serves the purpose of those few in power.

Kant was unashamedly optimistic and philosophically committed to his plan's success. 'Even if', he says, 'there is not the slightest theoretical probability of its realization, provided that there is no means of demonstrating that it cannot be realized' you have a duty to pursue it (p. 174). Indeed, he thought that, eventually, reason would overcome the antagonism between states and their resistance to the idea of a federation. This resolution may well be reached 'after many devastations, upheavals and even complete inner exhaustion of [state] powers', but is something that could have been reached and will be reached by the dictates of reason. Consequently, the 'barbarous freedom' of existing states will in time move toward a federation, a legal 'cosmopolitan system of general political security' (p. 49).

Kant saw economic factors as contributing to the long-term development of a peaceful and mutually dependent international order. He was very optimistic about the progressive impact of the spread of the capitalist commercial and financial system to those parts of the world not then affected by global capital and was convinced that making money would trump the desire to make war (p. 114). What Kant seems not to have realized is that it is perfectly possible to do both.[3]

In addition to placing his faith in the power of reason, the advice of philosophers, moral politicians, commerce and the natural and positive progression toward a better state of affairs, Kant also thought that it would only take one large state to begin the process of cosmopolitanism. Spurred on, somewhat ironically, by what he saw as positive revolutionary events in America and France, he noted that it only took the actions of one enlightened nation to provide a focal point for a new alliance of peace loving states.

Kant's theories continue to arouse much interest among scholars as the very processes of globalization that he identified as a positive factor in *Perpetual Peace* have continued unabated. But what should be clear from Kant's cosmopolitan 'political' theory is how much of the cosmopolitan order he envisages disarms the powers of ordinary citizens. His is a classically liberal social contract theory that is translated from 'republican states' to a global context, premised on the benign leadership of moral politicians and an ethically responsible hegemon.

His focus in *Perpetual Peace*, on states and the power of states, makes his analysis suspect given the increasing pressures upon the nation-state model from within and without. His faith in the benign and harmony inducing effects of commerce must also be questioned in the light of global inequities produced by the spread of economic liberalization. Whether the state needs to be strengthened to resist the vagaries of the market as well as providing a positive focus for local and ethnic identities is a point that is debated among scholars and activists.

Kant's reliance on the power of nature and the optimism of Enlightenment thinking also appears unduly hopeful. His teleological theory of nature, supplemented by a 'good will' said to be the possession of moral politicians, is equally unlikely to persuade particularly when placed in the context of current global crises and political scandals. His high opinion of leaders, his assumption that they are 'men of understanding' who will be humbled by the overwhelming weight of the responsibility of their office was a suspect view in the eighteenth century and is even less persuasive today.

5.2   The cosmopolitan citizen

To claim today that one is a 'citizen of the world' is to describe a moral aspiration, a legal fact and a political possibility. The ancient notion of the *kosmou politês* or world citizen was a description of a peculiar moral psychology. Cosmopolitan thinkers understood that individuals were members of more than one community and as such one's loyalties could not be completely confined by the accident of birthplace or one's local group memberships. The recognition of this fundamental contingency – that one could have been born outside the city gates – led thinkers to consider notions of universal justice. It also led them to describe the virtues of the cosmopolitan character.

Cosmopolitan agency required that flexibility of mind that enabled an understanding of others who were culturally different. Marcus Aurelius advised his fellow world citizens 'to give careful attention to what others are saying, and try...to enter into the mind of the speaker' (1964, p. 53). More importantly, cosmopolitanism required the difficult psychological admission that the state was not the world and that the current order of things was not necessarily the only order – something that still holds true. This admission might be liberating but the existential sacrifices demanded of world citizens could be considerable.

Diogenes knew that the invitation to think as a world citizen was an invitation to be an exile from the easy comforts of patriotism. And while this did not mean simply giving up attachments to the state, in actuality or idea, it did mean critically analyzing and placing those attachments in a broader context. The moral impetus to recognize another's 'humanity' wherever that person might come from changed the way one deliberated with oneself and one's compatriots. Cosmopolitan agency was a personal and political struggle.

The idea of multiple allegiances realized in the form of dual citizenship, while it might have been a legal fact in the Roman world, was frowned upon by the leading thinkers of the period. Cicero thought that the principles of residence and allegiance were fundamentally connected and could not be shared. If a Roman chose to sit as an Athenian and serve as member of a jury in that city then, argued Cicero, they had forfeited their own Roman citizenship as a result (Heater, 1999, p. 118). One could be Roman or Athenian but not both.

In the modern period the idea of multiple allegiances has suffered, until very recently, as a result of the heavily Romanticized idea of the nation. In the eighteenth century, Abbe Sieyes grabbed the nettle of nationality by recognizing the novelty of what 'the French' were trying to do in 1789 arguing that the French nation, while it was very new, was also very old 'prior to everything...the source of everything'. Johann Gottfried Herder, who studied with Kant, would argue for something similar, appealing to the notion of a *Volk*, casting the nation as an organic unity that ought to be protected from contamination. One's nationality was supposed to provide all the political identity that a citizen needed.

There were exceptions, of course. Kant, Voltaire, Paine and even John Stuart Mill, each one an internationalist in their own way, sensed the pathology in the nationalist sentiments of the period. Indeed, Mill did his best to redefine nationalism in his *System of Logic* to equate with the principle of sympathy: 'We need scarcely say that we do not mean nationality in the vulgar sense of the term; a senseless antipathy to foreigners; indifference to the general welfare of the human race, or an unjust preference of the supposed interest of our country; a cherishing of absurd peculiarities because they are national, or a refusal to adopt what has been found good by other countries. We mean a principle of sympathy, not of hostility; of union, not of separation' (1900, p. 369).

The qualifications for cosmopolitan agency during the eighteenth and nineteenth centuries, however, rested less on commitments to universal reason, morality or fellow feeling and more on the 'state-less' freedoms provided by what economists described as 'comparative economic advantage'. Cosmopolitans, noted the young Nietzsche, were those 'truly international, homeless, financial recluses' who 'misuse politics as an instrument of the stock exchange, and state and society as an apparatus for their own enrichment'. For Nietzsche, writing in *The Greek State* in 1871, a return to the womb of the polis and a form of aristocratic radicalism was the only answer (Nietzsche, 1999).

Marx shared a similar sentiment. Writing in *The Communist Manifesto* in 1848 he offered a prophetic vision of twentieth-century capitalist development. 'The bourgeoisie has through its exploitation of the world market given a cosmopolitan character to production and consumption in every country...old-established national identities have been destroyed or are daily being destroyed...we have intercourse in every direction, universal interdependence of nations...' (1985, p. 83). Little wonder that neo-Marxist interpretations of cosmopolitanism theories of global governance today consider the new cosmopolitans members of a corporate, technocratic, trans-national, capitalist class (Sklair, 2002).

The paradox of this period was that capital moved about freely and was essentially stateless, while politics seemed to be rooted to the spot. Marx's appeal to all working men to unite in the First International was a proper, political response to the economic revolution occurring around him. Yet both the International and the political revolutions that swept across Europe in the years following the Manifesto's publication were short-lived.

Indeed, by the end of the nineteenth-century the idea that political life should be rooted in the nation was a project undertaken deliberately and purposefully via military expansionism abroad and the institutions of education at home. The latter schooled individual citizens to speak a common tongue, to read a common history, to sing national anthems and pledge allegiance to the flag, with the express purpose of increasing stability and encouraging national distinctiveness (Hobsbawm, 1992).

The late twentieth-century preoccupation with the promise of cosmopolitanism shares many of the earlier commitments to a universal morality, and a renewed commitment to the basic rights and capabilities of individuals as many of those aspirations have been translated into precise legal safeguards and guarantees. Political experiments with federal structures, notably the ongoing experiment of the European Union, and the increasingly common phenomenon of dual citizenship have also made the idea of multiple allegiances a political reality. Citizenship, far from being the exclusive preserve of the state has been extended as the singular concept of citizenship 'bursts its bounds' (Heater, 1999, p. 117). This does not, however, mean that there is anything like a consensus over the meaning of 'world citizenship'. Indeed, the very idea has been dismissed in the past for being 'indefinable in theory, non-existent in practice and ... undesirable in any case' (p. 134).

To claim that world citizenship is currently 'indefinable', however, is hardly to condemn the notion. It is to accept, instead, that citizenship is a dynamic concept and that our ideas about world or cosmopolitan citizenship are only now catching up to current realities. Heater is surely correct to identify a continuum for cosmopolitan citizenship, ranging from a vague sense of connection with the rest of humanity, to a stronger feeling of responsibility for the planet and its inhabitants, a recognition of ecological interdependence, an acknowledgment of international law and standards of treatment for all human beings, and ultimately a commitment, sometimes an active commitment, to the design of truly cosmopolitan institutions of global, democratic governance (1999, p. 136). Cosmopolitan citizenship, unlike earlier forms rooted in ideas of a community/territory, is something that can be exercised by degree according to one's personal preferences.

This analysis points to a clearly 'consumerist' aspect of one's own cosmopolitan commitments. Bennett, for example, identifies 'global consumer activism' of the sort typified by anti-globalization campaigners such as Naomi Klein as signaling a change in the definitions of both citizenship and democracy. Consumer activism appropriates the techniques and images of global corporate advertising – as organizations like adbusters.org ably illustrate. Politics, far from being on the decline, is thriving, except that it is not recognized by traditional indicators – expressed by party affiliation or voter turnout. As Bennett notes:

> political engagement may be closer to home, less conventionally organized, and more likely to be defined in terms of struggles over evolving notions of rights, morals and lifestyle values. It is increasingly likely that engagement can occur at both local and global levels without traditional participation through traditional government or national institutions. In this view, the forms of public life, and the ways in which communication organizes them, are not only changing, but they require new concepts and methods of study.
>
> (Bennett, 2000, p. 308)

Theorizing citizenship in this context must account for a number of different factors. There is evidence that the distinction between consumer and citizen is being reconfigured and this is not something that should necessarily be resisted. Theorists of economic democracy have long equated politics with a marketplace of ideas with citizens as consumers of political advertising messages. Political consumerism in the postmodern period, however, encourages displays of social responsibility through a strange combination of highly individualized political decision-making expressed through the purchase or rejection of certain products. This individualized expression of political conscience is also often reiterated at a global level. Citizen-consumers recognize the connections between product and producer, very often a corporation that itself operates at a level of power beyond national representatives. Consumer-activists can express their disquiet with this state of affairs by limiting their personal expenditure on consumer goods; a phenomenon that Etzioni describes as 'voluntary simplicity' (1998); or by reappropriating corporate identity, as evidenced in the Nike sweatshop campaign, via the production of alternative printed and electronic media sources to counter the messages supplied by corporations (Goldman and Papson, 1998).

The second element of contemporary citizenship is decidedly existential. Deciding to what degree one endorses a particular cosmopolitan value and how one is to act is increasingly a matter of personal choice, but one set within a wider context of social and political responsibilities that are identified as 'shared'.

As Larry May has noted in his description of the notion of shared responsibility: 'When individuals recognize that they often share agency or subjectivity with the members of their group, when they recognize that their individual actions have repercussions on the lives of these others of both a direct and indirect sort, then they should also come to a recognition of the connectedness of their lives with other lives in the group' (1992, p. 170). Shared responsibility is a far more nuanced version of traditional theories of individual or collective responsibility, corresponding to the notion that the latter is diffused throughout a population contingent upon one's role or function within a group. Crucial to the social existential perspective is the choice one makes as an individual always-already in relation to others. This means, argues May, that a person can be held indirectly responsible for harms caused even though they may not have actually initiated those harms.

A person may share responsibility for a harm done simply by their inaction which resulted in an increase in the chances of those harms occurring again. Alternatively, they may have actively chosen to adopt an attitude that purported to remove them from any responsibility, adherence to a blinkered form of patriotism for example, that lends support to policies that are either illegal or unjust. In any case, the position of heightened awareness that citizens find themselves in invariably requires of them that they acknowledge their (in)action or that within this sense of shared responsibility they find the motive that leads them to identify their own concerns with those of others.

Beck (2000a) and Giddens (1991) describe this existential condition as a feature of 'reflexive globalization' and 'life politics' respectively. For both theorists, the period of 'simple modernity' which ran from the 1920s to the 1970s has come to an end. The collapse of political economic agreements at the global level has unleashed a period of instability on world economies and societies. Where people once 'knew their place', the precise role they occupied within the institutions of society, the workplace and the family, and the proper relation to their government and state, the situation now is much less clear and fraught with anxiety.

Beck's central claim is that the 'work society' hitherto defined as either a 'job for life' or 'full employment' is coming to an end. The result is that the career is being replaced by short-term contract work and that subjectivity is being forcibly reshaped by a management discourse of 'empowerment' and 'flexibility'. The results conspire to create worker insecurity. Flexibility can quite literally mean 'that when you go to bed at night, you don't know whether you have a job the next morning' (Chomsky, 1994, p. 143). Before the invention of the 'global economy' individuals could see their work within the context of a narrative that could be followed because work could be counted upon. In contrast, 'flexibility' introduces a sense of fragmentation to this notion of a self's narrative with the consequence that the worker is thrown back upon themselves as creators of meaning (Sennett, 1998, p. 99).

Beck's contention is that the result is a move away from 'work society' into 'risk society', where citizenship in Western democracies is increasingly defined by insecurity and where individuals are forced to market themselves to employers. As traditional authority is challenged so the individual is required to fashion a biography for themselves, to renegotiate their identity in the context of increased amounts of information, instability and choices.

The implications of this view for human relationships and for citizen–state relationships are considerable. Relationships are to be entered into, Giddens suggests, and sustained for their own sake only if they are perceived as bringing sufficient rewards. Once they fall below a certain threshold, they are ended (Giddens, 1995, p. 117).

Beck argues that what is required in such a situation is a reinvigoration of political life, a new kind of politics that draws on a conception of civil society that is both local and transnational, which in turn rests on a quite different conception of work and choice in human life. This must be, argues Beck, because full employment in idea and in practice is no longer possible. For social democrats like Beck, '[a] new politicized society is the only legitimate answer and the only answer capable of addressing ecological and social problems' that all people face irrespective of their particular biographies (2000b, p. 4).

For Giddens, the kind of politics required in response to globalization is 'life politics' where political issues arise from 'processes of self-actualization in post-traditional contexts, where globalizing influences intrude deeply into the reflexive project of the self, and conversely where processes of self-realization influence global strategies' (1991, p. 214). Life politics is about 'how we should live in a world where everything that used to be natural (or traditional) now has in some sense to be chosen, or decided about' (1994, p. 90). Life politics is inherently individual, social and political, as the decisions that have to be made must factor in global processes that were hitherto considered beyond the remit of private or national consciousness – a feature that looks set to accelerate as the meaning of national identities, of what it means to be American or British for example, comes under renewed scrutiny (see Huntington, 2004). The question is not only how one lives in a world of Chernobyls, BSE crises and 'flexible' work practices but how much responsibility one feels for a particular issue, which groups one identifies with and what one then chooses to do about it.

5.3   A new politics of cosmopolitanism?

Although it is possible to identify a need for global politics, the challenges facing such a notion are several. It is much easier to talk about institutional reform when the cosmopolitan institutional framework is, to some extent, already in place. Considering the model of citizenship most appropriate to the changed environment and the kind of citizen virtues appropriate to political action at different levels requires, I have suggested, an analysis of cosmorepublican agency.

This may sound contrived and it is no accident that, as both Pascal Lamy (2005) and Neera Chandhoke (2003) note, the challenge, above all, is one of vocabulary, of being able to find the words to best describe a new political vision for the future. If nationalism provided a 'grammar' of understanding and feeling that suited the political aspirations of a political elite in the nineteenth and twentieth centuries, cosmopolitanism has yet to provide an alternative that is as potent for global citizens. Discussions of 'world' citizenship, at least in their present form, are unlikely to inspire. 'Governance', suggests Lamy, sounds like a starchy Victorian value (2005).

Part of the problem, however, is the recognition of what is possible politically:

> Democracy is a big balloon filled with gas or hot air, and sent up so that you shall be kept looking up at the sky whilst other people are picking your pockets. When the balloon comes down to earth every five years or so you are invited to get into the basket if you can throw out one of the people who are sitting tightly in it; but as you can afford neither the time nor the money, and there are forty millions of you and hardly room for six hundred in the basket, the balloon goes up again with much the same lot in it and leaves you where you were before. I think you will admit that the balloon as an image of Democracy corresponds to the parliamentary facts.
>
> (Shaw, 1930, p. xii)

Written in 1929, this intentionally humorous description of George Bernard Shaw's does, nonetheless, correspond to 'the facts' as they appear to many. Indeed, there seems to be a failure of political imagination at the turn of the twenty-first century much as William James pointed to a failure of moral and aesthetic imagination at the turn of the twentieth century.[4]

Chandhoke notes that the generations of activists that grew up and participated in the turbulent events of the 1930s and 1960s somehow recognized the contingency of their own historical period because of a shared vocabulary of anti-imperialism, anti-colonialism and through the knowledge that ordinary people could change the political landscape. Gandhi's campaigns against the British in India used the vocabulary of *swaraj* (self-rule), 'ethical' nationalism and civilization to counter the 'irreligious' industrial civilization of the British (Gandhi, 1997). Martin Luther King's direct, mass, non-violent action in the United States during the 1960s was part of a complex strategy that mixed the personal with the political by drawing on vocabularies that were inspired by spiritual and quintessentially American traditions of freedom, revolution and emancipation. Although King toward the end of his life recognized the importance of the global dimension to his own discussion of economic inequalities in the domestic context – in a late speech he described himself as a 'citizen of the world' (1986, p. 238) – the same impetus behind these earlier movements is lacking from the vocabulary of global governance. Governance, rather than politics, has not added a new dimension to the language of contemporary politics but has emptied it of its radical potential.

The response from leading cosmopolitan political theorists to global issues has not resolved this dilemma. Their approach has tended to reflect a concern with institution building and reform, of adherence to universal moral principles rather than a call to political action, and the need for new treatises between nations and their peoples. Most see compliance to a new set of rules housed by a new set of institutions as the way forward. The character or virtues of global citizens are far less discussed and with good reason as we shall see in the next chapter.

Advocates of institutional reform argue for both the extension of institutional responsibility and/or the morphing of national political institutions (i.e. parties) into transnational ones. Pogge (1992) bases his suggestions for global reform on a reinterpretation of the thesis proposed by Kant in *Perpetual Peace*. He argues, for example, for global institutional reforms, coupled with the decentralization of power away from the state in order to check that power. Advocating what he describes as legal rather than moral (or for that matter, political) cosmo-politanism, Pogge suggests that individual human rights, rather than the state, should be taken as the primary unit of analysis and the ultimate unit of concern. A focus on institutions is required because everyone is in some way involved in a single 'global institutional scheme' and because states, however much their authority might be diminished, remain the enforcers of laws.

What is required, therefore, is the recognition and extension of insti-tutional responsibility. Following Kant, Pogge suggests that where a people cannot help but impact upon the lives of another, such interac-tions should be legally codified in some way for fairness sake but also because our lives, and the lives of future generations, depend on our reaching mutual agreements. Institutional reform of this kind, he argues, has the great advantage of blocking 'the rich and mighty in today's developed countries' from seeing themselves 'as disconnected from the fate of the less fortunate denizens of the Third World' (1992, p. 52).

Beck's (1998) focus on the novelty of a world order where the basic unit of analysis is no longer exclusively the nation-state leads him to propose a slightly different political arrangement intended to match the global flows of capital. Indeed, an equivalent context for political action, according to Beck, is the creation of transnational parties which will provide the key to solving the age-old problem of democratic legitimacy in the new era of globalization.

According to Beck, cosmopolitan parties will be sites of political activity and interaction that will come to represent transnational issues within the context of nation-states. These parties will exist as parties for 'global citizens' in the political sphere by mimicking the actions of corporations in the economic sphere and will operate as networks, sites of interaction that bring local concerns together with global issues.

At the very least, Beck thinks, more traditional, state-based parties will be forced to include something of a transnational agenda in their own programs. Cosmopolitan parties would have to develop 'cosmopolitan ethics and politics in their respective cultural milieux' to do this. Beck thinks that with a shift in the cultural values of many developed nations, these parties could be grounded on humanist traditions common to many of the world's religions and cultures, which would put global concerns at the center of their agenda.[5]

The interplay between the national and the international is a central cosmopolitan insight. Yet, relatively few attempts have been made to consider the interplay between structure and agency. One such attempt, advanced by Bohman (1997), updates Kant's original 'single people, single state' thesis to account for the existence of culturally plural states. He argues for cosmopolitan public spheres *within* republics, an active transnational civil society without, and the ongoing transformation of existing democratic institutions to account for what he envisages as a radically plural and, most importantly, critical cosmopolitan democracy. To be effective, to act as a counterweight to the activities of representatives, stop them from waging constant war, and provide solutions to economic and ecological crises, cosmopolitan democracy must be inclusive of the diversity of modern states and not limited to a privileged elite. The latter was, despite Kant's professed support for the public airing of views, extremely restricted. Even philosophers who ought to be allowed 'to speak freely and publicly on universal maxims of warfare and peacemaking', because their natures were supposedly incorruptible, had to do so in secret.

Discussion within the republic of letters was precisely the correct forum to air grievances, Kant thought, because this form of literary protest was limited to the educated and its effects were prescribed. The carefully worded criticisms of philosophers were never meant to overturn governments, only advise them. In *'What is Enlightenment?'* he was careful to note that King Frederick's subjects could argue as much as they liked and about whatever they liked, but they also had to abide by the monarch's will. In this regard, the function of philosophy and philosophers was twofold – to instruct the people upon their rights and duties to the state on the one hand, while always maintaining respectful tones to the state and its rulers on the other.

Bohman's commitment to the notion of a vibrant cosmopolitan democracy sits uneasily with this deferential attitude toward rulers. The demand that only the educated and literate participate is rejected as an unwelcome restriction on public contestation. Moreover, a public composed exclusively of philosophers would be incredibly conservative, 'entrenched and privileged enough not to want to use its public reason in dangerous or transformative ways' (1997, p. 187).

This reflects a broader concern Bohman has about the danger of institutions becoming entrenched and monolithic and it is one of his most valuable insights. Bohman asserts that world citizens should have the capability to make their opinions known in such a way that the authorities cannot avoid acknowledging them. In other words, they should be able to act always as a countervailing power to the institutions of governance that have a tendency to become monolithic.

However, he also notes that there are two main obstacles to this transformation of political life. First, there is the centrality of conflict that is part of cultural pluralism. Publicity for Kant and for Bohman means being able to give reasons publicly for why one holds certain opinions. It means 'enlarging your thought', changing your mind (p. 188). Citizens have to be sophisticated political actors when it comes to representing and defending their views. They cannot just criticize they also have to try to understand. This is an essential requirement of political agency.

Yet the second problem that Bohman brings up is how to practice democratic sovereignty on a global scale if you are actually to solve ecological and economic crises. Bohman does not want cosmopolitan public spheres to become homes simply for the chattering classes. He wants decisions to be made and cosmopolitan opinion to be politically influential. His recommendation, therefore, is that civil societies within republics should not be prone to community bias but be genuinely open to divergent opinion.

The need to find solutions to the world's crises has turned recent discussion of cosmopolitan reforms in a new direction. Theorists like David Held (1995, 2002, 2004a,b) have long noted the effects of the instability of global economics and the additional challenges to governments as they find it increasingly difficult to pursue their domestic agendas and deliver on campaign promises. Yet now Held has moved beyond stating the need for institutional reforms and a new commitment to democracy by suggesting that another pivotal moment has been reached, as important as the decision to establish the institutions of global governance during the 1940s and 1950s. 'We are at a turning point', he claims. 'It will not be measured by days or months, but over the coming few years between now and 2010, choices will be made that will determine the fate of the globe for decades to come. It is *that* serious' (2004a, p. 2).

Held notes the numerous failures by the global powers to address the imbalance in world trade (signified by the collapse of trade talks at Cancun in 2003), the chronic humanitarian crises that persist in some of the world's poorest regions, and the increasingly apparent consequences of global warming. Most recently, the actions taken by the United States and its allies through a series of foreign policy decisions following the 11 September 2001 attacks on the mainland United States have seriously undermined the basis of multilateral agreements and the credibility of the United Nations.

In response, Held is now calling for a new 'global covenant' including, but not limited to, reform of the UN, trade-related aspects of intellectual property rights, and expansion of the role of developing countries at the World Trade Organization, a reduction in the debt burden and so on. At the same time, Held notes that 'the most powerful nations are not dedicated to building an international order which delivers relief, hope and the opportunity to the least well-off and those most at risk, even though this in their own interests, as well as being in line with their expressed values' (2004b, p. 3).

Held's project is laudable. The means for improving the lot of the vast majority of human beings *is* available but there also appears to be a fundamental lack of political will to do anything significant to implement the systemic changes necessary to make life less of a burden and more of a possibility for the vast majority of people. For reasons similar to those identified by Amartya Sen (1999) who made the acute observation that poor people starve not because there is a lack of food but because of an unwillingness to share or distribute the food on the part of the 'haves', Held is now arguing that reform is desperately required not just in the institutions of global governance but in all areas of society. What is required is a transformation of political will.

Only those 'fundamentally' committed to a realist's view of political life would disagree that a greater degree of transparency, accountability and democracy in global governance combined with a genuine rather than instrumental commitment to international law and social justice is necessary for the safety of all citizens around the globe. Recognizing that the state is required to regulate global financial flows and that environmental safeguards are necessary safeguards in some instances and not simply impediments to the 'natural' operation of the 'free market' is necessary if the quality of life for the vast majority of people and their descendants is not to be severely diminished.

Increasingly, Held has moved from describing 'cosmopolitan democracy' as a self-consciously 'utopian' political project toward a list of recommendations that increasingly sound like a manifesto for a revolutionary cosmopolitan, global political movement. That may be what he desires in which case his theory has moved toward what, after Went (2004), we might describe as 'transformative cosmopolitanism'. Theorists of the latter persuasion recognize the need for fundamental change in the economic and social relations of power. Changing the system, argues Went, rather than managing it is what is required for a 'credible project for global democracy' (2004, p. 351).

5.4   Conclusion

Contemporary cosmopolitanism exposes the absurdity of the bounded community and the easy comfort of nationalism. It does this by drawing upon the new social and political realities of life in the early twenty-first century, realities made possible by commerce, much as Kant suggested, but with consequences that the stay-at-home cosmopolitan could not have foreseen. Like Kant, contemporary cosmopolitan theorists look to institutional solutions to solve the problems of the world's risk society. The individuals who populate these institutions are, moreover, described in classically liberal terms. The imagined cosmopolitan community of the future is home to enlightened individuals who exhibit those characteristics of the best liberal thinkers: autonomous, tolerant, open-minded and willing to change their opinions through reasoned debate.

Three questions arise as a result of this. First, how is this transition from state-centered to cosmopolitan democracy to come about? Second, who are the agents of change that will make this transition possible? And third, what kind of relationship should we imagine between global institutions of governance and global citizens? I believe that the answers to these questions are interrelated.

The most effective mechanism through which societies change is the education of future citizens. This has long been recognized by liberals and republicans and so it is to a discussion of education and specifically the basic requirements of education for citizenship in a global context that I will turn to in the following chapter.

The answer to the second question is more complex. I said at the outset of this book that what was required was a new political vision of citizenship, one that took the best elements of the republican tradition – a skepticism toward authority alongside a commitment to the substantive principles of human freedom and dignity – and combined it with the recognition that the context for political activity had changed.

No longer the polis, but the cosmopolis is the proper site of political action. Cosmorepublicans, I suggested, were not situated selves in the way that liberal citizens found themselves obediently bound to the leaders of an imagined nation, but ironic selves, bridge builders and networkers who participate virtually and actually in order to effect change locally and globally (Rheingold, 1994; Anheier and Katz, 2005).

This is a vision of citizenship that expands upon the notion of reflexive globalization and complements the institutional dimension of contemporary cosmopolitan thought. It is a model of citizenship that is intended to describe a new imaginary, a new way of political living in the postmodern world.

This model of citizenship also provides an important corrective to the institutional agenda of cosmopolitans by recognizing the essential openness of political debate and discussion. The vocabulary of republicanism prompts cosmopolitan theorists – who have hitherto chosen not to consider the dynamics of political agency – to consider the prerequisites necessary for political action if moral universalism is not to descend into a thinly disguised hegemonic project.

On the one hand, taking politics and deliberation seriously would require cosmopolitans to give more emphasis to the forms of civic life necessary to foster a political culture, promoting global civic virtues within a democratically oriented global society. What this further means is that the issue of global inequality, the enormous disparities of income and resources, the exploitation of vast numbers of the world's population which hampers their efforts to find a voice let alone use it, should become a primary political consideration. Inequality undermines any meaningful sense of well-being or enjoyment of human rights.

Institutional cosmopolitanism acknowledges processes of uneven development and the subsequent uneven distribution of power in the global system. The increasing availability of new technologies, which facilitate global communication between disparate groups both in terms of political projects, geographic location and the scale of activities, represents a dramatic development in the political impact of 'soft' power. This intensification of power is due to the capacity of the 'forces from below' to shape interests and agendas as well as making governments accountable for their actions and decisions.

Cosmopolitans that adopt an institutional perspective argue that the lack of transparency and accountability of suprastate governance is a crucial factor in limiting effectiveness and legitimacy. What is required, then, is reform rather than revolution. This institutional cosmopolitanism agenda seeks: (i) a desire for greater transparency, accountability and democracy in global governance; (ii) a commitment to social justice in the pursuit of a more equitable distribution of the world's resources and human security; (iii) the protection and reinvention of community at diverse levels and the regulation of the global economy through public management of global finances and trade flows; and (iv) the provision of global public goods.

Notions of republican political agency add to this mix the idea that global citizenship will always be oppositional. This would be the case even, and perhaps especially, if the global regulatory structures that Held *et al.* desire were actually effected.

Cosmorepublicans challenge the ideological ordering and institution-alization of power within societies. The struggles they engage in are not only concerned with issues of how economic and social resources are controlled and distributed in society. They are also struggles over the power to give meaning to the world by defining who the legitimate participants are, what the issues are and what the available alternatives might be. In other words, groups are engaged in a struggle for identity as well as for resources, which accounts for their mobility and extra-institutional posture.

This mobile or nomadic conceptualization of civic identity has only momentary congruencies with the discourses of global governance. Even in benign forms, institutions, we may assume following Weber, are likely to ossify into embedded structures that sacrifice deliberation for rationalization. Yet unlike Weber's state-centered assertion that only a charismatic parliamentary leader could provide the requisite counterweight to the growth of bureaucratic power, the proper goal is to aim for the paradox of *dynamic institutionalism*, where institutions remain open and responsive to extra-institutional pressures. In a global context, it would be a serious error to reduce questions of governance to the technical aspects of a new constitutionalism which is precisely why a cosmorepublican notion of political agency needs to be articulated.

6
The Case for Political Education

> Not only does society, as it is presently structured, keep people
> immature but every serious attempt to shift it ... towards
> maturity is immediately met with incredible resistances ...
> – Theodore Adorno, 1999, p. 32

If cosmorepublican citizens are to be understood as the necessary countervailing power to both state and suprastate institutions of governance
the question invariably arises, 'is it possible to educate for this kind of
citizenship?' The subject of political education has long remained a point
of contention between state-bound liberals and republicans, a hardly
surprising conclusion given their divergent philosophical aims and
political purposes. Theorists of a cosmopolitan persuasion have long
argued that educational systems need to be part of a platform for change if
a plan for international peace or a new global covenant is to be realized.
The problem with this admirable suggestion, however, is that the
specific requirements of a global citizen's education are, to quote one
authority on the subject, very much an area of 'grey uncertainty' (Heater,
1999, p. 169).

Kant argued just before he died that future citizens ought to be
educated in a manner which was adapted 'to the idea of humanity and
the whole destiny of man'. He pointed out, however, that this enlightened
view ran at crossed purposes from both parents and rulers. The former
were more concerned that children were able to 'make their way in the
world' the latter regarded their subjects as instrumental to their particular
political ambitions.

While it could hardly be claimed that education is denied to the vast
majority of citizens in modern nation-states, an explicitly 'political'
education, empowering citizens to question and even rebel against their

own governments, surely is. Joseph Schumpeter (1976) noted that one of the most significant features of modern states was the expansion in education, specifically higher education, something he took as the inevitable by-product of industrial development. What he also noted was the propensity for high unemployment among the educated who could not find satisfactory work. In fact, Schumpeter thought that universities were actually performing a disservice to society by creating unemployable persons, the consequence of which was an increase in discontent and resentment. In such a situation, Schumpeter suggested, with intellectuals unable to find the employment they so earnestly desired, feeling unhappy with the existing order of things was inevitable. It was only a matter of time before they would begin to criticize political institutions – a situation he thought should be avoided.

Education is a peculiar problem for modern states because it is unclear what the proper purposes of education are – another example, perhaps, of the paradox of liberalism, desiring both adherence to the laws of the market, obedience to legitimate political authorities, while also endorsing a progressive view of human development. The dilemma was captured most succinctly, however, not by a philosopher but by an official at the British Department of Education and Science in 1986 – a department that was soon to be merged with the Department of Employment. 'We are beginning to create aspirations', he noted, 'which society cannot match...When young people...can't find work which meets their abilities and expectations, then we are only creating frustration with...disturbing social consequences. We have to ration...educational opportunities so that society can cope with the output of education... People must be educated once more to know their place' (cited in Cohen, 1986, p. 6).

The sentiment behind these words reflects the widespread view that education is critically important, in many cases the primary means of transmitting an accepted view of history and politics from government to citizen. This is not a controversial point and not a particularly modern one either. Aristotle thought that education within a state should match its constitution, the primary purpose of which was the maintenance of social and political stability. Today, however, education within modern liberal societies is, principally, education to work (Barlow and Robertson, 1994).

This modern educational algorithm is, however, coming under strain because of changing work patterns nationally and transnationally (Rifkin, 1995). The end of the career and the new era of the 'McJob'[1] challenges the rationale of state education to a considerable degree.

Competing identities to traditional 'national identities' and a surplus of information about government activities, both official and independent, pose additional challenges to educational policy. The question 'what is education for?' may therefore be raised once again.

6.1   Liberalism: Educating for minimal autonomy

Contemporary liberal writing on the subject of 'political' education or 'education for citizenship' focuses squarely (and unsurprisingly) on the concerns and needs of the state. Liberals examine the proper scope of democratic citizenship, a model that requires adherence to certain norms, and whether this model can accommodate the demands placed upon it by those seeking a multicultural curriculum, social diversity and group rights. The major issue that preoccupies the current generation of liberal theorists writing about education is whether the demands of minority groups can exist within a liberal framework. While these considerations could form part of a global citizen's curriculum, there is little mention within this body of work that speaks to greater participation or reflection upon politics beyond the state.

Within liberal political theory, it is possible to identify different liberalisms and their corresponding approaches, approaches that may be divided for ease of explanation into three categories: neutral, political and comprehensive. Each offers a different answer to the question: 'What is education for?'

According to what has been termed a 'neutralist' position, the purpose of the liberal state is to remain impartial among competing moral conceptions (Ackerman, 1981). A defense of liberal institutions, rights and liberties that gives each and every group the same protections, it is argued, allows for the possibility of the pursuit of 'the good life' whatever that happens to be. With respect to education, the concept of 'non-interference' is to be upheld as much as possible with the curriculum and teaching approach reflecting this primary theoretical orientation. In the words of one advocate:

> We have no right to look upon the future citizens as if we were master gardeners who can tell the difference between a pernicious weed and a beautiful flower. A system of liberal education provides children with a sense of the very different lives that could be theirs – so that, as they approach maturity, they have the cultural materials available to build lives equal to their evolving conceptions of the good.
>
> (Ackerman, 1981, p. 139)

The theoretical attractions of this position notwithstanding, liberal neutralism faces both theoretical and practical difficulties. On the one hand, it is difficult to see how an educational system that wishes to teach one subject over another can claim to be strictly 'neutral', or indeed how teaching can be neutral in any but the weakest sense. The now famous examples of parents who have removed their children from public schooling precisely because they feel threatened by a curriculum that seeks to provide them 'with a sense of the very different lives that could be theirs' poses a real dilemma to the liberal neutralist. Indeed, such an education has been rejected on the grounds that it 'undermines' children's religious convictions and, consequently, a community's traditional way of life (Stolzenberg, 1993).

Kymlicka's work on multicultural citizenship illustrates the dilemma of the neutralist position, though he would probably dispute that label. Kymlicka is convinced that contemporary liberal political cultures need reform so that 'people are more able and willing to put themselves in other people's shoes, and truly understand . . . their needs and interests'. For this to happen a change needs to be effected in education, in the media portrayal of various groups, and in the political process which should become, according to Kymlicka, more deliberative (1996, p. 141). He also maintains that the liberal notion of toleration needs to be updated to include a defense of illiberal minorities with the result that where individual rights are being violated within the minority community the liberal majority should not be able to prevent them (p. 168). The preservation of illiberal cultures, for Kymlicka, trumps the rights of liberals to intervene.

Kymlicka desires reform in a more substantive liberal direction while remaining neutral on the subject of interference. He assumes that if change is to be effected within illiberal minority groups it will come from 'liberal reformers' from within the illiberal culture who 'seek to promote their liberal principles, through reason or example' while their supporters from the liberal majority outside the community speak out in their defense. Yet, as critics have noted, none of what Kymlicka says takes account of how difficult it might be for 'liberal reformers' in an illiberal minority to speak out, whether they would have the opportunity to do so, or whether their education system provided them with the capacity to articulate their dissent in any way (Okin, 2002, p. 20).

In recognition of the limits to the liberal neutral position, a rather more bullish view has been advanced by those who see the pretence to neutrality as translating into, at best, indifference and at worst a theory that promotes an inability to question and learn from others. This undermines, if not civic virtue, then a requisite degree of liberal civility. Adherents of a more substantive notion of liberal education therefore see the neutralist approach as ignoring the demands of 'democratic justice'. Amy Gutmann points out, for example, that '[t]reating every moral opinion as equally worthy encourages children in the false subjectivism that "I have my opinion and you have yours and who's to say who's right?"' (Gutmann, 1987, p. 56).

Theorists sympathetic to the goals of the neutralist but who claim that liberalism is better off by admitting some form of non-neutrality fall along a conceptual line that ultimately leads to the sorts of comprehensive liberalism one finds in the writings of Immanuel Kant and John Stuart Mill. Yet these ideas are regarded as too controversial, potentially oppressive and generally unsuitable for modern 'reasonably pluralist' societies.

This, at least, is the view of 'political' liberals who argue that liberalism is not claiming moral neutrality as such, but acts on the basis of a core or common morality, which is likely to form the basis of reasonable agreement.[2] Further, some political liberals argue that there is a subtle difference in liberal educational theory between educating for full autonomy and minimal autonomy (Reich, 2002) or autarchy (Macedo, 1990).

On the one hand, all political liberal citizens are assumed to share an understanding of political institutions, the ideals behind them, a sense of where they came from and a common understanding of justice. On the other, it is taken as given that if a choice arises between adherence to a personal belief and to the tenets of political justice, a believer in a comprehensive belief system will be able to revise their beliefs to allow for political liberal theories to take effect.

Needless to say, this is a demanding doctrine for those who do not wish to be 'reasonable'. Those who do not share or incorporate in their own way, for example, either liberal political conceptions of justice, or those who are unwilling or incapable of setting their religious selves to one side when political liberals require them to so do. Perhaps this is why some 'political liberals', unlike those that defend or advocate neutralism or diversity, assert that if children of religious or other persuasions are intolerant of others then they must be taught to be tolerant and that this assertion necessarily overrides the notions of neutrality and diversity.

What takes precedence for political liberals is the political settlement and if some groups have to adjust their belief structures to fit in with liberal public policies then this is justified on the assumption that religious groups are invariably engaged in public activities of one sort or another, activities that bring them into contact with wider elements of society. In other words, among the many roles that people adopt in their lives, whenever they venture into the public realm and make claims as citizens then they should adjust their behavior accordingly, speak in a language that all can understand and 'play the game'. For those groups who wish to protect/preserve their own way of life from the effects of diversity and consider reasonable liberalism too high a price, withdrawal from society has its costs.

Political liberalism 'invites' individuals to lay aside their most fundamental beliefs when it comes to 'laying the groundwork for common political institutions' (Macedo, 1995, p. 475). Requiring individuals of a comprehensive religious faith to place their beliefs to one side in a public and morally plural world has a certain theoretical neatness to it and the outcome, were it possible, might be desirable. Yet this form of liberalism faces the charge that what it regards as 'basic' to all citizens is simply not the case.

The problem for political liberals and liberals broadly in discussions about civic education is the problem of deciding what a *basic* education or an 'education up to a certain standard' actually entails and how it is to be agreed upon.[3] According to one prominent commentator this is a pressing need whose realization appears most unlikely:

> The pluralism of free societies makes urgent the task of creating citizens who share a sufficiently cohesive political identity. At the same time, the sheer range and power of pluralism make it hard to see how reasoned agreement on the content of that identity and the educational practices that would make it safe for the future could be more than an idle wish.
>
> (Callan, 1997, p. 21)

Theoretically, comprehensive and political liberalisms are distinct, with political liberalism attempting to offer a theory independent of deeper and hence controversial moral claims. Shorn of a fundamental philosophy it seeks to base its validity on practical, contingent considerations while comprehensive liberalism uses contestable notions like autonomy and its related metaphysical supports upon which to base its claims. The advantage of political over comprehensive approaches is that the former by appealing to the notion of an 'overlapping consensus' seems to avoid the undesirable requirements of the latter – the imposition of supposedly unwelcome ideals upon views of life in political and in private life.

The trouble with the distinction is that it stands or falls on a host of assumptions not the least of which is the acceptability of public *reasonableness* by people who are otherwise unreasonable in private. To put the point another way, public and private must remain distinct and unreasonable people must be convinced that it is an iron-clad distinction if political liberalism is to avoid collapsing into some closet form of comprehensive liberalism which they would most likely reject.

What political liberalism requires of citizens of all persuasions is that they be capable of political engagement that is 'fair minded'. Rawls' assumption is that most comprehensive doctrines in a liberal society can already be said to exhibit these qualities. Yet it is unclear whether he is making a strictly empirical claim here – which could be proven false – or whether he is 'rigging the model' in the same manner in which he openly admitted to working at his theory of justice 'from both ends' in order to arrive at an answer that accorded with his own assumptions (Rawls, 1971, p. 20).

Rawls claims that the major difference between comprehensive and political liberalisms lies in their scope. Comprehensive liberals require the exercise of autonomy in private. Political liberals do not. Yet, interestingly, in one of the few places where Rawls addresses the consequences of political liberalism for education, he contends that in order for the political virtues to exist – these include civility, tolerance, cooperation, fair-mindedness, a willingness to meet others half way – they may need to be taught. For people to be independent and fully cooperating members of society, they need to know that apostasy is not a crime (1996, p. 199).

Political liberalism might require far less theoretically than a Mill or a Kant might demand. Both theorists would argue for full autonomy in all spheres of life. Yet in practice the consequences of teaching political virtues might well spill over into private, non-political realms with undesirable consequences for the comprehensive doctrines concerned. The best that Rawls can offer is a sense of regret (1996, p. 200). If political virtues need to be taught and if political liberalism, on Rawls' own admission, begins to look increasingly like a version of Kant or Mill's arguments for autonomy then ultimately one might ask what the difference between the two liberalisms actually is.

Perfectionist liberals like Mill argued that autonomy was a good in itself, part of what it meant to be a 'progressive being' but that it also provided individuals with the wherewithal to participate in political life. This might come about through schooling but also activity in those public organizations – juries were a favorite example – that encouraged a proper sense of fellow feeling. The developmental view of liberalism, as we saw in an earlier chapter, was the most radical element of liberalism.

It was an argument, ultimately, about political opportunity, about the ability to gain access to state power.

Such arguments are almost, if not entirely, lacking from contemporary liberal discussion about the proper purposes of education. The focus of concern has shifted from a concern with exploitation and access to power, to accommodating illiberal minorities by constraining traditional arguments for autonomy. As a consequence, the thrust of the argument is distinctly apolitical. The focus of liberal education is in developing the best tools for coexistence such that illiberal minorities will not feel alienated from the mainstream political environment.

6.2 Republicanism: Educating for citizenship

The driving force behind Rawls' theory was a concern with toleration and the minimization of conflict. Yet for a self-styled 'political' liberalism, critics point out, there is little mention of politics in any real sense in any of his works. Rather, Rawls and others who share his views are concerned with stability, avoiding the thornier issues of conflict that permeate political societies by studiously choosing to avoid them (Mouffe, 1993).

It is somewhat curious, then, to find that Rawls himself defends civic republicanism of the kind originally developed by Machiavelli and reinterpreted most recently by Quentin Skinner – a theory that advocates widespread involvement in public life – because, he suggests, it differs from political liberalism only to the extent that different sorts of institutions would have to be designed to satisfy civic republicanism's aims. Indeed, Rawls suggests that there is 'no fundamental opposition' between political liberalism and classical republicanism because it does not 'presuppose a comprehensive religious, philosophical, or moral doctrine' (Rawls, 1996, p. 200).

It is debatable whether Machiavelli's thesis, as this is developed in his *Discourses*, actually conforms to what Rawls has in mind. The preference for a civic cult which would be used as a force for social stability and virtue seems to suggest otherwise. And although Skinner's instrumental or 'procedural' approach to politics has much more in its favor, from Rawls' perspective, than the more substantive demands of character placed upon Aristotle's citizens, the argument for 'public freedom' is still a demanding one.

Indeed, what both Aristotle and Machiavelli share is a concern with political practice as part of a suitable civic education.[4] Sherry has suggested that 'a responsible republican education would give children both the knowledge and the inclination to act in accordance with the common culture' (1995, pp. 171–2). Even 'critical thinkers', argues Harvey Siegel (1988), must be disposed to do so. The incentive to think and act critically comes, in part, from constructive exposure to the world. One contemporary argues that any effort to make politics 'real' should focus squarely on action rather than the accumulation of facts about the political system: 'The answer to political apathy is not classroom education but action' (Ridley, 1982, p. 41).

Perhaps the single greatest difference between the political liberal and civic republican approach to education, however, is the concern over corruption. To be educated as a republican citizen was to be able to defend oneself against abuse from powerful political elites.[5] There is little reason to think this tendency in political life has changed. 'There has never been a social stratum', noted Max Weber, 'which did not do this [i.e. perform corrupt actions] in one way or another' (1994, p. 319).[6]

Civic education in the republican tradition ensures that the citizenry maintain, along with a healthy respect for their leaders, an equally healthy distrust. Indeed, one might argue that the ability to defend oneself as a citizen against corruption in political life is, in effect, one of the basic abilities of a citizen in any decent society. As Jefferson noted in his 'Bill for the More General Diffusion of Knowledge':

> experience hath shewn, that even under the best forms, those entrusted with power have, in time, and by slow operations, perverted it into tyranny; and it is believed that the most effectual means of preventing this would be to illuminate, as far as practicable, the minds of the people at large, and more especially to give them knowledge of those facts, which history exhibiteth, that, possessed thereby of the experience of other ages and countries, they may be enabled to know ambition under all its shapes, and prompt to exert their natural powers to defeat its purposes...
>
> (1963, p. 149)

Along with the formal rights and protections furnished by liberalism, critical thinking – so necessary when there are so many different sources of information to choose from – and 'educational tough-mindedness', as Orwell once put it, are required for the republican. Without those abilities, the very basis of the social order in which one continues to enjoy membership is challenged.

That this has not been the major line of argument concerning 'civic education' pursued by theorists who fall under the umbrella of republicanism is surprising. In fact, what is notably absent from the discussions advanced by many contemporary 'republicans' is anything like a developed theory of education at all.[7] While the concepts of 'community', 'virtue' and 'liberty' have received exhaustive treatments by scholars, education has garnered far less attention. And where a discussion of education has appeared those brave enough to venture forth have added to the consternation of liberal critics by emulating Rousseau's description of the educative process as 'the manipulation of minds' and by asserting that 'to create community one must first create citizens' (Oldfield, 1991, p. 173).

It is not without consequence that Hannah Arendt, perhaps the most famous republican of recent times, penned a scathing attack upon educating children for politics. In her essay 'Reflections on Little Rock' concerning discrimination in schools in the segregated southern United States, she suggested that the separation of political and social spheres was imperative and that the enforcement of civil rights was inappropriate in a situation that demanded not the protection of political or human rights but social and private ones – the social right to free association and the private right of parents to send their children where they pleased (1959). The question for Arendt was not how to abolish discrimination but rather 'how to keep it confined within the social sphere, where it is legitimate, and prevent its trespassing on the political and personal sphere, where it is destructive' (p. 51).

The 'misunderstanding' of her position, as she put it, reflected both a theoretical and a practical difficulty commentators had with her quasi-Aristotelian distinctions. Modern commentators sympathetic to Arendt tend to suggest that Arendt's *polis*-inspired vision of public space resulted in a ' "blind spot in her thought", one that led to her failure to make the "fine distinction" between an issue of public justice – equality of educational access – and an issue of social preference – who my friends are or whom I invite to dinner' (Benhabib, 1990, p. 157).

However, Arendt's underlying concerns, though they were poorly expressed, continue to resonate. Children, for Arendt, represented a new beginning, containing the promise of the realization of a political vision. But as such, they were always likely to be abused in the process of realizing that vision by authoritarian educators.

> The role played by education in all political utopias from ancient times onward shows how natural it seems to start a new world with those who are by birth and nature new. So far as politics is concerned, this involves of course a serious misconception: instead of joining

with one's equals in assuming the effort of persuasion and running
the risk of failure, there is dictatorial intervention, based upon the
absolute superiority of the adult, and the attempt to produce the new
as fait accompli, that is, as though the new already existed.[8]

(1987, p. 176)

Arendt's evident concern is with a form of 'political education' that is
authoritarian in outlook. Yet because she was inclined, after Jefferson,
to believe that a 'natural aristocracy of mankind' ought to govern and
because the laboring poor did not have the time, the inclination or the
money to do so, she did not say too much else on the matter. For there
to be more politics, there had to be less poverty, not more education,
which meant, in Arendt's opinion, 'giving the poor more money'.

Republican educators like Rousseau, of course – the sort that would
have troubled Arendt – possessed a highly developed theory of education and political education in particular, one that was designed to have
serious practical consequences. For Rousseau, the formation of national
character was something that was necessary not only because it moved
modern societies closer to an ancient ideal of citizenship but because it
made people in the modern world, a world that was becoming increasingly cosmopolitan, distinctive. The educational system that he
describes in *The Discourse on Political Economy* and *The Government of
Poland* isolated what he considered to be the most important connection between education and the state: 'love of country'.

Republican scholars remain divided on this issue. Viroli, for example,
argues that the *patria*, while it may refer to a particular place also refers
to the practice of public freedom, the defense of rights and political
institutions, and (even) the condemnation of corruption (1995, p. 16).
On the other hand, David Miller in his discussion of nationality asserts
that a civic identity, inculcated via schooling, is required before political discussion in diverse multicultural societies like our own can even
begin. Rather than an imaginary 'overlapping consensus' providing the
glue that holds a diverse society together, nationalism is the core
commitment, Miller argues, that permits conversation to take place.

For Miller, the republican conception of citizenship demands from
everyone, irrespective of their group affiliations, the ability to translate
private commitments into a public language that all citizens both those
within and, more importantly, those outside one's particular group can
understand. The advantage with this approach is that it assumes that
the world is not neatly divided into private and public spheres, a schiz-
ophrenic tendency that has been attributed to the liberal approach

(Mulhall and Swift, 1992, p. 212). Indeed, what it suggests is that for there to be a public world at all, education should provide a counterbalance to the particular influence and loyalties of family and group membership and also to the trivializing and sensationalizing tendencies of the mass media and the rhetoric of politician; a useful intellectual tool as politicians 'sincerely deceive' their constituents.[9]

Jefferson's major claim for republican education was that a 'natural aristocracy among men' would emerge, in contrast to the 'artificial aristocracy, founded on wealth and birth, without either virtue or talents...' that he regarded as a threat to the republic (1963, p. 517). Active political involvement was encouraged by dividing each county into districts of five or six miles called 'hundreds', with a school established in each. From these schools one individual each year would be sent on to grammar school. From grammar schools over a period of one or two years, the best individual would be selected to continue for six further years. Half would eventually proceed to William and Mary College. In this manner, Jefferson hoped, 'the geniuses will be raked from the rubbish' and society would be divided into two classes, the 'laboring and the learned' (1963, pp. 207, 528).

However, as Eva Brann notes in her analysis of republican education in this period, Jefferson was also keen to justify censorship and thereby to make certain that 'the learned' would learn from only the correct, and corrected, materials (Brann, 1984). Jefferson sought to justify the selective, and vehemently anti-federalist, choice of political materials made available for students at his own University of Virginia and also censored certain texts according to his own liking – the *Jefferson Bible* being perhaps the most famous example.

Jefferson's coercive measures toward freedom have tended to make republicanism a poor candidate for educational reform. Yet, the central purpose of his educational theory remains relevant – to provide citizens with the intellectual resources to protect themselves from government that will invariably degenerate into corruption. The paradox, of course, is that without enlightened leaders to begin with the motivation for providing an education for citizens that would likely cause a government a good deal of trouble is likely to be minimal. Moreover, the degree of 'coercion' – or liberation, depending upon one's point of view – involved in a republican education will also transgress the basic requirements of both liberal solidarity and multicultural coexistence. Republicans would have to justify their intrusive educational requirements – a commitment to a more substantive notion of autonomy seems unavoidable – by reference to active involvement within the political community. At the same time, they would have to hope for sufficient commitment to a 'common identity' *qua* Miller or the principles of political freedom *qua* Viroli to stop the exercise of citizenship from degenerating into factional dispute.

6.3 Cosmopolitanism: Educating for world citizenship

Contemporary liberal and republican thinkers root their understanding of the citizen and the proper scope of civic education within the space of the modern, sovereign state. Yet that understanding is being challenged by formal obligations in the form of rights (and protections) that transcend national boundaries and by informal attachments that can now be formed and maintained with much greater ease due to increased mobility and ease of communication. What this entails for 'world citizenship education' is by no means clear. Educational experiments that have attempted to teach 'global values' have produced mixed results – from those attempts to construct universal languages like Esperanto or Volapiik in the nineteenth century to UNESCO's 'Education for International Understanding, Co-operation and Peace Education relating to Human Rights and Fundamental Freedoms' (Heater, 1999).

Clarity of purpose, the ability to define clear pedagogical objectives for the education of world citizens, is extraordinarily difficult because the requirements of world or global citizenship continue to be so indeterminate. We saw in an earlier chapter how difficult it was to define world citizenship and how a meaningful sense of belonging to a 'world community' falls outside the range of either traditional liberal or republican understandings of that term.

That contemporary cosmopolitan theorists should turn to familiar, state-centered proposals for reform in institutions like the mass media and state education – one of the latest of which is to require universal bi-lingualism (Weinstock, 2001) – is not surprising given that education has consistently been regarded as *the* institution that transmits the main tenets of a political culture from one generation to the next. At the heart of such cosmopolitan claims is not only an acceptance of the continued relevance of the state but an attempt to go beyond it, to expand the concept of civic loyalty and provide the motivation to become a transnational actor. In short, educating for 'world citizenship' in any meaningful sense requires an understanding of the philosophies and institutions of cosmopolitan justice but also the development of cosmopolitan notions of agency. As with embedded citizenship, the principles of world citizenship would need to be taught *and* practiced.

However, the challenges that face the idea of an education for world citizenship are several. First, there is not the inconsiderable opposition to educating for citizenship within states *at all*. Writing in the late 1950s, Michael Oakeshott noted that an explicitly 'political education' was likely to be rejected for the following reasons:

> in the wilful and disingenuous corruption of language which is characteristic of our time it has acquired a sinister meaning ... it is associated with that softening of mind, by force, by alarm, or by the hypnotism of the endless repetition of what was scarcely worth saying once, by means of which whole populations have been reduced to submission.
>
> (1962, p. 112)

The suspicion of government-sanctioned education, particularly one for 'political education', translates in the minds of critics from the left and right of the political spectrum into an exercise in ideological indoctrination, either reinforcing or destabilizing the hierarchies within a national political culture.

Government officials tend to see the idea of citizen education as 'woolly minded' and undermining of the traditional constitutional relationships between ruler and ruled. One observer notes that it is for precisely this reason that an explicit goal of educating for citizenship within a national setting, let alone a European or global context, was long resisted in the U.K. While an emphasis on educating for 'values' – normally meaning moral and spiritual values – was embraced, educating for citizenship was avoided: '[t]he emphasis on "values" ... [was] an explicitly de-politicizing move in the debate about the future of political education' (Frazer, 2000, p. 89).

Assuming that the need for a political education is accepted in principle, however, educating for citizenship today is complicated today by the notion of educating not for one but for 'multiple citizenships' – a term that has not only a descriptive but legal significance for the 456 million citizens of the European Union. Nonetheless, the idea of 'multiple citizenship' is often regarded with suspicion, something that places too high a burden upon the political psyche of individuals. It is claimed that citizens, who have a natural antipathy toward politics, when suddenly confronted with competing political identities and the overwhelming complexity of world problems will face a kind of cognitive collapse. Faced with the burden of the world's woes to which there is no easy solution together with the psychic strain of divided and occasionally conflicting loyalties, the 'multiple citizen' will suffer from a kind of cosmopolitan overload and become an unhappy, fragmented creature.

Moreover, if citizenship is taken to be an embedded concept, the absence of a substantive community at a European or global level provides little to counter the feelings of psychological and cultural rootlessness (Heater, 1999, p. 151). Global citizens while they might be recognized legally as human beings who are deserving of legal and political protections are unable to attach themselves in any significant way to the global village.

Leaving aside the difficulty of deciding upon a suitable curriculum for an education in multiple citizenships there is a deeper, philosophical problem when it comes to teaching future citizens of the world. Charles Taylor has pointed out that there is an enduring tension within modern liberal societies between an abstract version of liberalism which embraces universalism by denying particularity on the grounds of equal respect and a postmodern 'politics of difference' which embraces it on precisely similar grounds. Whereas contemporary liberals have tried to address this issue by minimizing autonomy, and redefining the basic requirements of citizenship by thinning out the liberal notion of the good to a point where it becomes almost non-existent, cosmopolitan educators who seek to empower global citizens have yet to respond to the charge of cultural insensitivity. For some multiculturalists, the unreflective life *is* worth living – whereas for world citizens a radical reflexivity is likely to be a core component.

One might respond to some of these challenges by pointing out that, the psychological challenges of multiple citizenships notwithstanding, the idea that education should provide a 'fence against the world'[10] is hardly an attitude that is likely to prepare citizens for the effects of globalization. A 'defensive' nationalist education could, conceivably, be equally if not more psychologically distressing if an exclusive focus on the nation-state, its history and the glorious achievements of its political and military leadership were conducted at the expense of any meaningful and balanced discussion of other cultures, polities and economies. Citizens would have but few resources to draw upon in order to understand the reasons for the conflicts that inevitably arise between nations or the global policies that effect their livelihood and well-being.

The gradual acceptance of the idea of dual citizenship within the European Union is of particular interest in this regard and reflects an important culture shift in attitudes toward multiple allegiances. Checkel (1999) argues that the introduction of the European Convention on Human Rights combined with the efforts of members of the

Council of Europe resulted in a marked normative shift in opinion regarding multiple allegiances over the past two decades. In May 1997, the Council approved the 'Convention on Nationality' which specifically addressed issues of European citizenship and immigrant naturalization, by revising the norms of citizenship that were described in an earlier Council-sponsored treaty. While the earlier treaty had been hostile to the idea of dual citizenship, the new treaty took a neutral view. Checkel notes that this change of opinion reflected a trend started at the state level by countries like Italy and Switzerland who had eased their prohibitions on dual nationality. It was also a response to the wealth of reports from NGOs and academics that had been produced during the intervening period which advocated models of dual citizenship. 'The old, anti-dual citizenship understanding', notes Checkel, 'has eroded, being replaced by a European-level norm that is neutral to slightly positive on questions of multiple nationality' (p. 96).

The implication of this move toward dual citizenship from a curricular perspective is that children will not only be taught about their rights and responsibilities as holders of dual citizenship but will increasingly be asked to compare and contrast the information they receive from official sources. Consider, for example, a website hosted by the BBC intended for both students and teachers named 'CitizenX'.[11] The site lists a number of EU myths purported to be true and printed in leading newspapers in the UK – such as the EU wanting to rename chocolate – which turned out to be false. Links from the home page lead to discussions of the founding of the EU, enlargement, membership rights and the introduction of the Euro. There is also an international chat room for students who swap stories about their own experiences of citizenship in their member states, including states from outside the EU, materials and discussion boards on legal rights, human rights, the global economy and video stories of refugees and asylum seekers.

The question, 'How do citizens choose between competing demands on their loyalty?', however, remains a valid one. How one chooses to respond to this question as a political theorist reveals much about whether one sees the diminution of state authority as something to be celebrated and potentially empowering or regretted because it undermines traditional authority structures and upsets the balance of world power.

The moral distress that comes from acknowledging that such a choice must be made is a central element of postmodern citizenship and one that cannot be avoided. Embedded citizens will fall behind their governments, confusing patriotism with love of government rather than the principles of political liberty.[12] Citizens who acknowledge their divided loyalties, however, are likely to recognize the fact that legitimate authority can make questionable, even illegitimate decisions in the name of the people.

Although there is no historically agreed upon set of texts to teach world citizenship, because of the division between the disciplines that forbid such agreement, recent research intended to determine a framework for thinking about a 'multinational curriculum' has produced some interesting results. A nine nation study that polled an international panel of participants from East Asia, Southeast Asia, Europe and North America identified both the major global trends over the next genera-tion, the citizen characteristics that would best cope with these trends and the education needed to develop these characteristics (Parker *et al.*, 1999).

Particular global challenges that world citizens would have to face over the next generation included: increasing economic disparity between and within countries; the reduction of individual privacy as a result of the increased sophistication of information technologies; a widening of the digital divide; and increased chances of conflict between developed and developing nations as environmental deterioration continues (p. 124). In response to these and other challenges the team of researchers were next able to identify the abilities that world citizens would require to face them. These included: the ability to approach the problems as members of a world society; to cooperate, understand and accept cultural differences; to think critically and systematically; to resolve conflict in a non-violent manner; and to possess the ability to participate in politics at a local, national and international level (p. 125).

The final set of recommendations described the educational strategies involved in transitioning from a state-centered to an international curriculum. Interestingly, the group recommended that what was required, above all, was a 'multidimensional' view of citizenship. World citizens were involved in a complex matrix of obligations, commitments, duties and responsibilities on personal, social, spatial and temporal levels.

The personal dimension included a commitment to nurture a citizen identity alongside other identities, ethnic or familial. Citizenship was a unique and valuable identity in its own right and should be conceived as such. The social dimension included a willingness to cooperate with other citizens especially those who belonged to social groupings different from one's own. The spatial dimension referred to the flexibility of mind required in acknowledging that one was involved in a series of overlapping communities at a local, municipal, regional, state and international level. Finally, a temporal appreciation was required so that citizens would recognize their place 'between past and future', without losing themselves in the present. Citizens should respect but not become trapped by past traditions and develop those skills that most assist with imaginative future-oriented problem-solving.

Perhaps the most interesting aspect of the researchers' recommendations, however, was the thoroughly open-ended nature of the curriculum. The principles motivating the design of world citizen curricula were all in the form of questions: 'What should be done in order to promote equity and fairness within and among societies?'; 'What should be the balance between the right to privacy and free and open access to information in information-based societies?' Rather than recommend that a world citizen's curriculum include a section on 'international relations' or 'human rights' the research provided the rationale for a different focus, one that was encouraging of deliberation. The authors cited Michael Sandel's view of multiple citizenship approvingly:

> Self-government today ... requires a politics that plays itself out in a multiplicity of settings, from neighborhoods to nations to the world as a whole. Such a politics requires citizens who can abide the ambiguity associated with divided sovereignty, who can think and act as multiply situated selves. The civic virtue distinctive to our time is the capacity to negotiate our way among the sometimes overlapping and sometimes conflicting obligations that claim us, to live with the tension to which multiple loyalties gives rise.
>
> (1996, p. 128)

Educating for world citizenship is education for risk analysis. The basic requirements for the exercise of this level of citizenship appear to be an ability to sift through the abundance of different information with which citizens are almost constantly bombarded, to 'crap detect' (Postman, 1968) as one educator put it, to exercise one's imagination, to be future-oriented and to exercise understanding. These, then, are the virtues of the postmodern citizen.

Echoing the findings of these researchers, Scheffler (1999) has argued that the choice we will increasingly face as humans and citizens is not whether we desire to be either culturally immured or cosmopolitan but whether there is not some way to be both. Cosmopolitans, he suggests, might do well to temper their enthusiasm for innovation, which can often resemble contempt for traditional ways of life. Yet equally, 'genuine allegiance to a tradition', he notes, 'can never be just a matter of blind adherence to past practices, but must always involve decisions about how earlier values and practices can best be applied in novel circumstances and about the form in which those values and practices can be extended and projected into an uncertain future' (p. 275).

That future is likely to be conflictual and one in which individuals will have to make difficult choices within (and between) complex modern societies. How far the principle of autonomy should stretch to equip citizens with moral and political skills they need to survive in a global context is likely to become a point of contention. A genuinely political education for world citizenship, rather than the kind of mind softening technique that Oakeshott was referring to would involve, in the words of one advocate, 'education in the structures of power – both formal political institutions and arrangements, and the informal. It would involve education in the skills necessary for engaging in conflictual encounters' but in a non-violent fashion (Frazer, 2000, p. 100).

6.4   Conclusion

The proper scope of educating for citizenship, the *basic* characteristics and aims, have always been highly charged political issues.

Liberal theories of education have changed from a preoccupation with political passivity and enforced economic activity to a discussion of the limits of liberal constitutionalism in a multicultural state. Yet, arguably, the idea of 'citizen workers', a defining feature of nineteenth-century discourse concerning the ends of education is not discussed because there is no perceived need to discuss it – though this has not stopped corporations from forcibly educating their workforce in the virtues of the free market (Fones-Wolf, 1994). Economic productivity and nationalism, historically, have gone hand in hand.

Republicanism offers an ambiguous approach to education which in an era marked by the end of work opens up a possibility for discussion about the appropriate civic virtues in a global context (White, 1997). Theorists seem torn between ignoring the subject altogether, proposing educational solutions to modernity that are utterly draconian or putting forward the notion that the best defense against the inevitable descent into the corruption that every government faces is the political education of the people. Freedom from dependency on government looks remarkably like an argument for civic autonomy. Republican educationists, we might say, force children to become free citizens.

A cosmopolitan self denies privileging one moral community over another. Cosmopolitan theories of education focus upon that which unites all people together, their membership in the human family. It is not difficult to see how someone who is committed to a multicultural politics of recognition would see this as a direct challenge to the distinctiveness of their own particular cultural values, values moreover that they may wish to preserve against outside interference. Nor is it difficult to appreciate how a cosmopolitan self in their eyes might be regarded as little more than a Steppenwolf, a weightless creature floating above cultural particularities without any enduring attachments.

While there have been significant shifts in attitudes toward notions like 'dual citizenship' within the context of the European Union, it is unclear whether the cosmopolitan model will be taken seriously by state governments who set the agenda for their own educational systems. World citizenship and the attempt to expand the notion of civic identity is not likely to be taken seriously within the current political climate by state powers who are actively seeking to defend their identities against enemies that are considered 'uncivilized'.

There is no doubt that the state could address the challenge of global citizenship. Education could be seen as a vehicle for the creation of a politically active and alert citizenry, one that was able to respond to the dilemmas of life in the global polity. Yet, it is unlikely that the state response to the challenges posed by globalization will move beyond the economic imperative that urges policy makers to create a 'flexible' and 'dynamic' work force toward a political one that enables citizens to conduct a little rebellion now and then.

7
The World Turned Upside Down

> To see what is in front of one's nose needs a constant struggle.
> – George Orwell, 1968, p. 125

Shortly before he died, Pierre Bourdieu had this to say about globalisation that as an economic doctrine it relied upon a false notion of the inevitability of economic laws, a 'reality' that, in turn, required a politics of depoliticization. In response, what was required was a new kind of politics, 'capable of addressing itself beyond the nation-state' (Bourdieu, 2002, p. 1). I began this book by suggesting that a defining feature of republicanism in a global age was the idea of resistance and of the formation of a politics, an active, participatory notion of politics which was being exercised beyond the nation-state. For that reason, I suggested that this kind of political freedom could be described as a form of liberty *after* liberalism, for while the latter was a theory of state bound government, today it was possible to see a different, active political liberty being exercised in a cosmopolitan context.

However, the reflexive experience of 'life politics' in postmodernity must now contend with a new world order that is being constructed both mentally and physically. The focus of this book has been on the notion of political space and its relation to political agency. In this final chapter, I will examine some of the new spatial mythologies that are currently being developed around the notion of the postmodern state, empire and network. If the post-1989 world produced a mythic 'end of history' then the world post-September 11, 2001 is producing its own ideology of space and politics. That new moral and political myths are being produced – 'theory doing imperial service' (Mann, 2003) – in order to cope with the consequences of rapid changes in domestic and foreign policy initiated by some of the world's most powerful governments is indisputable.

In response, in this final chapter I will reiterate the case for cosmore-publican agency but this time within and across the new context of empire. In so doing, I suggest that cosmorepublican liberty will sometimes mean the liberty to say no, to withdraw consent and to disobey state authority.

The liberty that Arendt identified as the freedom to resist oppression is no less relevant now than it was in her own 'dark times'. Yet, the figure of the active citizen will be different. What I want to provide here is a sketch of this new kind of agency, the cosmorepublican citizen as postmodern nomad, an *ironist*, who recognizes the contingency of their own identity and allegiance to the state. Such recognition, rather than cause for despair, is a knowledge that empowers politically.

The cosmorepublican citizen will exhibit a highly developed degree of reflexivity and a sense of impartiality that is 'many sided' and 'multi-dimensional'. Cosmorepublican selves are, inevitably, pulled in competing directions – the public sphere saying one thing, democratic institutions another and personal commitments, potentially, another.[1] This kind of oscillation while it might be problematic is a feature of civic life in the postmodern contexts of empire and network.

7.1   The anti-political space of empire

Since the end of 2001, there has been a fairly consistent effort to respond to the new world of 'terror' by reconfiguring politico-spatial ideologies on the part of policy makers and liberal theorists sympathetic to their aims. The consequence of the spread of 'global terror networks', themselves (in part) products of now defunct Cold War strategies and financial freedoms made possible by economic globalization and the deregulation of financial controls, is the perception that the territorial sanctuary of liberal democracy is under threat. Some analysts have suggested that, as a consequence, globalization which opened up new spaces for politics during the 1990s is over and that a period of 'regressive globalism' is now under way (e.g. Anheier *et al.*, 2003).

It has been argued that as a result of the tragic events of September 11, 2001 a fundamental challenge has been posed to one of the founding myths of the West, namely that modernity, the Enlightenment and its legacies of progress and scientific advance will eventually spread to every other nation. The idea that American-style 'democratic capitalism' was destined for export with the consequence that a universal civili-zation would come into being, and history come to an end is over (Gray, 2003). For many, the essential question to be asked now is how best the West might preserve itself and its freedoms against a global enemy that, it is suggested, cannot be reasoned with.

One response has been to argue that the state has 'grown honest' and that its powers, borders and raison d'être (to provide security and stability) need to be vigorously defended and reinforced. Events in the Balkans during the 1990s are taken as proof that the state still has an important role to play in the global theater of violence. National social and political orders cannot be taken for granted. The preponderance of failed states in Lebanon, Somalia, Armenia and Cambodia to name but a few and the concomitant rise of quasi-feudal warlords throughout many parts of the world in reaction to the absence of state power threaten, some argue, a return to the Middle Ages (Van Creveld, 2000; Ferguson, 2004). That such collapse is possible when there is an absence of concentrated state power makes the defining feature of the postmodern environment, less a sense of renewed political activity, democratic transformation and 'globalization from below', and more a sense of mutual vulnerability and risk. Ferguson gives the following dismal account of a future without coherent state powers:

> The worst effects of the new Dark Age would be felt on the edges of the waning great powers. The wealthiest ports of the global economy—from New York to Rotterdam to Shanghai—would become the targets of plunderers and pirates. With ease, terrorists could disrupt the freedom of the seas, targeting oil tankers, aircraft carriers, and cruise liners, while Western nations frantically concentrated on making their airports secure. Meanwhile, limited nuclear wars could devastate numerous regions, beginning in the Korean peninsula and Kashmir, perhaps ending catastrophically in the Middle East. In Latin America, wretchedly poor citizens would seek solace in Evangelical Christianity imported by U.S. religious orders. In Africa, the great plagues of AIDS and malaria would continue their deadly work. The few remaining solvent airlines would simply suspend services to many cities in these continents; who would wish to leave their privately guarded safe havens to go there?
>
> (Ferguson, 2004, p. 1)

To avoid such a scenario, Cooper (2002) divides the world of nation-states into three types: premodern, modern and postmodern. The premodern world is a world of failed states, where there is no legitimate monopoly of force. These are singled out as posing the greatest threat to the West, states that are identified, by contrast, as postmodern states, for while they may not match the military capabilities of the latter they provide a base for non-state actors to upset the delicate balance of world power. The West's response to Afghanistan in the immediate aftermath of the September attacks on the United States is viewed in this light as part of a postmodern program of 'defensive imperialism' (Cooper, 2002, p. 3).

Defensive imperialism consists of two components. The first is economic such that a benign imperialism assists those states that seek access to different sectors of the global economy through the mediation of institutions like the IMF. The latter provides help to states who wish to, 'find their way back into the global economy'. The second component is an 'imperialism of neighbors', the political dimension of the new program of empire building. Unlike the old colonialism of the nineteenth century the idea of empire today, it is argued, is very much a cooperative venture that develops common security procedures and responses which spreads the mutual risk.

A thoroughly postmodern world, for Cooper, would exhibit the following characteristics: a breakdown between domestic and foreign affairs; mutual interference in (traditional) domestic affairs and mutual surveillance; the rejection of force for resolving disputes and the consequent codification of self-enforced rules of behavior; the growing irrelevance of borders; principles of security that are based on transparency, mutual openness, interdependence and mutual vulnerability. 'Machiavelli's statecraft', argues Cooper, has been replaced by 'a moral consciousness that applies to international relations as well as to domestic affairs: hence the renewed interest in what constitutes a just war' (summarized from Cooper, p. 2).

The postmodern condition in international relations, however, demands also that the standards of behavior applied at home are different from the standards of behavior applied abroad when dealing with premoderns. The idea of double standards in political life, Cooper suggests, is something that ought to be accepted as an inevitable and necessary feature of the political culture (p. 3). Internally, postmodern states are honest and cooperative. But when these states collide with modern or premodern states, international regulation of state affairs should not hinder self-defense. When necessary, 'we need to revert' he argues, 'to the rougher methods of an earlier era – force, pre-emptive attack, deception, whatever is necessary to deal with those who still live in the nineteenth century world of every state for itself. Among ourselves, we keep the law but when we are operating in the jungle, we must also use the laws of the jungle' (p. 3).

In a recent book, the philosopher Michael Ignatieff (2004) makes a similar case for the defense of the liberal state and liberal freedoms against the threat of terrorism. Ignatieff describes liberal states as free spaces for democratic deliberation which set the limits to the coercive power of government. They stand, he says, against global violence while keeping the use of state-sanctioned violence to a minimum. Liberal states are the home of free institutions where policy is debated and decided freely. The liberal space of the nation-state needs to be protected physically *and* ideologically from terrorism, liberal democracy's nemesis in the twenty-first century.

It is not liberty that has escaped the container of the nation for Ignatieff, to be exercised transnationally, but evil that has escaped 'the prison house of deterrence' (p. 152). In order to stave off such a threat people need to know, he suggests, what they believe in – liberal values. They should, moreover, be prepared to defend those values. For Ignatieff, this means that liberals should not see their founding documents that guarantee individual liberty as suicide pacts if, in fact, some liberties need to be sacrificed for the greater good and continued existence of liberal states. What is required for such troubled times is a 'political ethic' that permits such actions as the use of pre-emptive attack on other nations and torture, provided the reasons for such decisions are made and justified publicly in the best liberal traditions.[2]

Ignatieff shares both Gray's and Cooper's premise that the West is facing a mortal threat, a threat which might prove the West's undoing, and that the task for theorists is to develop an approach which addresses what democratic states can and, indeed, should do in times of 'great evil'. The key questions of the age are how to choose to do 'lesser evils' and prevent them from becoming greater ones because democracies, Ignatieff notes, have a tendency to overreact (2004, p. 51).

The political ethic, described as an 'ethics of prudence' and 'ethical realism', is an unambiguously state-centric argument that makes the case, via the use of contemporary examples (i.e. the invasion of Iraq in March 2004) and hypothetical ones (like the use of torture) for the centrality of ethical compromise in postmodern political life. The complexity of the political environment requires less principle and more pragmatism if those liberal principles that all hold dear in liberal democracies are to be safeguarded. This is now necessary, because of the scale of the external threat involved. Provided that a state-sanctioned response to terror is made public and discussed in a public forum Ignatieff is convinced that actions which compromise the value commitments upon which liberal-democratic societies are based will, in fact, be justified. Public accountability is the linchpin of the argument. It is the defining element of difference, he suggests, between democracies and tyrannies.

What each of these theorists signal is a return to Hobbes, the anti-political philosopher of fear. While globalization posed particular problems to a liberalism that was 'land locked', drawing attention to the apparent failures of economic liberalism and the limitations of political liberalism, the perception of the threat of global terror isolates liberalism as a theory, containing its freedoms.

Such a reaction to the events of 11 September 2001 on the part of government is not surprising; but it is unfortunate. The relationship between the individual and the state has changed because laws have been enacted and organizations created (like Homeland Security in the United States in November 2002, the biggest reorganization of the US government in fifty years) that give governments new powers over the lives of their citizens. These powers have come into effect under the rubric of 'national security' by politicians whom, we may assume, are well-intentioned and do not wish to appear negligent in the face of external threats.

Sadly, a legacy of liberal states abusing the liberties of their citizens does not sit well with the notion that the state should now have somehow 'grown honest', that government powers should expand to previously unimaginable degrees and that the decisions of elected officials should be trusted, provided they are 'justified publicly' to citizens. The notion that citizens should only *now* consider the idea of double standards in public life acceptable flies in the face of three thousand years of theorizing which has openly advocated lying to captive populations. Attempts by administrations to conceal the truth or at least be economical with the actualité are only the latest manifestations of a tradition started by Plato, the virulently anti-democratic would-be philosopher king who invented the notion of the noble lie (Bok, 1978).

Those attempts to employ such a tactic openly, such as the creation of the Office of Strategic Influence (OSI) which the Pentagon announced in February 2002, have, mercifully, come to naught. As part of its war on terror, the OSI was established in order to deliberately feed misinformation to friendly nations. It was closed down within a week of its existence becoming public knowledge. As one commentator noted at the time, '[i]f our cause is just, why not just tell the truth' (Dowd, 2002, p. 21).

That deception is part of postmodern politics, just as it has been for modern political societies, is hardly surprising. The question for societies that claim to be democracies, however, is not whether but how the public at large are likely to be manipulated by the withholding of relevant information. The need for secrecy in a war against terrorists can exacerbate this which is why Ignatieff asserts that 'we can and should be told what we need to know' (p. 164) and that 'the practice of secrecy' if it is itself not kept secret 'can be controlled' (p. 11).[3]

On the one hand, one can appreciate why a thinker like Ignatieff would stake liberal democracy's moral credentials on the notion of public discussion in order to justify the morally dubious, but 'necessary', political actions. A 'political ethic' can only be achieved and sustained via public discussion. But on the other hand, Ignatieff seems to undermine his own case by acknowledging that governments tend to deceive their populations: '...the capacity of a ruthless government, bent on abridging freedoms, must never be underestimated, especially not in an age in which government has such power to shape public perceptions and manufacture consent through the media' (p. 53).

This is sage advice. The legacy of liberal-democratic governments, let alone tyrannies, that restrict information and abuse the liberties of their citizens in times of national crisis and necessity are too numerous to mention (Rackow, 2002). The idea that state officials should be trusted despite a tendency to conceal information from the public poses a real dilemma for citizens in a time of perpetual war.

The disappointing part of this postmodern tale, however, is that in all likelihood when liberal citizens are kept in an almost constant state of alarm their consent is unlikely to be anything but manufactured. Public justification in a time of perceived crisis, the very thing that justifies a 'political ethic', is likely to be compromised by national security issues which tend to trump institutional openness.

7.2   A different citizen?

Earlier chapters examined the different responsibilities of citizenship envisioned by theorists with different goals for the state. Liberals on the whole describe a passive citizen-subject-worker, and republicans an active-skeptical-patriot whose relation to the state authority is ambiguous at best. Cosmopolitan citizens display a flexibility of mind and a moral commitment to humanity rather than adopt arbitrary political moralities.

Invariably, any theory that deviates from the norms that currently exist within liberal-democratic societies faces the problem of transition. This is no less true now for cosmopolitan democratic theory than it has been for republican theorists who were keen to revive the glories of the theory's past. In the last chapter we saw an outline of the requirements of world citizenship, the sorts of questions to be addressed, and the global virtues encouraged that would, indeed, go a long way to fostering an education for the practice of world citizenship.

However, I also noted that while it might be possible to determine the questions/principles that motivate an education for global citizenship the likelihood of their being adopted as a program for state-sanctioned education was unlikely on pragmatic and philosophical grounds. Pragmatically, it is not clear why a political elite would be compelled to develop an educational program that would make life difficult for them. Philosophically, it is not clear how an education that is at once authoritative and non-conformist might be possible. Does this mean that this new version of republicanism fails because of the problem of transition yet again? I do not think so. If there are cosmorepublican citizens today, they have not been taught to be so.

The paradox of political revolutions for Hannah Arendt was that the revolutionary spirit they engendered inevitably found no permanent place of residence in the post-revolutionary community. The exercise of public freedom, which started out as a spontaneous gesture of 'human togetherness', was ultimately sacrificed in an attempt to secure the foundations for a new political order. Administration was an anathema to the spontaneity of political affairs.

As the only political spaces left in the post-revolutionary state where an individual might *be* a citizen and participate in the politics of the republic were representative institutions like Congress, which severely limited the number of participants, the majority of the people had no access to politics. Hence, taking their cue from Arendt, theorists of active politics have continued the search for the political space.

Yet Arendt offered an additional answer. Even if a new kind of state could be imagined and numerous public arenas existed it was clear to her that not everyone would be interested in politics. While each citizen might have the potential for political activity, outside of the extraordinary periods of revolutionary upheaval, only those individuals dedicated to the task of good government, those who cared more about the state of the world than their 'private happiness', would participate in political life (1963, p. 253; 1972, p. 232).

This meant that, for Arendt, politics would always be an elite project. Not the elite of liberal democracies, the 'social or cultural or professional elite', one that was composed of individuals who often cared less for the common good or 'the state of the world' and more for their own personal advancement and ambition. For her, there would always be an elite, but an elite composed of the genuinely public spirited, the kind of people identified by Jefferson as a 'natural aristocracy' – in contrast to the 'artificial aristocracy, founded on wealth and birth, without either virtue or talents' (1963, p. 517).

The difference today is that Arendt's and Jefferson's elite are much larger in number than either could have imagined. Today's elite are cosmopolitan in outlook and not afraid to act politically in defense of their freedom. They are bridge builders between disparate communities, mental and physical nomads who, paradoxically, act politically in some instances without moving at all. They are as the poet W. H. Auden noted writing at the beginning of World War II, 'dotted everywhere, ironic points of light'.[4]

They are ironic in the sense that they exist at all when all about them is darkness. They are ironic in the second sense that they choose to act politically in the knowledge that their goals may never be achieved. Finally, they are ironic in their approach to politics, acting in full recognition of the contingency of human institutions, their own memberships in political and other communities, and the folly and pomposity of experts and politicians. These ironists inhabit numerous political spaces, some real and some virtual. They have broken free from the mental universe of the state, the 'mind forged manacles', as Blake put it, of modern life.[5] In so doing, they have affected a cognitive revolution by permitting themselves to believe that another world is possible.

7.3   Public irony and political hope

Why irony? Auden's poetic description of ironists who 'show an affirming flame' in dark times is a very good description of the kind of 'elite' activity we see occurring on a global scale. Irony is a particular description of agency, an approach that is peculiarly and appropriately postmodern as the edifices of modern life are shown to be as much mental constructs as they are 'real'.

Yet the use of irony in political contexts is not without its problems. We see one form of irony in Machiavelli's discussion of politics in the *Prince* and another in his comedy, *The Mandrake Root*. For Machiavelli, who acknowledges the abyss between how one lives and how one ought to live, irony in politics is a necessity. It is predicated and dependent upon a sense of free will, the sense that one as an individual is separate and autonomous, that things could be otherwise than they are, and that the willingness to acknowledge this feature of the human condition is itself a kind of freedom. Irony walks hand in hand with the self-referential ability to place oneself not only within a given narrative or discourse but outside of it as well. In the dedication to the *Prince*, Machiavelli was careful to point this out through his use of metaphor. The example of the landscape artist who must place himself on the plain in order to see the mountain and on the mountain in order to see the plain is a good illustration of the ironic point of view (1981, p. 30).

The politics of irony is, however, problematic because it seems to be almost exclusively destructive. It serves as a rebuff toward the powerful but seems to offer no insight into a better way of organizing power. In fact its legitimacy appears to depend on power and on the corruption of the powerful. In *The Mandrake Root*, every character is the embodiment of the corrupt institutions of society, church, family, educated classes, lawyers and so on. Irony approaches this world with an air of irreverence, confident in the knowledge that that the emperor has no clothes, that the institutions of society are inefficient and corrupt. Machiavelli knows that the world is not fair, that folly is rewarded and that a world where what ought to be is, is rarely the norm.

Prima facie, the 'ironist' is a figure unlikely to inspire notions of public responsibility or political commitment. Muecke (1969), in one of the most comprehensive studies of the subject, describes the ironist as an artist and an intellectual who uses irony for a number of different purposes: rhetorically, to enforce her meaning; satirically, to expose vanity or hypocrisy; or heuristically, to reveal the complexity or otherwise of a particular situation. The ironist is a person who says something without really saying it, someone who victimizes and deceives, and someone who is prone to being corrupted by their own clever use of language.

Above all, once the ironist has become aware of 'the pathos of heaven's falling', as Kierkegaard put it, the ironist seeks and employs a 'negative freedom', a sense of detachment from the world and others. The ironist 'hovers' above the world, seeking refuge from it by proceeding to talk 'every phenomenon out of its reality in order to save himself, that is, in order to preserve himself in the negative independence of every-thing' (1965, p. 274).

Richard Rorty, in one of the most notable contemporary analyses and descriptions of the function of irony, moves beyond the classical definition of irony – 'saying one thing while meaning another' – only to reject its political potential altogether. His conclusion is that while an ironic approach to the overblown claims of traditional philosophy is entirely suitable, the ironist who embodies these claims is and ought to be private and that it is a category mistake to contemplate the notion of 'public irony' (Rorty, 1991).

Rorty embraces the elitist interpretation of irony, casting ironists as intellectuals, self-creative poets who stand in contrast to an alienated public which relies on notions like 'common sense' and looks to philosophical and metaphysical systems to justify their particular way of doing things. Ironists embrace the radical contingency of their situation and consider the search for philosophical foundations for the way they happen to live a flawed enterprise. Yet they are also acutely aware and disturbed by the fact that their own way of describing reality, their 'final vocabulary' may be the wrong one. Consequently, they are very good at redescribing their own vocabulary in unfamiliar terms and therefore consider 'truth' as something that may be created rather than discovered.

Rorty contends that the opportunities for avoiding both cruelty and humiliation, the very things that, as a committed liberal, he seeks to eliminate, may be enhanced by the ironist's poetic 'redescriptions' something that comes about through 'the imaginative ability to see strange people as fellow sufferers' (1991, xiv). The paradox with irony, however, as Muecke noted, is that ironists can humiliate through their redescription as much as they can sensitize us to harm.

The 'private ironist', consequently, is not and should not be concerned with justice. Indeed, the creative urges of private ironists are potentially damaging to the political realm and should be barred access. This is so because ironists undermine the beliefs of the public metaphysicians – the general and unsophisticated public – who *really* believe in the metaphysics of justice.

An ironist, Rorty tells us, '...cannot get along without the contrast between the final vocabulary she inherited and the one she is trying to create for herself...Ironists have to have something to have doubts about, and something from which to be alienated' (1991, p. 88). Non-ironists who lack poetry nonetheless fulfill an important function in the ironist's utopia. Indeed, the ironist is dependent upon them. Ironists need the unpoetic, the 'petty, bland, unheroic and calculating', in order to react against them and their ideas (1982, p. 269).

Politics is the domain of 'the liberal', the pragmatic, that area of life that is given over to accommodating often competing claims in 'banal, familiar terms' (1996, p. 17). The public realm is that area where we are more likely to meet strangers, with varying opinions and different outlooks on the world. It is a place in which John Rawls' model of justice exemplified by his 'original position' becomes practicable. According to Rorty, one must learn in such encounters to control one's feelings 'smile a lot, make the best deals you can, and, after a hard day's haggling, retreat to your club' (1991, p. 209).

Ironists, people who acknowledge the contingency of their situation and imagine new, poetic ways of dealing with it, would be terrible public philosophers but they might, suggests Rorty, be able to accommodate the private hopes of individuals in a way that makes them relate to liberal hopes. This last feature is the crux of the matter for Rorty. The 'liberal ironist', the strange combination of poet and pragmatist is his idea of the model postmodern citizen, is someone who:

> faces up to the contingency of his or her own most central beliefs and desires – someone sufficiently historicist and nominalist to have abandoned the idea that those central beliefs and desires refer back to something beyond the reach of time and chance. Liberal ironists are people who include among these ungroundable desires their own hope that suffering will be diminished, that the humiliation of human beings by other human beings may cease.
>
> (Rorty, 1991, xv)

As he puts it, all that is in question here is 'accommodation', the securing of liberty and equality *without* fraternity. An ironist is not a campaigner, not a dynamic social entity nor a revolutionary, merely someone who wants the chances of being kind expanded by 'redescription'. Rorty attempts to argue, then, that the freedoms that liberals fight for and the poetic redescriptions that ironists produce might be regarded in some instances as mutually beneficial and supportive.

It should be clear from the preceding discussion that this version of liberalism is directed toward the maintenance of an intellectual elite's – rather than an 'artificial aristocracy's' – cultural utopia; the realm of theorists intent upon self creation and edifying discourse. The public realm, by contrast, is the realm of 'thugs'; of untheoretical fellow citizens and empirical predictions (1987, p. 574). This division is a structural feature of societies, Rorty thinks, because irony itself is not something that can be taught. It is almost impossible to imagine a culture in which irony was advanced as an appropriate education for the young.[6]

Rorty's irony is part of a project that sets out to defend his own brand of North American postmodern bourgeois liberalism without relying on the eternal claims of philosophy to do so. Yet, as critics have pointed out, while one might agree with Rorty's premises – there are no secure

or irrefutable foundations for philosophical speculation or truth claims –
there is no logical reason why his attempts to update J. S. Mill's version
of liberalism should hold sway over any other theoretical preferences. If
ethical values are contingent, why not choose an Aristotelian or a
Marxist ethic from which to launch one's claims? If the minimalization
of cruelty is the aim, rather than an ungrounded and ultimately conservative defense of the status quo, then surely a compelling analysis of
how liberal institutions manage to do this is called for?

Indeed, it is important to note that others equally conversant with
the concept of irony have adopted a less individualistic and private
approach to the topic, emphasizing care over disdain, humility over
humiliation and community over separateness (Golomb, 1995; Pollard,
2005). In one of the most famous passages relating irony to compas-
sion, Anatole France noted:

> The more I reflect upon human life, the more I believe that it should
> be given, as witnesses and as judges, Irony and Pity, just as the
> Egyptians on behalf of their dead called upon the goddess Isis and
> the goddess Nephtys. Irony and Pity are two good counselors; the
> one in smiling, makes life agreeable for us; the other, weeping, makes
> it sacred. The irony I invoke is not cruel. It mocks neither love nor
> beauty. It is mild and benevolent. Its laughter calms anger, and it is
> this irony that teaches us to make fun of the fools and villains whom
> otherwise we might have been weak enough to hate.
>
> (cited in Muecke, 1969, p. 232)

France's description of irony offers the promise of release from a self-
imposed mental captivity while simultaneously challenging those who
hold sway over us politically. An irony that 'makes fun of fools and
villains' is an empowering idea. Recognizing one's own part in a political drama that could be otherwise were it not for one's own continued
and ill-considered consent is the first step toward releasing oneself from
subordination.

Irony in this sense *is* public irony, one that reminds us of the contingent position we occupy as citizens and the possibility we have of
changing that position. In contrast to despair, it is the most appropriate
expression of reflexive individuality and life politics in the postmodern
period and a description of a new kind of civic agency.[7]

Seery (1990) examines the concept from a motivational standpoint.
When there is no reason to care, no final reason to do anything, to do
so anyway is the true mark of the (public) ironist.

to affirm human community in the face of human mortality, to seek order against the background of chaos, to hold out for worldly justice even though death ultimately defeats or mocks all such efforts, to be dedicated when one is also deeply doubtful...entails what I think is best called an ironical attitude.

(Seery, 1990, p. 343)

Understood this way, irony understood simply as negative freedom, as detached and private can only be a partial reading (Soloft, 2001). While change and action come from the individual, individual freedom is always-already bound, always limited in some way. Individuals exist but not as monadic entities, however much they might wish to extricate themselves from the burdens of living in society. Individuals are always-already in relation and always born within a particular cultural and historical moment. It is this understanding that helps Kierkegaard *control* irony so that it does not fly off into abstraction overwhelmed by the sheer possibility of choice.

Indeed, when Kierkegaard spoke of irony he left his audience with little doubt about the significance of the concept to philosophy and life: 'Just as philosophy begins with doubt, so also a life that may be called human begins with irony.' In answer to the problem he posed, that irony detaches the individual from others in an attitude of radical independence, Kierkegaard argued that it was possible to deepen self-understanding, to master the feeling of existential weightlessness by expanding one's comprehension of the ultimate meaninglessness of existence to a single moment in history. To do this was to move from an understanding of the individual in isolation to the individual in relation with a view of deepening one's subjective understanding. A necessary move, he thought, for without others one could not develop as a self. It also meant that one assumed some responsibility for the times in which one lived, to be 'positively free in the actuality to which [the ironist] belongs'. This freedom is most challenging and not something for which one can merely apply pre-existing formulae or rules. Rather, '[the ironist] is compelled...to develop his own view, to discover for himself the possibilities and limits of his historical context' (Summers, 2001).

Most importantly, ironists can achieve this state of freedom only by relating to others *in freedom*, in situations that are removed from 'role playing' – much as Arendt's citizens experienced political freedom in the polis, away from the constraints of socially defined roles. It is the ever-present destructive power of irony that makes this possible, constantly unmasking, freeing people of illusions and pretensions so that they can experience their freedom together.

Kierkegaard's master ironists, even after recognizing the vanity and essential pointlessness of the world, choose nonetheless to live with the age, to engage with the world creatively. To do so is to live authentically, and courageously too, not to be swept away with despair in the knowledge that nothing matters. If one can do this, irony can become a potent force for good, a way of living in the world, a world that is full of contradiction, pomp and injustice. Understanding this, Kierkegaard assures us, means that individuals can live healthy lives by 'actualizing actuality' (1965, p. 341). Yet, understanding this also means that one will have to continuously employ irony in an attempt to overcome the ever-present buffoonery of political life and one's own tendency to slip back into the comfortable anesthesia of the everyday.

Seery argues that in times of acute crisis – his own work is premised on the threat of nuclear annihilation – irony emerges as a positive force, an ethical stance that is more suited to the complex demands of a politics that is essentially tragic and, ultimately, pointless. From a profoundly ironic perspective, neither politics nor substantive notions of community continue to matter in the face of overarching mortal threats. Any attempt to provide reasons for action by using the special qualities of political life or 'community' as theoretical leverage will be unconvincing.

Public ironists do act, but they act while recognizing the very futility of acting against such overwhelming obstacles. The very real possibility of annihilation, indeed, *does not* compel many people to take action to reduce that possibility. For many, the Grand Inquisitor's contention that few will voice their objections to life's disorders when they are well fed and happy seems entirely apposite which is why the public nature of irony will always be an elite project for those who are publicly spirited.

The lone student facing down a tank in Tiannemen square, anti-globalization protestors who employ 'Ewok' tactics against heavily armed police units in Kananaskis,[8] or those that hurl teddy-bears at police in Quebec are all ironists to some extent. The individuals involved in such demonstrations are being publicly ironic, recognizing that in all probability, they can do very little to change the world but they will try anyway and, occasionally, succeed.

The power of irony of this kind is twofold. On the one hand, ironic action, action that looks absurd in the face of overwhelming odds, actually reclaims some of the power from authority that prides itself on its seriousness, expertise and professionalism. On the other hand, those who observe such actions while they may not find themselves motivated to take action, at least initially, do think of themselves as part of a community that is far larger than any they were born into. The enormous significance of the verbal or non-verbal, publicly ironic demonstration lies in its appeal to 'the human community' – a 'community' that, I would argue, has become steadily easier to imagine as we have become aware of the earth's fragility and its uniqueness. Individuals who are capable of identifying with the actions of others in this manner find themselves detached and implicated at the same time. This ability is fundamental to public irony's purposes. Those who act on the basis of these events adopt a publicly ironic stance, in the full knowledge that their aims will perhaps never be achieved, but who choose to act nonetheless. They are ironists who, in a strictly Arendtian sense, love the world.

If cosmorepublican citizenship today is understood as an activity that is engaged in ironically largely for its own sake, an expression of existential choice in dark times, then the implications for the relationship between citizen and state power are significant. Recognizing that membership of a particular national culture is an accident of birth, ironic citizens will choose other communities with which to associate and develop duties and obligations accordingly. Traditionally, notions such as dual citizenship were, as noted earlier, frowned upon by theorists who considered ideas of divided loyalty a threat to the stability of a political order. Citizens of the world have always been rather unpopular with nationalists. Public ironists are likely to prove similarly troublesome for existing categories of political thought which is why a new way of thinking about politics and a new vocabulary for describing political action is required.

7.4 Conclusion

In his fictional work, *Invisible Cities*, the Italian author Italo Calvino writes of a once great city named 'Aglaura', the defining characteristic of which was that, for some unknown reason, it was impossible to 'go beyond the things its own inhabitants have always repeated' even if those stories and description jarred with the particular view of reality that you, the observer, held. 'You would like to say what it is', Calvino noted, 'but everything previously said of Aglaura imprisons your words and obliges you to repeat...' (1996, p. 61).

The idea of repeating the past and its mistakes by using the language of the past has been a distinctive concern of philosophers and theorists in recent times who recognize that the world of signs and symbols is as much a reality as the physical world. At times of crisis, language changes to accommodate and respond to unexpected events. At such moments, it shapes the world that comes after.

In this work, I have tried to suggest that republicanism no longer has to try to find reasons for its existence as a theory. Defining republicanism today is less about justifying its relevance to a liberal world and more about describing a new one. The sketch of cosmorepublican agency offered here is part of a new political vocabulary, one that is required to describe the experience and not just the legal reality of citizenship in a postmodern context. This is necessary, now more than ever, as a response to the mythic construction of empire, an imagined space that like the imaginary city of Aglaura will, before long, make it seem impossible to offer political alternatives.

I have tried to suggest that cosmorepublican citizenship is not simply a subset of theories of global governance, important though they are, but a description of a particular kind of human agency and part of an attempt to 'humanize' globalization (Brassett and Higgott, 2003). In this chapter, I described that agency as *publicly ironic* in an attempt to find the words to describe why global citizens act in the manner that they do when, seemingly, there is little that they can do to effect change. I also suggested that republicanism understood as a theory of resistance, political action, of skepticism toward authority is well suited to the new political circumstances of twenty-first-century living. The complexity and contingency of postmodern life demands a thoughtful and responsible approach to problems that can no longer be addressed effectively by any single actor in a global environment.

Writing in *Wind, Sand and Stars*, Antoine de Saint Exupéry noted that '. . . we lack a perspective for judgement of transformations that go so deep. . . To grasp the meaning of the world of today we use the language created to express the world of yesterday' (1975, p. 39). The battle for command of the political language of today is currently underway. What cosmorepublicanism begins to sketch out is a vocabulary for political change.

At the beginning of Hobbes' century, Shakespeare could write that regicide was an unnatural abomination.[9] Yet by the time of the English Republic, less than half a century later, Milton could ask what had hitherto been considered unthinkable: Why should a king rule a society simply because he has been born to a particular family? Similar questions are required today of those who would restrict what is possible politically by reducing the vocabulary of freedom to one of inside and outside, state power and terrorism, civilization and barbarism.

Permitting ourselves to exercise our political imaginations, to refrain from using tradition, as the young Marx noted, to weigh 'like a nightmare on the brain of the living' ought to be the task of political theory. It should, in its own way, threaten to disturb the political peace.[10]

Recognizing the complexity and partiality of official information, the contingency of governmental power while acknowledging one's own part to play in the unfolding drama is, I have suggested, a mark of the public ironist. Like the ironist, the revolutionary is someone who recognizes the contingency of power (Monbiot, 2004, p. 253). Yet an ironist is also someone who recognizes that revolutions do not and should not end. Republican thinkers like Arendt and Jefferson recognized this which is why they called for a little revolution now and then so that people would not slip back into the comforts of avoidable dependency.

Citizenship today, in addition to the formal legal guarantees of state membership, is also a choice. To be a citizen is to recognize the fragility of political power and to choose to act on a number of different spatial levels, in order to influence or restrain that power. For the ironist, one of the most pressing questions today, in light of the experience of 'life politics' and an expanded sense of responsibility, mutual risk and mutual vulnerability, is whether or not one should obey government when questionable decisions are taken in the name of the people.

8
Conclusion: After Liberalism?

> Politics is a surface in which transformation comes about as much because of pervasive changes in the depths of the collective imagination as because of visible acts, though both are necessary. And though huge causes sometimes have little effect, tiny ones occasionally have huge consequences.
>
> – Rebecca Solnit, 2004, p. 2

This book started life as an attempt to think about a tradition of political freedom that, supposedly, had no place in the modern world. As I finished the book, it occurred to me that the title 'Liberty after Liberalism', while it might refer to a reconstructed and revised form of this ancient liberty, might just as well refer to a period in the history of the West in which there is hardly any liberty at all. Nonetheless, I have refrained from placing a question mark after the title because it is my belief that although these are dark times for political freedom there are always possibilities for its realization.

The consequences of the ironic interpretation of citizenship that I began to sketch in the previous chapter call into question the twin theoretical pillars of liberalism in modern times – consent and obedience. Neither concept is entirely satisfactory from a democratic standpoint and is in tension with thoughtful and responsible citizenship in a global context.

As we noted in Chapter 2, rather than a duty to participate in politics in order to safeguard the public good, the relevant issue for liberal thinkers came to be how individual citizens might consent to those in power who represented legitimate authority. Consent, which is an essentially passive response to initiatives taken by someone else, was supremely important historically to liberal theorists seeking to justify the societal arrangements in which they lived because it was the intellectual mechanism whereby citizens could be said to belong and be obliged to a society. And if individuals consented to the order of society they ought, therefore, to obey that same order.

Modern defenders of this notion argue that consent to the political institutions of a society is guaranteed by one's using a public library, sending one's children to public school or voting, for example. Yet just as the notion of tacit consent was used by Locke in an attempt to justify a portion of the existing, elite order of seventeenth-century English society so the modern version of this ancient sleight of hand is equally unconvincing. To advance the argument today on the premise that voting somehow constitutes consent ignores the fact that people vote for all sorts of reasons – out of a sense of resignation, or simply to keep the least likable candidate from gaining office.

Politicians assume that consent is present when, in fact, acquiescence can mean something altogether different. More disturbing, of course, is the fact that consent can also be manufactured by those in power. In short, a situation of dependency arises and is perpetuated in modern liberal societies, a situation that is then exploited by politicians who claim to act in the name of the people.

Threatening the withdrawal of consent, on the part of the citizens, is an absurdity from the government's point of view as it threatens the whole fabric, imagined and otherwise, of state authority. Becoming a 'majority of one', as Thoreau put it, poses a threat to the supreme power of the state (1983, p. 397). Yet, for consent to be meaningful, rather than a mere rationalization for a poorly managed plutocracy, it would have to be achieved through participation in the political process which permitted the exchange of ideas between citizens and their governments. A notion of consent worthy of a democratic people would require free and open discussion, and a level of social understanding that would require restricting the influence of corporations on the media, for example (Arblaster, 1994). In the absence of these elements, however, and with the information gap decreasing between governors and the governed the notion of consent becomes a real theoretical problem for liberals as the existence of groups such as 'Not in our Name' testifies.[1] Consequently, consent in the postmodern period is something that is much more likely to be withdrawn.

If this analysis is correct, then a second feature of modern citizenship – obedience to legitimate authority – is also challenged. If the age old question of political theory was 'how do the few control the many' the postmodern version is surely 'how do the many control the few' (i.e. how do global citizens control the actions of their elected representatives and unelected officials)? An ironist position that recognizes the contingency of power will complicate the notion of obedience to authority. Public ironists will choose to be obedient (or not) given the particular merits of a particular policy.

For Hobbes, civic obedience was tied to fear, a position that he thought was consistent with liberty, while Hume noted that the most potent source of continued obedience to authority was the belief that there was no other way of organizing society. Custom or habit induces obedience. Yet, given the numerous 'crimes of obedience' committed in the last century perhaps citizens today are likely to be far more circumspect before pledging unquestioned allegiance to political authority. The legacy of the legitimate rise to power of the Nazis in Germany in the early 1930s has, at the very least, problematized the notion that it is *always* one's duty to obey government (Sharp, 1973, p. 45).

In political life it is not always obvious when a legitimate authority has started to issue illegitimate decisions, particularly if government is remote from the majority of the lives of the population, or when it decides to withhold information or send mixed messages about a particular policy or issue. Most people will, in all probability, follow the dictates of government, confusing patriotism with loyalty to the administration rather than the principles of liberty. As Etienne de la Boetie noted nearly five hundred years ago, most people obey government because they want to, not because they have to. A condition of voluntary servitude is preferable for many than a condition of freedom (Boetie, 1997). Yet for others this will not be the case. For them, freedom is something taken, never given.

Notes

1 Introduction: From polis to cosmopolis

1. J. Nye writes: 'The challenge for the United States will be to learn how to work with other countries to better control the non-state actors that will increasingly share the stage with nation states' (2002, p. 3).
2. I return to examine this issue in some detail in Chapter 5 of the present work.
3. Rousseau had suggested that it was, in fact, possible for 200,000 people to gather together in an assembly. He later argued in *The Government of Poland* that '[l]arge populations, vast territories!' were the 'first and foremost reason for the misfortunes of mankind, above all the calamities that weaken and destroy polite peoples' (1985, p. 25).
4. In *Wasted Lives*, Zygmunt Bauman notes that, thanks to centuries of colonization and modernization, there is no place left that is free from the reach of state administrations. 'Our planet,' he asserts, 'is full' in a political sense (2004, p. 5).
5. In *After Virtue*, Alasdair MacIntyre saw virtue as possible only within local traditions and hierarchies and not as a universal moral principle (1994, pp. 260–80). Martha Nussbaum (1990) and Onora O'Neill (1996), on the other hand, approached the subject from distinctively Aristotelian and Kantian perspectives respectively and suggested that human reason could identify human needs and thus some universal human virtues.
6. See Wootton's 'Introduction' to *Republicanism, Liberty and Commercial Society, 1649–1776*, particularly pp. 14–16. Where republicanism up to the mid-seventeenth century had signaled a participatory form of politics, Wootton suggests that 'Harrington marks the death, not the continuation, of this classical republican tradition' due to a new emphasis on republican constitutionalism (1994, p. 14).
7. There is also the additional problem, as Wootton points out in his 'Introduction', that '[republican] authors are not as consistent as historians might like. Toland, writing the life of a leading figure in the republican pantheon, John Milton, pauses to praise Locke. Cato's *Letters*, like Sydney's *Discourses*, draws alternatively on civic humanist and natural rights arguments, without any sign of strain or awareness of inconsistency. How are we to describe the interpenetration of languages, this confusion of paradigms?' (1994, p. 18).
8. While the reasons for the rejection of misogyny are too obvious to mention, the reason for the rejection of 'military virtues' is, perhaps, less so. At least one contemporary author sympathetic to republican aims has argued for the revitalization of military virtue as part of a program for 'reconstructing' republicanism. Janowitz (1983) advances a version of patriotism as civic consciousness tied to military national service. However, for pragmatic reasons alone, a theory that operates at a level beyond the state, and sometimes in opposition to it, cannot use the language of the state – that is controlled

violence – which is why so many transnational groups explicitly use the language of non-violence in their approach to political action (see Zunes, 1999). Hence, cosmorepublicanism is a theory of non-state, non-violent political resistance.

9. For further discussion, see Maurizio Viroli's (2002) biography, *Machiavelli's Smile*.

2 The transformation of political space

1. See Seneca's *I Made The Crooked Straight*, in Clarke (1994).
2. In *De Clementia*, Seneca proclaimed that the city was embodied not in the people but in the figure of the ruler: 'All those many thousands of swords which my peace restrains will be drawn at my nod; what nations shall be utterly destroyed, which banished, which shall receive the gift of liberty, which have it taken from them ... this is mine to decree' (cited in Wolin, 1961, p. 93).
3. One of the earliest views of sovereignty was advanced by William Tyndale in 1530. Writing in *The Obedience of a Christian Man and How Christian Rulers Ought to Govern*, he noted that there was 'One King, One Law is God's Laws in every realm' or, in other words, the wishes of the Bishop of Rome did not apply to the monarch of England.
4. This claim should not overshadow the fact, however, that societies during this period were severely divided into different strata based on, as Daniel Defoe notes, 'wealth and consumption'. In fact, Defoe noted that Georgian society in England at the turn of the eighteenth century could be divided in the following manner: 'The Great, who live profusely; The Rich, who live plentifully; The Middle Sort, who live well; The Working Trades, who labour hard, but feel no Want; The Country People, Farmers etc. who fare indifferently; The Poor, that fare hard; The Miserable, that really pinch and suffer Want' (cited in Porter, 2001, p. 53).
5. Jefferson noted in a letter to James Madison, dated 30 January 1787, 'I hold it, that a little rebellion, now and then, is a good thing, and as necessary in the political world as storms in the physical' (cited in Fries, 1963, p. 258). His most famous proclamation on this subject appears, however, in a letter written later in the same year to William Stephen Smith, 13 November 1787: 'The tree of liberty', he noted, 'must be refreshed from time to time with the blood of patriots and tyrants' (pp. 263–4).
6. See Lincoln's wonderful speech, 'The Perpetuation of Our Political Institutions', in Basler (ed.) (1990, pp. 76–85).
7. For a more ambiguous view of 'work' in the Greek world, see H. D. F. Kitto's *The Greeks*, pp. 239–43.
8. S. Lynd notes in his analysis of Paine's *Rights of Man* that market capitalism and republican government were compatible for Paine and would, moreover, 'inherently tend toward peace' (1969, p. 154). Benjamin Franklin noted that both 'Industry' and 'Frugality' were the chief means for 'procuring Wealth and thereby securing Virtue' (1986, p. 106).

9. See Book 5, Part III, Article II of *The Wealth of Nations*.
10. For a sample of the information available to activists see OneWorld.net and Civicus.org, organizations that act as a hub for civil society groups worldwide.
11. While the effects of the Internet upon society are only now being quantified, its transformative political effects are undeniable. For an example of the former see the 2004 report prepared by the Stanford Center for the Quantitative Study of Society: 'Ten Years after the Birth of the Internet, How do Americans Use the Internet in Their Daily Lives'. For an example of the latter, see James Rosenau's (2002) essay, 'Information Technologies and the Skills, Networks, and Structures that Sustain World Affairs'. Rosenau makes the acute observation that '...the significance of virtually free access to the Internet by ever greater numbers of people can hardly be underestimated. Already it has facilitated the formation and sustenance of networks among like-minded people who in earlier, pre-Internet times could never have converged. The result has been...a vast proliferation of associations – from environmental to human rights activists, from small groups of protestors to large social movements, from specialized interest associations to elite advocacy networks, from business alliances to interagency governmental committees, and so on across all the realms of human activity wherein goals are sought. This web-like explosion of organizations has occurred in territorial space as well as cyberspace, but the opening up of the latter has served as a major stimulus to the associational proliferation in the former' (p. 282).

3   The state we are (no longer) in

1. Hobbes' famous description, from Chapter 13 of his *Leviathan*, of states as 'gladiators...their weapons pointing, and their eyes fixed on one another' in a constant 'posture of war' remains the dominant 'realist' interpretation of the international order of states.
2. From Bentham's *Principles of the Civil Code* (cited in Macpherson, 1977, p. 27).
3. See Book IV of his *Principles of Political Economy* where he notes how the interests of the working classes were often at odds with those of their employers.
4. Mill was elected to The British House of Commons in 1865 but failed to retain his seat in the 1868 election.
5. However, Mill qualified this assertion by suggesting that mass education could, in fact, work in the interests of an aristocratic leadership for without education the uneducated masses were more likely to effect a violent revolution.
6. Mill noted in *On Liberty* that bondage to the state bureaucracy would extend to the members of the government as well as the general population: 'For the governors are as much slaves of their organization and discipline as the governed are of the governors' (1985, p. 184).
7. The absence of such qualities, Weber feared, would lead to 'a polar night of icy darkness and hardness, no matter which group wins the outward victory...' (1994, p. 368).

8. In contrast to what might be termed the 'maximally perfectionist' liberalism of someone like Joseph Raz (1984), for example, who upholds the liberal notion of 'autonomy'.
9. See E. Countryman (1985), *The American Revolution*. I would like to thank Professor Hugh Brogan of the Department of History, University of Essex, for drawing my attention to this book.
10. Tocqueville, 1994, pp. 236, 274, 444, 511, 513, 528, 602.
11. Some of which are discussed by Iris M. Young (1995).

4 Republicanism revisited

1. See John Carvel (1998) and Bikhu Parekh (1997) for an argument that is similar to Miller's.
2. In this sense, Pettit's model falls somewhere between what the political theorist David Held (1987) has described as 'protective' and 'developmental' models of state functions. Where the former is associated most readily with classical liberal theorists who advocated a largely apolitical arrangement between governors and those governed, the latter advocated political participation and state promotion of principles of political and economic equality.
3. For an Aristotelian interpretation, see Jurgen Habermas (1977); for a Nietzschean interpretation, George Kateb (1984); for a Heideggerian version, Dana Villa (1996). On the influence of Saint Augustine, see Arendt (1999) *Love and Saint Augustine*.
4. Arendt continued to remain suspicious of the partisanship of such organizations, however. In 'Public Rights...', she noted the following: '...but it [the public right] has degenerated into lobbying, that is, into the organization of private interest groups for the purpose of public, political influence' (p. 105).
5. Hannah Arendt once remarked that the trouble with historians and political scientists was their growing incapacity for making distinctions. See Arendt (1953).
6. A suggestion she did not altogether dismiss. See Arendt (1979, p. 326).
7. http://www.amnesty.org.uk/news/briefing/ai.shtml (1 August 2004).
8. See L. Quill and H. Uluorta (2004) for an extended discussion of this topic.
9. See A. Liptak (2003).
10. United States vs Greenpeace, Inc. Case No. 03-20577-CR-ALTONAGA.
11. As is well known, the Internet grew out of the initial efforts of the United States Defense Advanced Research Project Agency in the wake of the Sputnik affair of 1957. The ARPANET team was a community of computer scientists whose task was to design a wide area network communication system using computers.
12. See also H. Rheingold (1994) and I. Budge (1996).
13. See the data on the numbers of people identifying themselves as global citizens in the 'Introduction to Global Civil Society', in Anheier and Katz (2005).
14. This ability increasingly extends to developing nations as software developers lower prices to expand their markets. See G. Peck (2004).

15. P. Tyler (2003). This, the most 'global' of the mass action movements of recent years followed earlier protests in Birmingham in May 1998 (60,000), Hyderabad in the same month (200,000), Seattle in November 1999 (10,000), Genoa in March 2001 (20,000), New York in January 2002 (10,000), Tel Aviv, Israel in February 2002 (200,000), Barcelona, Spain in March 2002 (300,000), Oslo, Norway in June 2002 (15,000). A complete chronology of protest actions is available from the Centre for Global Governance, London School of Economics: http://www.lse.ac.uk/ Depts/global/index.htm (1 August 2004). Prior to this event, even Joseph Nye was forced to concede that the (then) anti-globalization movement was forcing a reappraisal of the political agenda: 'The challenge for the United States will be to learn how to work with other countries to better control the non-state actors that will increasingly share the stage with nation states' (2002, p. 3).

5 On the ancient and modern origins of cosmopolitanism

1. This is surprising given that a key feature of the global political environment is the interdependence between structure and agency. As Keck and Sikkink note: 'When we ask about who creates networks and how, we are inquiring about them as structures – as patterns of interactions among organizations and individuals. When we talk about them as actors, however, we are attributing to these structures an agency that is not reducible to the agency of their components' (1998, p. 5).
2. Together with LaPlace.
3. See A. Sampson (1988) for a detailed discussion.
4. See W. James (1911).
5. For a related discussion on the need to transform party structure to accommodate the new 'global' demands of citizens, see G. Papandreou (2004).

6 The case for political education

1. The 11th edition of Merriam-Webster's Collegiate Dictionary defines a 'McJob' as 'a low-paying job that requires little skill and provides little opportunity for advancement'.
2. This provides for C. Lamore (1990) part of what he describes as 'the minimal moral conception of liberalism'.
3. The reference is to J. S. Mill's discussion of education in *On Liberty*. For more on 'the basics' of a liberal education, see R. E. Flathman (1996).
4. Aristotle stated that 'the things we have to learn before we can do them, we learn by doing them e.g. Men become builders by building and lyre players by playing the lyre; so too we become just by doing just acts, temperate by doing temperate acts, brave by doing brave acts' (1976, p. 91). See also Machiavelli (1970, p. 114).
5. M. Viroli has contributed to this reading of Machiavelli, noting that '...the citizens' ordinary willingness to serve the common good and their strength

to resist the ambition of the powerful...is the only ideal of political action that is still appealing even in our times...' (1998, p. 174).
6. See http://www.transparency.org/.
7. Richard Dagger (1997) is one notable exception.
8. Aristotle, whom Arendt draws on extensively, gives a slightly more nuanced view of education. While the young should not be forced into making political judgements for which they would be ill equipped they should, nonetheless, be able to perform 'good acts' and be provided with an education that corresponds to the government of their state (1994, p. 185).
9. The phrase is taken from a headline in *The Economist*, July 17, 2004, p. 11.
10. The phrase is taken from Locke (1947).
11. http://www.bbc.co.uk/schools/citizenx/ (1 August 2004).
12. In 1996, Bill Clinton made a similar error when he noted in a speech that: 'There is nothing patriotic about pretending that you can love your country but despise your government.' Cited in G. Vidal (2002, p. 12).

7 The world turned upside down

1. The writer-activist Arundhati Roy (2002) describes this sense of 'schizophrenia' in the opening to her book, *Power Politics*.
2. This is a common argument used in defense of institutionalized torture. See Alan Dershowitz's (2002) influential discussion.
3. Yet how, one might ask, is the practice of secrecy to be regulated? In March 2002, it was announced that a parallel government in the United States had been in operation since September 2001, part of a secret government operation known as the Continuity of Operations Plan (COP). High ranking officials from various departments had rotated in and out of two secret locations on the East Coast. There was no public discussion of this remarkable revelation.
4. From Auden's poem, 'September 1, 1939'.
5. From William Blake's poem, 'London'.
6. This point, assumed by Rorty, is debated by others. Linda Hutcheon (1994), for example, argues persuasively that what is at issue today is the fact that people are in possession of different cultural knowledges simultaneously and that different communities develop their own ironic styles – styles that, moreover, can be learnt and taught by others with sufficient inclination to understand them. Hutcheon advances a far more sophisticated and less exclusionary version of irony than Rorty's by playing on the notion that societies are far more fractured into different knowledge communities than even Rorty imagines, and that the primary task of education is to navigate across these communities.
7. For a related discussion, see David Harvey's (2000) description of the 'insurgent architect'.
8. For more information, see http://www.tao.ca/~wrench/dist/g8/ewok.html (1 August 2004).
9. The reference is to *Macbeth*, Act Two, Scene 4.
10. The importance of this cannot be overemphasized. As John Maynard Keynes noted in the 1930s: 'the ideas of economists and political philosophers, both

when they are right and when they are wrong, are more powerful than is commonly believed. Indeed, the world is ruled by little else. Practical men, who believe themselves to be exempt from any intellectual influences, are usually slaves of some defunct economist. Madmen in authority, who hear voices in the air, are distilling the frenzy of some academic scribbler of a few years back' (1936, p. 383).

8   Conclusion: After liberalism?

1. www.notinourname.net.

Bibliography

Ackerman, B. *Social Justice in the Liberal State* (New Haven: Yale University Press, 1981).

Adorno, T. 'Education for Maturity and Responsibility – Theodore W. Adorno and Hellmut Becker', *History of the Human Sciences*, 12, 1999, pp. 21–34.

Anderson, B. *Imagined Communities: Reflections on the Origins and Spread of Nationalism* (London: Verso, 1991).

Anheier, Helmut and Katz, Hagai 'Network Approaches to Global Civil Society', in *Global Civil Society 2004/5* (eds) Helmut Anheier, Marlies Glasius and Marty Kaldor (London: Sage Publications, 2005), pp. 206–22.

Anheier, H., Glasius, M. and Kaldor, M. (eds) *Global Civil Society* (Oxford: Oxford University Press, 2001).

Anheier, H., Glasius, M. and Kaldor, M. (eds) *Global Civil Society* (Oxford: Oxford University Press, 2002).

Anheier, H., Glasius, M. and Kaldor, M. (eds) *Global Civil Society* (Oxford: Oxford University Press, 2003).

Annas, J. 'My Station and Its Duties: Ideals and the Social Embeddedness of Virtue', *Proceedings of the Aristotelian Society* (Oxford: Blackwell, 2002), pp. 109–23.

Appleby, J. *Liberalism and Republicanism in the Historical Imagination* (Cambridge, MA: Harvard University Press, 1992).

Arblaster, A. *Democracy* (Buckingham: Open University Press, 1994).

Arendt, H. *Love and Saint Augustine* (eds) Judith Chelius Stark and Joanna Vecchiarelli Scott (Chicago: Chicago University Press, 1999).

Arendt, H. 'Rejoinder to Eric Voegelin's Review of the Origins of Totalitarianism', *The Review of Politics*, 15, 1953, pp. 76–85.

Arendt, H. *The Human Condition* (Chicago: Chicago University Press, 1958).

Arendt, H. 'Reflections on Little Rock', *Dissent*, 5, 1959, pp. 45–56.

Arendt, H. *On Revolution* (New York: The Viking Press, 1963).

Arendt, H. *Men in Dark Times* (New York: Harcourt Brace and World, 1968).

Arendt, H. *Crises of the Republic* (New York: Harcourt Brace, 1972).

Arendt, H. *The Origins of Totalitarianism* (New York: Harcourt, Brace, Jovanovich, 1973).

Arendt, H. 'Public Rights and Private Interests', in *Small Comforts for Hard Times – Humanists on Public Policy* (eds) Michael Mooney and Florian Stuber (New York: Columbia University Press, 1977), pp. 103–9.

Arendt, H. *The Life of the Mind* (New York: Harcourt Brace & Company, 1978).

Arendt, H. 'On Hannah Arendt', in *Hannah Arendt: The Recovery of the Public World* (ed.) Melvyn Hill (New York: St Martin's Press, 1979).

Arendt, H. *Lectures on Kant's Political Philosophy* (ed.) Ronald Beiner (Chicago: Chicago University Press, 1982).

Arendt, H. *Between Past and Future* (New York: Penguin, 1987).

Aries, P. *A History of Private Life, from Pagan Rome to Byzantium* (trans.) Arthur Goldhammer (Cambridge, MA: Belknap Press, 1987).

Aristotle 'Moral Goodness', *Nicomachean Ethics*, Book II (ed.) J. A. K. Thompson (London: Penguin, 1976), pp. 91–110.

Aristotle *The Politics*, Book VIII (ed.) Stephen Everson (Cambridge: Cambridge University Press, 1994), pp. 185–97.

Auge, M. *Non-Places: Introduction to an Anthropology of Supermodernity* (London: Verso Press, 1995).

Aurelius, M. *Meditations* (London: Penguin, 1964).

Bailyn, B. *The Ideological Origins of the American Revolution* (Cambridge, MA: Belknap Press, 1967).

Balen, M. *The Secret History of the South Sea Bubble: The World's First Great Financial Scandal* (London: Fourth Estate, 2003).

Ball, T. (ed.) *Transforming Political Discourse* (Oxford: Basil Blackwell, 1988).

Barber, B. *Strong Democracy* (Berkeley: University of California Press, 1984).

Barber, B. *An Aristocracy of Everyone – The Politics of Education and the Future of America* (New York: Ballantine Books, 1992).

Barlow, M. and Robertson, H. *Class Warfare: The Assault on Canada's Schools* (Toronto: Key Porter Books, 1994).

Bauman, Z. *Liquid Modernity* (Cambridge: Polity Press, 2000).

Bauman, Z. *Wasted Lives* (Cambridge: Polity Press, 2004).

Beck, U. *Risk Society: Towards a New Modernity* (London: Sage, 1992).

Beck, U. 'The Cosmopolitan Manifesto', *New Statesman and Society*, March 20, 1996, pp. 38–50.

Beck, U. 'The Cosmopolitan Manifesto', *New Statesman and Society*, March 20, 1998, pp. 28–30.

Beck, U. *What is Globalization?* (Cambridge, Polity Press, 1999).

Beck, U. 'Living Your Own Life in a Runaway World', in *On the Edge, Living with Global Capitalism* (eds) Will Hutton and Anthony Giddens (London: Jonathan Cape, 2000a), pp. 164–74.

Beck, U. *The Brave New World of Work* (Cambridge: Polity, 2000b).

Beck, U. 'The Cosmopolitan Perspective: Sociology of the Second Age of Modernity', *British Journal of Sociology*, 51, 2000c, pp. 79–105.

Beiner, R. *What's the Matter with Liberalism* (Berkeley: University of California Press, 1992).

Beitz, C. 'Rawls's Law of Peoples', *Ethics*, 110, 4 (July, 2000), pp. 669–96.

Bellah, R. *Beyond Belief: Essays on Religion in a Post Traditional World* (New York: Harper & Row, 1970).

Benhabib, S. 'Hannah Arendt and the Redemptive Power of Narrative', *Social Research*, 57, 1, 1990, pp. 167–97.

Benhabib, S. *Situating the Self: Gender, Community and Postmodernism in Contemporary Ethics* (Cambridge: Polity Press, 1992).

Bennett, W. L. 'Communication and Civic Engagement in Comparative Perspective', *Political Communication*, 17, 2000, pp. 307–12.

Bentham, J. *A Fragment on Government* (Cambridge: Cambridge University Press, 1988).

Berlin, I. *Four Essays on Liberty* (Oxford: Oxford University Press, 1969).

Black, A. *Guilds and Civil Society in European Political Thought from the Twelfth Century to the Present* (London: Methuen & Co. Ltd, 1984).

Bohman, J. 'The Public Spheres of the World Citizen', *Perpetual Peace: Essays on Kant's Cosmopolitan Ideal* (Cambridge, MA: MIT Press, 1997), pp. 179–201.

Bohman, J. 'Cosmopolitan Republicanism: Citizenship, Freedom and Global Political Authority', *The Monist*, 84, 2001, pp. 3–22.

Bohman, J. 'Republican Cosmopolitanism', *The Journal of Political Philosophy*, 12, 2004, pp. 336–52.

Bok, S. *Lying – Moral Choice in Public and Private Life* (New York: Pantheon Books, 1978).

Bourdieu, P. 'The Politics of Globalization', http://www.opendemocracy.net (1 August 2002).

Brann, E. *The Paradox of Education in a Republic* (Chicago: Chicago University Press, 1984).

Brassett, J. and Higgott, R. 'Building the Normative Dimension(s) of a Global Polity', in *Governance and Resistance in World Politics* (eds) David Armstrong, Theo Farrell and Bice Maiguashca (Cambridge: Cambridge University Press, 2003), pp. 29–57.

Braunfels, W. *Urban Design in Western Europe* (Chicago: Chicago University Press, 1988).

Budge, I. *The New Challenge of Direct Democracy* (Cambridge: Cambridge University Press, 1996).

Burtt, S. 'The Good Citizen's Psyche: On The Psychology of Civic Virtue', *Polity*, 23, 1990, pp. 23–8.

Burtt, S. 'The Politics of Virtue Today: A Critique and Proposal', *American Political Science Review*, 87, 1993, pp. 360–8.

Burtt, S. 'Response', *American Political Science Review*, 89, 1995, pp. 148–51.

Callan, E. *Creating Citizens – Political Education and Liberal Democracy* (Oxford: Clarendon Press, 1997).

Calvino, I. *Invisible Cities* (London: Secker & Warburg, 1996).

Caney, S. 'Liberalism and Communitarianism: A Misconceived Debate', *Political Studies*, XL, 1992, pp. 273–90.

Canovan, M. 'Politics as Culture: Hannah Arendt and The Public Realm', *History of Political Thought*, 1, 1985, pp. 617–42.

Carrell, S. 'UK Troops in Iraq Face New Court Threat', *The Independent on Sunday*, November 28, 2004, p. 2.

Carvel, J. 'Muslim Schools Get Grants', *The Guardian*, January 10, 1998, p. 7.

Castells, Manuel 'European Cities, the Informational Society, and the Global Economy', *New Left Review*, 204, 1994, pp. 18–32.

Chandhoke, N. 'Global Civil Society: A Text Without a Context', in *Global Civil Society* (eds) Helmut Anheier, Marlies Glasius and Mary Kaldor (Oxford: Oxford University Press, 2003), pp. 411–12.

Chandhoke, N. 'Global Civil Society: A Text Without a Context', http://www.lse.ac.uk/Depts/global/Yearbook/PDF/PDF2003/Chapter%20Updates.pdf (1 August 2004).

Chatwin, B. 'The Nomadic Alternative', *Anatomy of Restlessness: Selected Writings, 1969–89* (New York: Viking, 1996).

Checkel, J. T. 'Norms, Institutions, and National Identity in Contemporary Europe', *International Studies Quarterly*, 43, 1999, pp. 83–114.

Chomsky, N. *World Orders, Old and New* (London: Pluto Press, 1994).

Clarke, P. A. B. *Citizenship* (London: Pluto Press, 1994).

Clarke, P. A. B. *Autonomy Unbound* (Aldershot: Ashgate Press, 1999).

Cohen, G. A. 'No Habitat for a Shmoo', *The Listener*, September 4, 1986, p. 6.

Connolly, W. E. *Identity/Difference* (Ithaca: Cornell University Press, 1991).

Cooper, R. 'The Post-modern State', in *Reordering the World: The Long Term Implications of September 11* (eds) E. Barak and M. Leonard (London: Foreign Policy Centre, 2002), pp. 11–21.

Cornford, F. 'The Invention of Space', *Essays in Honour of Gilbert Murray* (Cambridge: Cambridge University Press, 1936).

Countryman, E. *The American Revolution* (London: I.B. Taurus & Co. Ltd, 1985).

Crick, B. *In Defence of Politics* (London: Butler & Tanner Ltd, 1992).

Critchley, S. (ed.) *Deconstruction and Pragmatism* (London: Routledge, 1996).

Dagger, R. *Civic Virtues* (Oxford: Oxford University Press, 1997).

Dahl, R. *A Preface to Economic Democracy* (Berkeley: University of California Press, 1985).

Dallmayr, F. 'Cosmopolitanism: Moral and Political', *Political Theory*, 31, 2003, pp. 421–42.

Deibert, R. *Parchment, Printing and Hypermedia* (New York: Columbia University Press, 1997).

De la Boetie, E. *The Politics of Obedience: The Discourse of Voluntary Servitude* (London: Black Rose Books, 1997).

Derrida, J. *On Cosmopolitanism and Forgiveness* (London: Routledge, 2001).

Dershowitz, A. *Why Terrorism Works* (New Haven: Yale University Press, 2002).

De Tocqueville, A. *Democracy in America* (ed.) J. P. Mayer (London: Fontana Press, 1994).

Dowd, M. 'The Office of Strategic Mendacity', *New York Times*, February 20, 2002, A, p. 21.

Dunn, J. *Western Political Theory in the Face of the Future* (Cambridge: Cambridge University Press, 1993).

Dworkin, R. 'Liberalism', in *Public and Private Morality* (ed.) Stuart Hampshire (Cambridge: Cambridge University Press, 1978).

Etzioni, A. 'Voluntary Simplicity: Characterization, Select Psychological Implications, and Societal Consequences', *Journal of Economic Psychology*, 19, 1998, pp. 619–43.

Everdell, W. *The End of Kings – A History of Republics and Republicanism* (Chicago: Chicago University Press, 2000).

Falk, R. 'The World Order between Inter-State Law and the Law of Humanity: The Role of Civil Society Institutions', in *Cosmopolitan Democracy – An Agenda for a New World Order* (eds) Daniel Archibugi and David Held (Cambridge: Polity Press, 1995).

Fallon, R. J. 'What is Republicanism, and is it Worth Reviving?', *Harvard Law Review*, 102, 1989, pp. 1695–735.

Faulks, K. *Citizenship* (London: Routledge, 2001).

Ferguson, N. 'A World Without Power', *Foreign Policy*, 143, 2004, pp. 1–4.

Finley, M. *Politics in the Ancient World* (Cambridge: Canto, 1983).

Fishkin, J. *The Voice of the People* (New Haven: Yale University Press, 1995).

Flathman, R. E. 'Liberal Versus Civic Republican, Democratic, and Other Vocational Educations', *Political Theory*, 24, 1996, pp. 4–32.

Fones-Wolf, E. A. *Selling Free Enterprise* (Chicago: University of Illinois Press, 1994).

Foucault, M. 'Space, Knowledge and Power', in *A Foucault Reader* (ed.) Paul Rabinow (Harmondsworth: Penguin Books, 1986), pp. 239–56.

Foucault, M. 'Of Other Spaces', *Diacritics*, 16, 1986, pp. 22–7.

Franklin, B. *The Autobiography and Other Writings* (Harmondsworth: Penguin, 1986).

Fraser, N. 'Rethinking the Public Sphere: A Contribution to the Critique of Actually Existing Democracy', in *Habermas and The Public Sphere*, Craig Calhoun (ed.) (Cambridge: MIT Press, 1992).

Frazer, Elizabeth 'Citizenship Education: Anti-political Culture and Political Education in Britain', *Political Studies*, 48, 2000, pp. 88–101.

Fries, A. (ed.) *The Essential Jefferson* (New York: Collier Books, 1963).

Galston, W. *Liberal Purposes* (Cambridge: Cambridge University Press, 1991).

Galston, W. 'Two Concepts of Liberalism', *Ethics*, 105, 1995, pp. 516–34.

Gandhi, M. K. 'Civilisation', in *Hind-Swaraj* (ed.) Anthony Parel (Cambridge: Cambridge University Press, 1997), pp. 34–8.

Gerth, H. H. and Wright-Mills, C. (eds) *From Max Weber: Essays in Sociology* (New York: Oxford University Press, 1946).

Giddens, A. *Central Problems in Social Theory* (London: Macmillan, 1979).

Giddens, A. *Modernity and Self Identity* (Stanford: Stanford University Press, 1991).

Giddens, A. *Beyond Left and Right* (Stanford: Stanford University Press, 1994).

Giddens, A. *Runaway World: How Globalization is Reshaping Our Lives* (London: Routledge, 2000).

Goldman, R. and Papson, S. *Nike Culture – The Sign of the Swoosh* (Thousand Oaks, CA: Sage Publications, 1998).

Golomb, J. *In Search of Authenticity* (London: Routledge, 1995).

Gray, J. 'Can We Agree to Disagree?', *New York Times Book Review*, May 16, 1993, p. 35.

Gray, J. 'The Sad Side of Cyberspace', *The Guardian*, April 10, 1995, p. 18.

Gray, J. *False Dawn – The Delusions of Global Capitalism* (London: Granta Books, 1998).

Gray, J. *Al Qaeda and What it Means to Be Modern* (New York: W.W. Norton & Co., 2003).

Guthrie, W. K. C. *The Sophists* (Cambridge: Cambridge University Press, 1995).

Gutmann, A. 'Communitarian Critics of Liberalism', *Philosophy and Public Affairs*, 14, 1985, pp. 309–22.

Gutmann, A. *Democratic Education* (New Jersey: Princeton University Press, 1987).

Gutmann, A. 'Civic Education and Social Diversity', *Ethics*, 105, 1995, pp. 557–79.

Habermas, J. 'Hannah Arendt's Communications Concept of Power', *Social Research*, 44, 1977, pp. 3–24.

Hamilton, A. *The Federalist Papers* (New York: Mentor Books, 1961).

Hartz, L. *The Liberal Tradition in America: An Interpretation of American Political Thought Since the Revolution* (New York: Harcourt Brace, 1955).

Harvey, D. *The Condition of Postmodernity* (Oxford: Blackwell, 1989).

Harvey, D. *Spaces of Hope* (Edinburgh: Edinburgh University Press, 2000).

Heater, D. *What is Citizenship?* (Cambridge: Polity Press, 1999).

Held, D. *Models of Democracy* (Cambridge: Polity Press, 1987).

Held, D. *Democracy and the Global Order: From the Nation State to Cosmopolitan Governance* (Stanford: Stanford University Press, 1995).

Held, D. 'Cosmopolitan Democracy and the Global Order: A New Agenda', in *Perpetual Peace – Essays on Kant's Cosmopolitan Ideal* (eds) James Bohman and Matthias Lutz-Bachmann (Cambridge, MA: MIT Press, 1997), pp. 235–51.

Held, D. *The Global Transformations Reader* (Cambridge: Polity Press, 2000).

Held, D. 'Globalization: The Dangers and the Answers', http://www.
openDemocracy.net (1 September 2004a).
Held, D. *Global Covenant: The Social Democratic Alternative to the Washington
Consensus* (Cambridge: Polity Press, 2004b).
Held, D. and McGrew, A. *Globalization/Anti-Globalization* (Cambridge: Polity
Press, 2002).
Heller, A. 'The Concept of the Political Revisited', in *Political Theory Today* (ed.)
David Held (Stanford: Stanford University Press, 1991).
Herodotus *The History* (trans.) David Grene (Chicago: University of Chicago
Press, 1987).
Hobbes, T. *Leviathan* (ed.) Richard Tuck (Cambridge: Cambridge University Press,
1992).
Hobsbawm, E. *Nations and Nationalism Since 1780* (Cambridge: Cambridge
University Press, 1990).
Hobsbawm, E. *The Invention of Tradition* (Canto: Cambridge University Press, 1992).
Horwitz, M. J. 'Republicanism and Liberalism in American Constitutional
Thought', *William and Mary Law Review*, 29, 1987, pp. 57–74.
Hume, D. 'The Origin of Government', in *Theory of Politics* (ed.) Frederick
Watkins (Edinburgh: Thomas Nelson and Sons, Ltd, 1951), pp. 81–6.
Huntington, S. *Who Are We? The Challenges to America's National Identity*
(New York: Simon and Schuster, 2004).
Hutcheon, L. *Irony's Edge – The Theory and Politics of Irony* (London: Routledge, 1994).
Ignatieff, M. 'The Attack on Human Rights', *Foreign Affairs*, 80, 2001, pp. 102–16.
Ignatieff, M. *The Lesser Evil: Political Ethics in an Age of Terror* (New Jersey:
Princeton University Press, 2004).
Inglehart, R. *Culture Shift in Advanced Industrial Society* (New Jersey: Princeton
University Press, 1989).
Isaac, J. 'Republicanism vs. Liberalism? A Reconsideration', *History of Political
Thought*, IX, 1988, pp. 349–77.
James, W. 'The Moral Equivalent of War', *Memories and Studies* (New York:
Longman Green and Co., 1911), pp. 267–96.
Jameson, F. *Postmodernism* (London: Verso, 1991).
Janowitz, M. *The Reconstruction of Patriotism – Education for Civic Consciousness*
(London: University of Chicago Press, 1983).
Jardine, L. *Worldly Goods* (London: Macmillan, 1996).
Kant, I. 'The Metaphysics of Morals', in *Basic Political Writings* (ed.) H. S. Reiss
(Cambridge: Cambridge University Press, 1991), pp. 131–75.
Kateb, G. *Hannah Arendt: Politics, Conscience, Evil* (Oxford: Martin Robertson, 1984).
Keck, M. E. and Sikkink, K. *Activists Beyond Borders: Advocacy Networks in
International Politics* (Ithaca: Cornell University Press, 1998).
Keenan, A. 'Promises, Promises: The Abyss of Freedom and the Loss of the Political
in the Work of Hannah Arendt', *Political Theory*, 22, 1994, pp. 297–322.
Kelman, H. C. and Hamilton, V. L. *Crimes of Obedience: Toward a Social Psychology
of Authority and Responsibility* (New Haven: Yale University Press, 1989).
Kenny, M. 'Global Civil-society: A Liberal-republican Argument', in *Governance
and Resistance in World Politics* (eds) David Armstrong, Theo Farrell and Bice
Maiguashca (Cambridge: Cambridge University Press, 2003), pp. 118–45.
Keynes, J. M. *General Theory of Employment Interest and Money* (London:
Macmillan, 1936).

Kierkegaard, S. *The Concept of Irony – With Constant Reference to Socrates* (trans.) Lee M. Capel (New York: Harper & Row, 1965).

King, M. L. K. 'A Time to Break Silence', in *A Testament of Hope* (ed.) James Melvin Washington (San Francisco: Harper, 1986), pp. 231–44.

King, A. *Running Scared – Why America's Politicians Campaign Too Much and Govern Too Little* (New York: The Free Press, 1997).

Kitto, H. D. F. *The Greeks* (London: Penguin, 1951).

Kloppenburg, J. T. 'The Virtues of Liberalism: Christianity, Republicanism, and Ethics in Early American Political Discourse', *The Journal of American History*, 74, 1, 1987–8, pp. 9–33.

Koyre, A. *From the Closed World to the Infinite Universe* (Baltimore: John Hopkins University Press, 1957).

Kramnick, I. *Republicanism and Bourgeois Radicalism: Political Ideology in Late Eighteenth-Century England and America* (New York: Ithaca, 1990).

Kymlicka, W. *Multicultural Citizenship* (Oxford: Oxford University Press, 1996).

Laclau, E. and Mouffe, C. *Hegemony and Socialist Strategy* (London: Verso, 1996).

Lamore, C. 'Political Liberalism', *Political Theory*, 18, 1990, pp. 339–60.

Lamy, P. 'Harnessing Globalisation: Do We Need Cosmopolitics?' http://www.lse.ac.uk/collections/globalDimensions/lectures/harnessingGlobalizationDoWeNeedCosmopolitics/transcript.htm (27 June 2005).

Laughlin, J. M. 'Nation-Building, Social Closure and Anti-Traveller Racism in Ireland', *Sociology*, 33, February 1, 1999, pp. 129–51.

Lewis, C. S. *The Discarded Image* (Cambridge: Canto Press, 1995).

Limbaugh, P. and Rediker, M. *The Many Headed Hydra: The Hidden History of the Revolutionary Atlantic* (Boston: Beacon Press, 2001).

Lincoln, A. 'The Perpetuation of Our Political Institutions', in *Abraham Lincoln, His Speeches and Writings* (ed.) Roy P. Basler (New York: Da Capo Press, 1990).

Liptak, A. 'Greenpeace Faces Federal Charges', *New York Times*, October 11, 2003, A, p. 9.

Lloyd, M. 'In Tocqueville's Shadow: Hannah Arendt's Liberal Republicanism', *Review of Politics*, 57, 1995, pp. 31–58.

Locke, J. 'Some Thoughts Concerning Education', *On Politics and Education* (New York: Walter J. Black, 1947).

Lynd, S. *Intellectual Origins of American Radicalism* (London: Faber, 1969).

Macedo, S. *Liberal Virtues* (Oxford: Clarendon Press, 1990).

Macedo, S. 'Liberal Civic Education and Religious Fundamentalism: The Case of God v. John Rawls?', *Ethics*, 105, 1995, pp. 468–96.

Machiavelli, N. *The Prince* (London: Penguin, 1981).

MacIntyre, A. *After Virtue – A Study in Moral Theory* (Guilford: Duckworth Press, 1994).

Madison, J. *The Federalist Papers* (New York: Mentor Books, 1961).

McChesney, R. W. *Corporate Media and the Threat to Democracy* (New York: Seven Stories Press, 1998).

McClure, K. 'On the Subject of Rights: Pluralism, Plurality and Political Identity', in *Dimensions of Radical Democracy* (ed.) Chantal Mouffe (London: Verso, 1992), pp. 108–28.

Machiavelli, N. *The Discourses*, Book 1, 4 (ed.) Bernard Crick (London: Pelican Books, 1970), pp. 113–15.

Macpherson, C. B. *The Life and Times of Liberal Democracy* (Oxford: Oxford University Press, 1977).

Makimoto, T. and Manners, D. *Digital Nomad* (London: John Wiley and Sons, 1997).

Manin, B. *The Principles of Representative Government* (Cambridge: Cambridge University Press, 1997).

Mann, M. *Incoherent Empire* (London: Verso, 2003).

Marx, K. *The Communist Manifesto* (London: Penguin, 1985).

Massey, D. 'Politics and Space/Time', *New Left Review*, 196, 1993, pp. 65–84.

May, L. *Sharing Responsibility* (Chicago: Chicago University Press, 1992).

Meyrowitz, J. *No Sense of Place. The Impact of Electronic Media on Social Behaviour* (New York: Oxford University Press, 1985).

Michelman, F. 'Foreword: Traces of Self Government', *Harvard Law Review*, 100, 1986, pp. 4–77.

Mill, J. S. *A System of Logic* (New York: Harper and Brothers, 1900).

Mill, J. S. *On Liberty* (ed.) Gertrude Himmelfarb (London: Penguin Books, 1985a).

Mill, J. S. *Principles of Political Economy; With Some of Their Applications to Social Philosophy. Books IV and V* (London: Penguin, 1985b).

Mill, J. S. *Autobiography* (London: Penguin, 1990).

Mill, J. S. *On Liberty and Other Essays* (ed.) John Gray (Oxford: Oxford University Press, 1991).

Mill, J. *Political Writings* (ed.) Terence Ball (Cambridge: Cambridge University Press, 1992).

Miller, D. (ed.) *Liberty* (Oxford: Oxford University Press, 1991).

Miller, D. 'Deliberative Democracy and Social Choice', *Political Studies*, XL, 1992, pp. 54–67.

Miller, D. *On Nationality* (Oxford: Clarendon Press, 1995).

Miller, D. 'Bounded Citizenship', in *Cosmopolitan Citizenship* (eds) Kimberly Hutchings and Ronald Dannreuther (New York: Macmillan Press Ltd, 1999), pp. 60–80.

Monbiot, G. *The Age of Consent: A Manifesto for a New World Order* (London: Harper Perennial, 2004).

Morley, D. and Robins, K. *Spaces of Identity. Global Media, Electronic Landscapes and Cultural Boundaries* (London: Routledge, 1995).

Mouffe, C. *The Return of the Political* (London: Verso Press, 1993).

Muecke, D. C. *The Compass of Irony* (London: Methuen & Co Ltd, 1969).

Mulhall, S. and Swift, A. *Liberals and Communitarians* (Oxford: Blackwell, 1992).

Mumford, L. *The City in History: Its Origins, Its Transformations and Its Prospects* (New York: Harvest Books, 1968).

Munkler, H. 'Kant's "Perpetual Peace": Utopia or Political Guide', http://www.open democracy.net (27 May 2004).

Nedelsky, J. *Private Property and the Limits of Constitutionalism* (London: University of Chicago Press, 1990).

Nietzsche, F. 'The Greek State', in *On the Genealogy of Morals* (ed.) Keith Ansell-Pearson (Cambridge: Cambridge University Press, 1999), pp. 176–86.

Norris, P. (2003) 'Deepening Democracy through E-Governance', http://ksghome.harvard.edu/~.pnorris.shorenstein.ksg/ACROBAT/e-governance.pdf (1 August 2004).

Nussbaum, M. C. 'Aristotelian Social Democracy', in *Liberalism and the Good* (eds) R. Bruce Douglass, Gerald M. Mara and Henry S. Richardson (New York: Routledge, 1990).

Nussbaum, M. C. 'Human Functioning and Social Justice', *Political Theory*, 20, 1992, pp. 202–46.

Nussbaum, M. C. 'For Love of Country', in *For Love of Country – Debating the Limits of Patriotism* (ed.) Joshua Cohen (Boston: Beacon Press, 1996), pp. 3–17.

Nye, J. 'A Whole New Ball Game', *Financial Times Weekend*, December 28/29, 2002, pp. 1 and 3.

O'Neill, O. *Towards Justice and Virtue* (Cambridge: Cambridge University Press, 1996).

Oakeshott, M. 'Political Education', *Rationalism in Politics* (London: Methuen & Co., 1962).

Okin, S. 'Mistresses of Their Own Destiny: Group Rights, Gender, and Realistic Rights of Exit', *Ethics*, 112, 2002, pp. 205–30.

Oldfield, A. *Citizenship & Community: Civic Republicanism and The Modern World* (London: Routledge, 1991).

Oldfield, A. 'Political Education', in *Defending Politics. Bernard Crick and Pluralism* (eds) Iain Hampshire-Monk and Anthony Arblaster (London: British Academic Press, 1993).

Orwell, G. 'In Front of Your Nose', in *The Collected Essays, Journalism and Letters of George Orwell* (eds) Sonia Orwell and Ian Angus (New York: Harcourt, Brace and World, Inc., 1968), pp. 122–5.

Orwell, G. 'Review of Power: A New Social Analysis by Bertrand Russell', in *George Orwell The Complete Works, Vol. 11, Facing Unpleasant Facts 1937–1939* (ed.) Peter Davison (London: Secker & Warburg, 1998).

Papandreou, G. 'Go Ahead George, Change it All', http://www.opendemocracy.net/debates/ (1 July 2004).

Parekh, B. *Contemporary Political Thinkers* (Oxford: Martin Robertson, 1982).

Parekh, B. 'The Cultural Particularity of Liberal Democracy', in *Prospects for Democracy – North, South, East, West* (ed.) David Held (Stanford: Stanford University Press, 1993), pp. 156–75.

Parekh, B. 'When Religion Meets Politics', *Demos*, 11, 1997, pp. 5–7.

Parker, W. C., Ninomiya, A. and Cogan, J. 'Educating World Citizens: Towards Multinational Curriculum Development', *American Educational Research Journal*, 36, 1999, pp. 117–45.

Peck, G. 'Microsoft Cuts Prices to Court Developing Countries', *Information Week*, June 7, 2004, http://informationweek.com/story/showArticle.jhtml?articleID=21401815 (1 September 2004).

Perec, G. *Species of Space* (New York: Penguin Books, 1998).

Pettit, P. *Republicanism – A Theory of Freedom and Government* (Oxford: Oxford University Press, 1999).

Pinker, S. *The Blank Slate: The Modern Denial of Human Nature* (London: Allen Lane, 2002).

Pitkin, H. *The Concept of Political Representation* (Berkeley: University of California Press, 1967).

Pitkin, H. 'Justice: On Relating Public and Private', *Political Theory*, 9, 1981, pp. 327–47.

Pitkin, H. *Fortune is a Woman: Gender and Politics in the Thought of Niccolo Machiavelli* (Berkeley: University of California Press, 1984).

Plamenatz, J. *Man & Society Volume 1* (London: Longman, 1992).

Pocock, J. G. A. *The Machiavellian Moment* (New Jersey: Princeton University Press, 1975).

Pocock, J. G. A. 'Virtues, Rights and Manners – A Model for Historians of Political Thought', *Political Theory*, 9, 1981, pp. 353–69.

Pogge, T. W. 'Cosmopolitan and Sovereignty', *Ethics*, 103, 1, 1992, pp. 48–75.

Pogge, T. W. 'An Egalitarian Law of Peoples', *Philosophy and Public Affairs*, 23, 3, 1994, pp. 195–224.

Pogge, T. W. 'Rawls on International Justice', *The Philosophical Quarterly*, 51, 2001, pp. 246–53.

Pollard, J. 'Authenticity and Inauthenticity', in *Existential Perspectives and Human Dilemmas* (eds) Emmy van Deurzen and Claire Arnold Baker (London: Palgrave Macmillan, 2005), pp. 288–304.

Porter, R. *The Creation of the Modern World: The Untold Story of the British Enlightenment* (London: W.W. Norton & Co., 2001).

Posner, R. *Law, Pragmatism and Democracy* (Cambridge, MA: Harvard University Press, 2003).

Postman, N. *Teaching as a Subversive Activity* (New York: Delacorte, 1968).

Power, S. 'The Lesson of Hannah Arendt', *The New York Review of Books*, April 29, 2004, pp. 34–7.

Quill, L. and Uluorta, H. 'Rethinking Global Citizenship', Paper delivered at the annual *Peace and Justice Studies Association Conference*, San Francisco, California, October 15, 2004.

Rackow, S. H. 'How the USA Patriot Act Will Permit Governmental Infringement upon the Privacy of Americans in the Name of "Intelligence" Investigations', *University of Pennsylvania Law Review*, 150, 2002, pp. 1651–96.

Rawls, J. *A Theory of Justice* (Oxford: Oxford University Press, 1971).

Rawls, J. *Political Liberalism* (New York: Columbia University Press, 1996).

Rawls, J. *The Law of Peoples* (Cambridge, MA: Harvard University Press, 2001).

Raz, J. *The Morality of Freedom* (Clarendon: Oxford University Press, 1984).

Reich, R. *Bridging Liberalism and Multiculturalism in American Education* (Chicago: Chicago University Press, 2002).

Rheingold, H. *The Virtual Community – Finding Connection in a Computerised World* (London: Secker & Warburg, 1994).

Ridley, F. F. 'Political Education or Education for Life?', *Political Quarterly*, 53, 1982, pp. 32–45.

Rifkin, J. *The End of Work: The Decline of the Global Labor Force and the Dawn of the Post-Market Era* (New York: Putnam, 1995).

Robin, C. 'Fear Itself', *The Chronicle of Higher Education*, August 13, 2004, B, pp. 11–12.

Rodrik, D. *Feasible Globalizations*, 2002, available at http://ksghome.harvard.edu/~drodrik/Feasglob.pdf (27 June 2005).

Rorty, R. *Consequences of Pragmatism* (Brighton: Harvester Press, 1982).

Rorty, R. 'Thugs and Theorists: A Reply to Bernstein', *Political Theory*, 15, 1987, pp. 564–80.

Rorty, R. *Contingency, Irony and Solidarity* (Cambridge: Cambridge University Press, 1991).

Rorty, R. 'Remarks on Deconstruction and Pragmatism: Is Derrida a Private Ironist or a Public Liberal', in *Deconstruction and Pragmatism* (ed.) Simon Critchley (London: Routledge, 1996), pp. 13–18.

Rosenau, J. N. 'Information Technologies and the Skills, Networks, and Structures that Sustain World Affairs', in *Information Technologies and Global Politics*, J. E. Rosenau and J. P. Singh (eds), 2002, pp. 275–87.

Rosenau, J. N. *Distant Proximities: Dynamics Beyond Globalization* (New Jersey: Princeton University Press, 2003).

Rousseau, J. J. *The Social Contract and Discourses* (trans.) G. D. H. Cole (London: Everyman, 1973).

Rousseau, J. *The Government of Poland* (trans.) W. Kendal (Indianapolis: Hackett Publishing Company, 1985).

Roy, A. *Power Politics* (Cambridge, MA: South End Press, 2002).

Saint Exupéry, A. *Wind, Sand and Stars* (trans.) Lewsi Galantière (New York: Harcourt, Brace and World, 1975).

Sampson, A. *The Arms Bazaar* (London: Hodder and Stoughton, 1988).

Sandel, M. J. *Liberalism and the Limits of Justice* (Cambridge: Cambridge University Press, 1988).

Sandel, M. J. 'The Procedural Republic and the Unencumbered Self', *Political Theory*, 12, 1984, pp. 81–96.

Sandel, M. J. *Democracy's Discontent: America in Search of a Public Philosophy* (Cambridge, MA: Belknap, 1996).

Sandel, M. J. 'Democrats and Community', *The New Republic*, February 22, 1998, pp. 20–3.

Sauermann, B. (ed.) *2/15 – The Day the World Said No to War* (New York: Hello, 2003).

Scheffler, S. 'Conceptions of Cosmopolitanism', *Utilitas*, 11, 1999, pp. 255–77.

Schatzki, T. R. 'Theory at Bay: Foucault, Lyotard, and Politics of the Local', in *Postmodern Contentions. Epochs, Politics, Space* (eds) John Paul Jones, Wolfgang Natter and Theodore R. Schatzki (New York: The Guildford Press, 1993), pp. 39–64.

Schofield, M. *The Stoic Ideal of the City* (Cambridge: Cambridge University Press, 1991).

Scholte, J. A. 'Globalization: Prospects for a Paradigm Shift', *Politics and Globalization – Knowledge, Ethics and Agency* (London: Routledge, 1999), pp. 9–23.

Schumpeter, J. *Capitalism, Socialism and Democracy* (London: Allen & Unwin, 1976).

Scruton, R. *Kant: A Very Short Introduction* (Oxford: Oxford Paperbacks, 2001).

Seery, J. E. *Political Returns – Irony in Politics and Theory from Plato to the Antinuclear Movement* (San Francisco: Westview Press, 1990).

Sen, A. *On Ethics & Economics* (Oxford: Basil Blackwell, 1987).

Sen, A. *Development as Freedom* (New York: Anchor Books, 1999).

Sennett, R. *The Conscience of the Eye* (New York: Alfred Knopf, 1990).

Sennett, R. *The Corrosion of Character: The Personal Consequences of the New Capitalism* (London: Norton & Co., 1998).

Sharp, G. *The Politics of Nonviolent Action: Part One* (Boston, MA: Porter Sargent Publishing, 1973).

Shaw, G. B. *The Apple Cart: A Political Extravaganza* (London: Constable and Company Ltd, 1930).

Sherry, S. 'Responsible Republicanism: Educating for Citizenship', *University of Chicago Law Review*, 62, 1995, pp. 131–208.

Shklar, J. 'Montesquieu and the New Republicanism', in *Machiavelli and Republicanism* (eds) Gisela Bok, Quentin Skinner and Maurizio Viroli (Cambridge: Cambridge University Press, 1990), pp. 265–80.

Siegel, H. *Educating Reason – Rationality, Critical Thinking, and Education* (London: Routledge, 1988).

Skinner, Q. *Foundations of Modern Political Thought* (Cambridge: Cambridge University Press, 1978).

Skinner, Q. 'On Justice, the Common Good and the Priority of Liberty', in *Dimensions of Radical Democracy* (ed.) Chantal Mouffe (London: Verso, 1992), pp. 211–25.

Skinner, Q. *Liberty before Liberalism* (Cambridge: Cambridge University Press, 1998).

Skinner, Q. and Van Gelderen, M. (eds) *Republicanism: A Shared European Heritage. Volume 2, The Values of Republicanism in Early Modern Europe* (Cambridge: Cambridge University Press, 2002).

Sklair, L. 'Democracy and the Transnational Capitalist Class', *Annals of the American Academy of Political and Social Science*, 581, 2002, pp. 144–57.

Soja, E. *Postmodern Geographies* (London: Verso, 1989).

Soloft, P. 'Ethics and Irony', in *International Kierkegaard Commentary* (ed.) Robert Perkins (Georgia: Mercer University Press, 2001), pp. 265–87.

Solnit, R. *Acts of Hope*, www.oriononlne.org/pages/oo/sidebars/Patriotism/index_Solnit.html (1 August 2004a).

Solnit, R. *Hope in the Dark* (New York: Nation Books, 2004b).

Stanford Center for the Quantitative Study of Society 'Ten Years after the Birth of the Internet, How do Americans Use the Internet in Their Daily Lives', http://www.stanford.edu/group/siqss/SIQSS_Time_Study_04. pdf (1 March 2005).

Stokes, G. and Carter, A. (eds) *Democratic Theory Today: Challenges for the 21st Century* (Cambridge: Polity, 2002).

Stolzenberg, N. M. 'He Drew a Circle That Shut Me Out: Assimilation, Indoctrination, and the Paradox of a Liberal Education', *Harvard Law Review*, 106, 1993, pp. 581–667.

Storing, H. J. *What the Anti-Federalists Were For: The Political Thought of the Opponents of the Constitution* (Chicago: University of Chicago Press, 1981).

Sullivan, K. M. 'Rainbow Republicanism', *The Yale Law Journal*, 97, 1988, pp. 1713–23.

Summers, R. 'Controlled Irony and the Emergence of the Self in Kierkegaard's Dissertation', in *International Kierkegaard Commentary* (ed.) Robert Perkins (Georgia: Mercer University Press, 2001), pp. 289–317.

Sunstein, C. 'Beyond the Republican Revival', *The Yale Law Journal*, 97, 1988, pp. 1539–90.

Taylor, C. *Multiculturalism and the Politics of Recognition: An Essay* (New Jersey: Princeton University Press, 1992).

The Essential Jefferson (ed.) Albert Fried (New York: Collier Books, 1963).

Thomas, A. 'Liberal Republicanism and Civil Society', *Democratization*, 4, 1997, pp. 26–44.

Thoreau, H. D. *Walden and Civil Disobedience* (New York: Penguin, 1983).

Thrower, N. *Maps and Civilization: Cartography in Culture and Society* (Chicago: Chicago University Press, 1999).

Tilgher, A. *Work: What It Has Meant to Man Through the Ages* (trans.) D. C. Fisher, (New Jersey: George G. Harrap & Company Ltd, 1931).

Tyler, P. 'A New Power in the Streets', *New York Times*, February 17, 2003, A, p. 1.

Van Creveld, M. 'The New Middle Ages', *Foreign Policy*, 119, 2000, pp. 38–40.

Vernant, J. *The Origins of Greek Thought* (London: Methuen & Co., 1982).

Vidal, G. *Perpetual War for Perpetual Peace – How We Got to Be So Hated* (New York: Thunder's Mouth/Nation Books, 2002).

Villa, D. *Arendt and Heidegger – The Fate of the Political* (New Jersey: Princeton University Press, 1996).

Virilio, P. *Speed and Politics* (trans.) Mark Polizzotti (Columbia University: Semiotext(e), 1977).

Viroli, M. *For Love of Country* (Oxford: Oxford University Press, 1995).

Viroli, M. *Machiavelli* (Oxford: Oxford University Press, 1998).

Viroli, M. *Machiavelli's Smile – A Biography of Machiavelli* (trans.) Anthony Shugaar (New York: Farrar, Strauss and Giroux, 2002).

Waldron, Jeremy 'Theoretical Foundations of Liberalism', *Philosophical Quarterly*, 37, 1987, pp. 127–50.

Walker, R. B. J. 'Challenging the Debate – Citizenship after the Modern Subject', in *Cosmopolitan Citizenship* (eds) Kimberly Hutchings and Ronald Dannreuther (New York: Macmillan Press Ltd, 1999), pp. 171–200.

Walzer, Michael 'The Communitarian Critique of Liberalism', *Political Theory*, 18, 1992, pp. 6–23.

Weber, M. 'Parliament and Government in Germany under a New Political Order', in *Political Writings* (ed.) Peter Lassman (Cambridge: Cambridge University Press, 1994), pp. 130–271.

Weinstock, D. 'Prospects for Transnational Citizenship and Democracy', *Ethics and International Affairs*, 15, 2, 2001, pp. 53–66.

Went, R. 'Economic Globalization Plus Cosmopolitanism', *Review of International Political Economy*, 11, 2, 2004, pp. 337–55.

White, J. *Education and the End of Work* (London: Cassell, 1997).

Wolin, S. *Politics and Vision* (London: Allen & Unwin, 1961).

Wood, G. S. *The Creation of the American Republic, 1776–1787* (Chapel Hill: University of North Carolina Press, 1969).

Wootton, D. (ed.) *Republicanism, Liberty and Commercial Society, 1649–1776* (Stanford: Stanford University Press, 1994).

Worden, B. 'Marchamont Nedham and the Beginnings of English Republicanism, 1649–1656', in *Republicanism, Liberty and Commercial Society, 1649–1776* (ed.) David Wootton (Stanford: Stanford University Press, 1994), pp. 45–81.

Wuthnow, R. *Between States and Markets* (New Jersey: Princeton University Press, 1991).

Yates, R. *Bicentennial Edition of the Secret Proceedings and Debates of the Convention Assembled at Philadelphia, in the year 1787 for the Purpose of Forming the Constitution of the United States of America by Robert Yates Albany, New York, 1821* (Birmingham, Alabama: Southern University Press, 1987).

Young-Bruehl, E. *For Love of the World* (New Haven: Yale University Press, 1982).

Young, I. 'Mothers, Citizenship, and Independence: A Critique of Pure Family Values', *Ethics*, 105, 1995, pp. 535–79.

Zinn, H. *Declarations of Independence. Cross-Examining American Ideology* (New York: Harper-Collins Publishers, 1990).

Zunes, S. *Nonviolent Social Movements: A Geographical Perspective* (Oxford: Blackwell Publishers, 1999).

Index